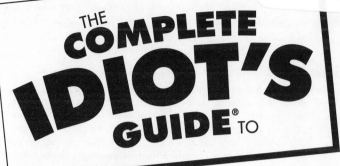

THE **COMPLETE IDIOT'S GUIDE®** TO

Pet Psychic Communication

by Debbie McGillivray and Eve Adamson

ALPHA

A member of Penguin Group (USA) Inc.

To all the animals everywhere, including the human ones. That we may all someday learn to live in harmony, communicate with love, and recognize our common spirit.
Also to Buffy and her human Gloria, who, with love from spirit, nurture and protect.

International Standard Book Number: 1-59257-214-6
Library of Congress Catalog Card Number: 2004103226

06 05 04   8 7 6 5 4 3 2 1

Interpretation of the printing code: The rightmost number of the first series of numbers is the year of the book's printing; the rightmost number of the second series of numbers is the number of the book's printing. For example, a printing code of 04-1 shows that the first printing occurred in 2004.

Printed in the United States of America

Publisher: *Marie Butler-Knight*
Product Manager: *Phil Kitchel*
Senior Managing Editor: *Jennifer Chisholm*
Senior Acquisitions Editor: *Randy Ladenheim-Gil*
Book Producer: *Lee Ann Chearney/Amaranth Illuminare*
Development Editor: *Lynn Northrup*
Production Editor: *Megan Douglass*
Copy Editor: *Molly Schaller*
Illustrator: *Chris Eliopoulos*
Cover/Book Designer: *Trina Wurst*
Indexer: *Tonya Heard*
Layout/Proofreading: *Angela Calvert, Mary Hunt*

Contents at a Glance

Appendixes

Contents

Appendixes

Foreword

Interspecies communication? Animal psychics? Animals talking to people and people talking to animals? Do people really expect others to believe there is some kind of human-animal communication going on? Is it really possible that animals have the cognitive abilities to relate to us? For most people, it sounds a little too much like Dr. Doolittle, but the truth is that interspecies communication is a reality.

As children, we all believed that animals talked and communicated—to each other and even to us. Most children know when things are wrong with their pets and often bring those communications to the attention of adults. Adults, unfortunately, usually treat them as cute and imaginative, sending a message that what children sense and experience from their animals is not real. And the barriers begin to go up.

Fortunately, though, we are living in a time when the barriers are being broken down. People are returning to a part of themselves they had forgotten about. Animal communicators and animal psychics are showing up everywhere and it is a wonderful sign. It marks a growing return to what has been so often ignored in modern society. As people begin to explore their more creative aspects, they find themselves reconnecting to Nature and to animals in new and powerful ways. People are beginning to remember that there is a spirit to everything, regardless of what kind of form it might have in this life.

Every loving pet owner knows that his or her pet talks to him or her. They know that the animal, even though it may not understand the words, does understand the tone and the emotion behind the words. Every pet owner knows that he or she also communicates in unspoken ways with the animal. Whether we call it intuition, telepathy, understanding of subtle body language—it doesn't matter. What matters is that there is communication going on.

One of the most frequent questions I get in workshops and lectures is, "Do you actually talk to animals?" And the answer is, "Yes I do." I have never gone by the terms "animal communicator" or "animal psychic" but I have always communicated with animals. They talk to me. I talk to them. They seek me out—both domestic and wild animals. But I am not that unusual, special, or gifted. I do what many others have been doing throughout the ages and it is something anyone can learn to do. Debbie McGillivray and Eve Adamson have put together a tremendous tool to help you recognize your own innate ability to relate animals as creative, cognitive, and intelligent beings.

Because we are part of Nature, we each are born with the innate ability to communicate with everything of the natural world. As humans in this modern society though, we often rely solely upon verbal communication. We forget that there are many other ways of communicating. I have worked with animals for most of my life. I still do wildlife rescue and rehab. I hold federal and state permits to work with birds of prey. I teach wildlife education in classrooms throughout the school year. My home is residence to horses, dogs, cats, hawks, owls, rats, a scarlet macaw, and a Jandaya conure. And they each speak in their own unique ways and a lot of times they speak more than what I want to hear.

But animals do communicate, and if we wish to communicate with them and to have them communicate with us, we need to understand how we can do such a thing. To communicate with anyone requires that we listen and attend quietly. The same is true of communication with animals. Just as no two people ever communicate quite the same, so it is with animals. *The Complete Idiot's Guide to Pet Psychic Communication* provides fun and effective techniques to help you listen and attend more easily to your animal brothers and sisters and actually begin to communicate with them.

As we remember our connection to Nature, we soon realize that we can communicate with animals as friends, allies, brothers, and sisters. Interspecies communication begins with realizing that all animals have spirits and that all animals communicate through their spirits as well as their bodies. Loving pet owners have known this throughout history.

In our modern world it is easy to get so wrapped up in fulfilling our daily obligations and responsibilities that we forget that we can starve as much from a lack of wonder as we can from a lack of food. If only for this reason, it is important to reconnect with Nature—to find what has been lost. Nature—and animals in particular—awaken our sense of wonder. And this wonder keeps our inner magic alive and our spirit strong. Through this book, you will learn to experience animals in a fresh way. You will learn to see and experience with a child's eyes. And in the process, you will find that part of you which is still magical, mysterious, and filled with wonder.

Ted Andrews

Ted Andrews is the award-winning and best-selling author of *Animal-Speak*, *Animal-Wise*, and *The Animal-Speak Workbook*.

Introduction

So you thought Dr. Doolittle was just a fun story? You, too, can talk to animals, deepening your relationship with your pets, gaining an understanding of animals in the wild, and strengthening your sense of place in the natural world. Professional animal communicator Debbie McGillivray shares her many experiences and stories in consulting with animals and their humans, and shows you how you can learn to communicate with animals, too.

Animals talk to each other telepathically all the time. If you want to join in on the conversation, you might just find your animals know a lot more about you, your life, and the world around you than you ever imagined. Talking to animals can delight you, sadden you, and heighten your understanding of what your pet needs, wants, and loves about you.

Through psychic communication, you can keep your pet feeling calm and safe when you are away. You can help your animal heal. You may be able to find your lost pet, and when you struggle with issues like whether or not it is time for you to help your pet pass on, you can actually talk to your pet about it, which helps you act according to your animal's wishes.

Join us on our journey into the minds and heart of our animal friends. It is an amazing journey, a journey that starts and ends in love. We can all learn a lot, so let's start listening together.

NOTE: All examples used in this book are based on actual people, pets, and experiences in Debbie's practice. However, other than Debbie, Eve, and the animals that live with Debbie and Eve, all other names of clients, interviewees, and their pets are changed to protect their privacy.

About This Book

This book has five parts, each designed to introduce you to a different aspect of animal communication:

Part 1, "The Intuitive Wisdom of Your Pet," introduces you to the basic concepts of animal communication: how animals communicate with each other telepathically all the time, how humans have featured animals in their spiritual lives throughout history, and how you can begin to understand your animal better by opening your heart, trusting your intuition, and learning how to listen.

Part 2, "Sending and Receiving Psychic Messages," gets into the nuts and bolts of how to communicate with your animal. You'll learn how to send messages, how to really listen for the answers, how to tune in to your own intuition, and how to build a closer relationship with your animal. You'll also learn how to communicate with your animal long-distance.

Part 3, "How Much Do You Know Intuitively About *Your* Pet?" will help you to know your pet better, not just as a species or a breed but as an individual with a unique personality and singular spirit. You'll learn about the importance of names, how to find and heal your animal's emotional scars, and how much your animals want and need to know what is going on in the family.

Part 4, "Welcome to Your Pet's World: The Animals Speak," helps guide your ear to what your pet most desperately wants you to know. Debbie will share the common complaints she's heard from countless animals that share their lives with humans. You'll also learn how to directly address behavior problems, overcome communication blocks, and locate a lost pet.

Part 5, "The Sacred Bond Between Animals and Humans," explores the many ways animals heal humans, the ways we can return the favor by helping heal them, how to cope with and continue communicating with an animal who has passed into spirit, and finally, the sacred bond between humans and animals: how to honor it, strengthen it, and become a stronger link in the great chain of life.

Extras

Each chapter in this book contains boxes with interesting information that will add to your knowledge and your sense of wonder about animal communication:

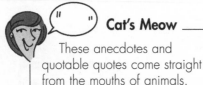

Cat's Meow

These anecdotes and quotable quotes come straight from the mouths of animals.

Pet Speak

Brand new terms you've never heard? These boxes will define them for you.

Horse Sense

These boxes give you tips and other useable information about how to communicate better with animals.

Doggone!

These boxes give you cautions about things to watch out for or be aware of while you learn more about and practice animal communication.

Acknowledgments

Debbie McGillivray: I would like to thank all of the many animals who have been my teachers and guides throughout this process and my life. Finnegan, my horse and hardest critic yet most persistent teacher; Jimmy James for his teachings and love; Champ for his compassion and joy of life; Tyler the goat for allowing me to have my first "validated" conversation with an animal; Sonny, Scarlett O'Hara, Ernie, Mamma Kitty, Mrs. T, Cindy Lou, Freddie, Sophie, Blueberry, Maxx, Orion, Fattie, Sam, and The Kid, as well as the many other animals that have graced my life.

I want to thank my husband, Scott, for his love and support. He is my biggest fan and continues to surprise me with the scope of his love and understanding. Thanks to my parents, for nurturing and respecting my deep love of animals. And many thanks to my friends and earth angels, Anne and Nancy, for always being there. I want to thank my first teacher, Dawn Hayman. She is a gift to the animal world. Thanks also to Penelope Smith of www.animaltalk.net, the leading pioneer of this vision. A special thanks to the clients and animals whose stories are used as examples in this book.

Thank you to God, my angels, and spirit guides, for giving me the courage and ability to do what I love to do so that I can make a difference in the lives of animals. A special thank you to Alpha Books, to Lee Ann Chearney of Amaranth, to Rita Berkowitz for pointing the way to Lee Ann, and to Eve Adamson, for making this book possible.

And finally to the reader: Thank you for your interest and enthusiasm in learning how to communicate with your animals on a deeper level. I hope that you enjoy the journey!

Eve Adamson: Thanks to my most devoted helper, Sally ("Bella"), who sits under my desk while I work to help keep me focused. She is a very, very good dog. Thanks to little Jack, for his joyful puppy energy and the aesthetic pleasure he brings to us all with his arctic-fox good looks. Thanks to Budge Buddy (who recently passed to spirit), Snugglebunny, Mr. Hampy, and Little Fishies 1, 2, and 3, for bringing life, energy, and music into the household. Thanks to my children, Angus and Emmett, for their unbridled enthusiasm about the subject of this book and for the great love they have for animals. Thanks to my parents, for teaching me how much it means to have relationships with animals. Thanks to Lee Ann, for bringing us this book and for always reminding me why I do this work. Thanks to Debbie, for sharing her incredible gift with the world. Thanks to all the wonderful folks at Alpha Books for keeping me so busy. And finally, thanks, love, admiration, and awe to all the beings that share this planet, sentient and nonsentient, two-legged, four-legged, eight-legged, winged, finned, furred, and scaled, the trees, rocks, oceans, for their great unity, and diversity. May we all wake up and pay attention, so we can remember who we really are.

Trademarks

All terms mentioned in this book that are known to be or are suspected of being trademarks or service marks have been appropriately capitalized. Alpha Books and Penguin Group (USA) Inc. cannot attest to the accuracy of this information. Use of a term in this book should not be regarded as affecting the validity of any trademark or service mark.

Part 1

The Intuitive Wisdom of Your Pet

Can you really talk to your animal? People have wondered about and longed for this skill for centuries. Yet you have that skill inside you, even if you have buried it with intellect and logic. The chapters in this section explore how much your animal already understands about telepathic communication; how for centuries, humankind has featured animals in its sacred traditions and religious rituals, sensing the connection animals have with the natural world; and how you can begin to open your mind and heart, reclaiming your own inner intuitive skills. You *can* talk to your animals, and this section ends with a chapter that sets the groundwork for exactly how to do it.

Chapter 1

How Do Pets Speak Telepathically?

In This Chapter

- ◆ The wisdom of animals
- ◆ You already "talk" to your pets!
- ◆ The nature of intuition and telepathy
- ◆ How to begin tuning in

Have you ever wondered what your dog is thinking as he looks at you quizzically, or barks at the air, or lies with his eyes half shut in apparent meditation? Have you ever contemplated your cat's consciousness as she stretches into a luxurious arch before batting at the tassels on the sofa, or presses her head into your palm for a stroke-on-demand? What is your horse thinking when he suddenly refuses to jump, or stops eating, or nuzzles you affectionately?

Pet owners long to know what goes through the heads of the animals they love. Are animals simple-minded creatures operating on instinct? Or do they know more than we ever imagined about the world around them and the humans who share their lives?

If only we could ask them! If only we could somehow find a way to communicate with them in a way that is clear and easy for us to understand.

It's no wonder people are fascinated with the idea of pet psychic communication! Just about everybody who watches cable television has at least heard of pet psychics, and many of us watch the *Pet Psychic* on the Animal Planet network, the show where pet psychic Sonia Fitzpatrick psychically connects with pets, both those living and those who have passed on, and "translates" to their people.

Many of us even know of a pet psychic or two. We wonder if calling a pet psychic would be worth the money, or just a frivolous expense. Some of us have already called a pet psychic for a consultation once, twice, or all the time. *We want to believe!* But some of us just aren't sure.

Does that sound like you?

Converted Skeptics

If you had asked either of us 10 years ago what we thought about *animal communication*, or pet psychic communication, we aren't sure how we would have answered. Maybe we would have laughed, or rolled our eyes, or said something sarcastic. Maybe we would have reacted the same way you, our readers, might be tempted to react right now. But that was then.

Today, in her work as a professional animal communicator, Debbie McGillivray has experienced thousands of validated communication sessions with animals from all over the globe.

Pet Speak

Animal communication is the process of communicating psychically or telepathically with an animal. Because of the negative connotations sometimes attached to the word "psychic," some prefer to call themselves "animal communicators" instead of "pet psychics," but the terms essentially mean the same thing. Animal communication is the preferred term of many for psychic communication between animals and humans, but we will use these terms interchangeably throughout this book.

In her work as a veteran dog writer, Eve Adamson has heard hundreds of first-hand stories from breeders, trainers, and pet owners about the amazing ways animal communicators have made contact with pets, discovering medical problems, unveiling the causes behind mysterious behaviors, and generally ironing out human/animal communication problems to great effect.

Debbie has even discovered some amazing things about Eve's dogs, Sally and Jack! But we'll tell you more about that later.

Animal communication might not have double-blind controlled scientific studies to back it up, but it does have thousands of satisfied, enlightened, and forever-changed humans and animals with inspirational, even shocking stories to offer as proof. We are among them, and that is why we've chosen to write this book.

We believe that although some people have a gift for animal communication, anyone can learn how to communicate with their own animals and with animals they might meet along life's journey. All it takes is some focused practice, something we will help you to do for yourself throughout the course of this book. We'll show you what we've learned, and how to get started "talking" to your own pets.

> **Horse Sense**
>
> If you don't believe in pet psychic communication, your brain will erect barriers to your own telepathic abilities, the abilities that you already possess. Opening your mind to the possibility is the first step to achieving success in pet psychic communication. If you believe it, and you practice, you can do it, too!

What Your Pet Already Knows

Sometimes, our pets know more about us, and about the world around them, than we realize. They tune in to our thoughts and emotions. They pick up our feelings and reflect them back to us. And they have some pretty specific ideas all their own. Some pets humor us by answering to the names we give them, but have other names in mind, names they know are their *real* names. (Sally tells us her real name is "Bella.")

Pets tend to know how we are feeling, understand the dynamics of family relationships, and sense whether someone has good or bad intentions. Some animals come to us to teach us something, and some come to us to learn. Still others come to share lessons with us.

Some pets watch over us to keep us on the right path. Some mirror our actions to help us change our paths. Or they may simply be with us in order to share their lives with us, to simply love us and be loved by us. We know many humans who have learned how to love because of a pet.

Of course, we don't always *know* how wise or knowledgeable or needy or interested our pets are. We might guess that a pet is happy or distressed, feeling energetic or feeling pain. We might assume our pets are fond of us, or that they don't care much for the mailman, but unless we find a way to speak to them, how will we ever know for sure?

Cat's Meow

Eve's little Rat Terrier, Sally, told Debbie that she helps Eve to concentrate on her writing by lying quietly under her desk while she works. When Sally senses that Eve needs to refocus, she gets up and asks to be let out, even if she doesn't really need to go out. She helps keep Eve grounded and centered on what she needs to do by redirecting counter-productive energy flow. Eve agrees that Sally is just what she needs, a point of focus against distraction, a companionable presence, and a welcome break when the words just aren't flowing.

When people do finally get to "talk" to their pets through pet psychic communication, they often become inspired at how their very own pets have overcome adversity or displayed courage. They are often inspired by their pet's great capacity for love.

Many animals face obstacles that test their life purpose and still they never lose sight of why they are here. Debbie's dog, Champ, is one such soul. Champ came with the first house Debbie and her husband, Scott, purchased. When Debbie and Scott went to view the house, the pit bull/German shepherd mix came bounding into the yard to greet them, and it was love at first sight. Debbie and Scott soon found out that the owners of the house couldn't find a home for him, due to his pit bull origins. They believed their only option was to take him to the animal shelter. Debbie and Scott told their agent that they would take the house … if Champ came with it.

When Debbie and Scott took possession of the house, they saw that Champ had been living outside in a small yard without shelter. Underweight and craving attention, Champ quickly adapted to his new family. Champ had a reputation in the neighborhood for chasing cars, but everyone admired his unquenchable enthusiasm. Debbie and Scott quickly took Champ to the vet, got him some premium food, and brought him inside to live. He was still the mayor of the neighborhood, and soon became a great source of joy for Debbie and Scott, thriving with shelter, care, lots of attention, and plenty of love.

Cat's Meow

In the face of adversity I stand tall. In the face of fear, I roar loud. In the presence of love, we all become one.

—Champ McGillivray, a Pit Bull/German Shepherd mix

Everyone knows Champ. He is greeter to all, and he always has a smile on his face and a ball in his mouth. He is much older now, but still the most amazing being Debbie and Scott have ever met. He guards over Debbie's cats, and on many occasions will break up the confrontations between some of them. He will be in a deep sleep and if he senses Ernie, a stray cat Debbie took in, going after Scarlett, Champ's beloved cat, Champ immediately rouses himself and interrupts.

Champ has become a big part of Debbie's workshops on animal communication, and many people enjoy talking to him. Champ never dwells on his past, but chooses to live in the present, without resentment or sadness. Debbie confirms that Champ does tend to ramble on about his many "girlfriends."

Despite a rough past, Champ never lost his gift to love, trust, and rejoice in the wonder of life. Humans had neglected him up until the day he adopted Debbie and Scott, but he has never let his past stop him from loving them completely. He teaches us all that living in the past only inhibits the gifts of the present and the joy of the future. Debbie feels lucky every day to know him.

Amazing Animals All Around

Champ isn't the only wise animal soul Debbie—and indeed, many of us—have met. The more we get to know our animals, and the more we use our own intuition to better understand our animal friends, the more many of us have been continually astounded by the depth, the perception, the compassion, and the understanding animals possess.

Because dolphins are among the few animals on the planet with brains of similar size and complexity to humans, some scientists believe that dolphins are as intelligent as humans and communicate with each other in ways just as complex as those humans use. Some scientists have devoted their lives to developing interspecies modes of communication so dolphins and humans can finally fully get to know each other. Perhaps animal communication will be the ultimate tool that helps us finally commune with the dolphins!

Once Debbie had the opportunity to communicate with some dolphins located in Key Largo, Florida. It was a memory she will cherish forever, and she describes the experience as being like a child in the company of master teachers. Dolphins, says Debbie, are incredible beings that touch our heart and soul at its deepest level. One dolphin shared her message with Debbie:

> *The human world is so noisy, so cluttered with meaningless sounds. The water is a buffer for me, tranquility like no other. Humans need to swim more to experience this "silence." Humans need to experience this tranquility whenever they start to lose control of their true selves. Humanity is in search of healing from within. Their energy is high. A change is occurring, but we must not put the responsibility of this change on anything other than ourselves. The dolphins are here to teach and to help, but humans must take what they learn and apply it to everyday life. We serve to remind humans of how attainable pure joy is. It is your responsibility to make it happen. Open your hearts, and breathe in this love and peace.*

It may surprise some people to learn how interested animals are in the human species, and how invested they are in helping us. On many occasions, an animal has confided in Debbie that the reason he or she was misbehaving (or that the human perceived the actions as misbehavior) was because the animal was trying to help his or her person. Our pets sometimes try to teach us, even compel us into better, healthier, or more loving action.

Once Debbie did a consultation with a cat named Norah who was neglecting to use her litter box. Norah was normally a very clean kitty, so this was out of character for her. After Debbie asked her if she felt all right, Norah said she did. Debbie asked her why she exhibited this undesirable behavior and Norah stated that she would not stop until her person, Jackie, stopped smoking. Jackie confirmed that she was, indeed, a smoker. Debbie explained Norah's "conditions" for her person—the disciplinary action she was taking to "help" her human's health. Abashed, Jackie said she would make an effort to cut back, but this half-hearted effort was unacceptable to Norah! She wanted Jackie to quit completely, and only then would she return to her litter box. (They are still struggling with this issue—Jackie still trying to quit, Norah still trying to "remind" her. That Norah is a stubborn one … but only because she loves her human!)

Doggone! _____

It's easy to idealize animals, but every animal is an individual, just like every human. They each have their different personalities, attributes, faults, and personality clashes. Some are kind, some are vivacious, and some are naturally giving. Others are victims of neglect or abuse, or so spoiled by their people that they develop rude behavior, just like a spoiled child. Seeing the animals in your life as unique individuals will help you to understand them more authentically.

In many cases, love is a much simpler, more straightforward affair for animals than for humans. Humans tend to put conditions on everything. We sometimes live too much in the past, or the future. We might think this makes us smarter, but perhaps it only makes us more confused!

Animals tend to have a knack for cutting through the many excuses, justifications, and over-thinking to which humans are so prone. Animals are pretty good at telling it like it is, doing what is healthiest and most productive, living in the moment, loving unconditionally. No, they aren't perfect. But we do think that sometimes they see things a little more clearly than we do. It's pretty helpful to have friends like that!

Teaching Us, Saving Us

One of Debbie's most moving consultations was with a wonderful couple, Tom and Jessica, who had lost their black Labrador, Cassidy. They wanted Debbie to connect with him in spirit. At first, Debbie had no idea how Cassidy had died, but as she located him and asked him what had happened, he described an impact injury to his chest. He had transitioned quickly and had not suffered, something his humans were relieved to know.

And then, Cassidy explained to Debbie that he had actually caused his own death to teach the family how to better protect their children. The images he showed Debbie gave her chills.

Cassidy showed Debbie that the father of the family, because he was a police officer, often unloaded and then cleaned his gun at home. Tom was always extremely careful while doing this, and Cassidy often sat in the room with Tom during the process, always waiting calmly for him to finish. Cassidy and Tom were particularly bonded and had a very close relationship.

But this day, something was different. As Tom was preparing to unload the gun so he could clean it, Cassidy suddenly, for no apparent reason, jumped up onto Tom and the gun went off. The bullet hit Cassidy, fatally, in the chest. Tom held Cassidy in his arms as the dog passed.

The event was traumatic and heart wrenching for the family, and they mourn Cassidy's loss because he was truly a member of their family. They wanted desperately to know what had happened, how such a bizarre sequence of events could have transpired.

Cassidy explained to Debbie that he understood how dangerous guns could be, and he was very worried that one of the children might get hurt in a gun accident. Cassidy decided to sacrifice himself to show his family that no matter how careful they were, they must know that something could happen. When Debbie explained this to Tom and Jessica, they realized the amazing unconditional love Cassidy had displayed, a great sacrifice designed to teach the family, no matter how painfully, that they could never, never allow the same thing to happen to one of their children.

Animals save humans again and again—physically, emotionally, and spiritually. The ways animals love us is almost beyond our understanding, a love few humans are ever able to return in equal proportion. If more humans had the ability to love animals, or even each other, as deeply as animals love us, maybe the world would be a much different place. We have a lot to learn from our animal friends, and they are eager to teach us.

Learning to speak to animals, and perhaps more importantly, to *listen*, gives us access to a profound source of wisdom and natural intelligence that can enrich all our lives. We can learn how to love better, and in so doing, we may also learn how to treat our fellow sentient beings with greater respect and care—not as possessions, but as friends.

Keep Talking!

Animals relate to each other through verbal, physical, and telepathic communication (communicating mind to mind, without words) all the time. To animals, these three modes of communication are probably equally helpful, and none more unusual than any other. We've had friends comment, "Doesn't an animal think it's strange to suddenly hear a voice in its head?" Actually, not at all! To animals, this is one of several normal, perfectly commonplace modes of communication. One wonders if human "speech" seems a little bit crude and elementary to them!

Horse Sense

Contrary to what you might have read in science fiction books, telepathic communication isn't an advanced skill that only a few highly evolved people can access. It's a primitive skill, and intellectual advancement is exactly what has buried our natural ability to communicate telepathically with each other. The primitive part of our brain has been so outweighed by the higher parts that we've forgotten this most basic form of communication, one that is based on subtleties, nuances, and impalpable energies.

Humans also possess the ability to communicate this way. Yet because our ability to communicate telepathically with animals as well as with each other still waits deep within us, we can reclaim this instinct with a little focused work. We understand verbal communication, of course, and even many of the subtleties of physical communication—body language, hand signals, a gentle stroking versus a slap. We know what these mean, and we can (and do) use these vehicles to communicate with our animal friends.

They communicate with us in these ways, too—a growl, a purr, a whinny, a wagging tail, rippling skin, a buck or lunge, or a joyful wiggle. We see our animals' body language and often, we know, instinctively, what feelings the animals mean to convey.

But what about telepathic communication?

Actually, we communicate telepathically with our animals, and with each other, all the time! We just don't realize it, most of the time, on a conscious level. When you tell your dog, "Good dog!" with joy and enthusiasm, you are saying the words. Your body reflects your feelings. And, as you speak, your mind also broadcasts your thoughts, your intentions, and your emotions. You say "Good dog" with respect or appreciation or enthusiasm or awe with your voice, and you also say "good dog" with emotions behind it in your mind.

We, and many other animal communicators and clients, believe your pets read these mental broadcasts just as clearly as they hear your words or understand your body language. To them, it is simply one more facet of communication, and an important facet. How much we miss when we neglect to communicate with our pets this way! And how much we gain when we finally remember how.

Cat's Meow

Living in the joy of the moment, we expose ourselves to uncondensed fun!
—Rudy, a gregarious black seal

When we limit ourselves to verbal and physical communication, we can often get our pets to understand what we want them to do. We teach them certain "commands" and give them positive or negative feedback, depending on their "performance." We might also be able to tell that our animal is happy or unhappy, fearful or excited or lonely, or any number of feelings, by observing our pets' physical communication or body language.

Yet it is telepathic communication that will allow us to understand *why* our pets feel the way they do. Telepathic communication can give us the story behind it all. It can tell you that your dog is unhappy because his left rear paw hurts, or because he thinks you haven't been paying enough attention to him since you started your new job. It can tell you that your cat particularly enjoys that game you play with the flashlight beam on the wall, but that she doesn't like that new food you just started to feed her. Your pet can tell you how he ended up in the animal shelter, which family routines disturb her, or even whether he has suffered long enough from old age or infirmity and is ready to be let go.

Telepathic communication allows us to communicate with our animals, talking to them and hearing their answers. It even allows us to communicate with our animals from far away, to explain why your return from a trip is delayed or to assure them that everything is okay. It also allows a professional pet psychic to talk to your animal while on the phone with you, even if you live in different states, or different countries, because in psychic communication, geography is irrelevant.

In other words, psychic communication helps us to understand our pets on a deeper level. It is the key to unlock all that is untold. Even though you do it all the time, once you begin to do it with consciousness and intention, you can discover an entire new level of communication with your pet.

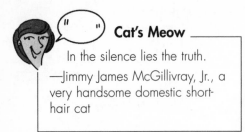

Telepathy is like a muscle, and with regular exercise you can improve your telepathic skills, so you can not only send messages to your animals, you will also be able to receive messages back from them. Animals have so much to teach us, all we need to do is listen. Just as with any human relationship, communication is the key to understanding, and telepathic communication can help to make this more possible than ever before.

What Is Telepathy?

Telepathy is the exchange of energy over distance. When Debbie asks an animal a telepathic question, she might get back from them an answer in pictures, words, feelings, or emotions. In some cases, she experiences a general knowing. Or the answer might be a combination of all of these.

When Debbie first started telepathically communicating with animals, she received most of her messages from them in the form of words, a mode that surprised her because she had always thought of herself as a visual person. However, Debbie found that as she became more and more experienced and comfortable with telepathic communication, she began to receive information in the form of moving pictures in addition to words.

The Five Psychic Senses (and a Sixth Sense)

As you begin to develop and refine your own telepathic ability, you might discover that you receive messages from animals in any or all of the following modes:

◆ Visual: Seeing pictures or scenes with your mind's eye. For example, an animal might show you a scene or reenactment of something that happened.

◆ Aural: Hearing words and thoughts with your psychic ear. You might actually hear your pet speaking to you in your mind, or you might hear sounds your pet heard.

◆ Tactile: Experiencing physical or emotional sensations in your body that are coming directly from the animal, such as pain or vigor, strength or fatigue. Or you might experience a sensation your pet experienced such as a shock, a chill, or heat.

- ◆ Olfactory: Experiencing aromas as the animal would experience them. You might smell what your animal smelled: something burning, something delicious, something foul.

- ◆ Gustatory: Experiencing tastes as the animal would experience them: the great taste of your dog's favorite food, the horrible taste of those treats you thought your cat would love, or even a taste that could lead to uncovering a mystery about what your animal might have ingested.

- ◆ A general "knowing": You ask a question, and you just know the answer, without being directly told through any of the five senses. Call it the "sixth sense" mode.

Furthermore, psychic communication, in its many forms, can occur at any distance. Telepathy may occur between two beings that are face to face, or across the globe. Geography is irrelevant to telepathy, which is why animal communicators can talk to animals telepathically from any distance. For long-distance communications, animal communicators may use the telephone to relate to you their telepathic conversations, mind to mind, spirit to spirit, with the animals, but the phone is as irrelevant as the actual distance for the human-animal communication.

Although some people become even more skeptical when they hear that telepathic readings happen "over the phone," that's not exactly how it works. The telepathic communication doesn't happen over the phone line. This is simply the best way for the pet psychic to communicate with the animal's human, because most humans aren't so adept at communicating telepathically with each other.

When Debbie communicates with an animal in Australia or France, the connection certainly doesn't feel far away. We wish we could say the same for international telephone connections!

Using the Body Scan to Pinpoint Pain

In her practice, Debbie has become more in tune to each animal's body. When the animal hurts, she feels the pain in her own body. This has become a common part of her consultations, scanning the body for pain or discomfort.

However, when people ask Debbie to *look* at their animals to find out where they are hurt, Debbie usually asks *not* to see the animal first. Tuning in telepathically to "feel" where the pain is located works better for Debbie than looking right at the animal because Debbie knows her eyes can play tricks on her.

If a leg hurts and she looks at the animal, she might lose "second sight" of where the pain is located, but if she focuses only on the feeling, the body scan, then she can feel exactly where the pain is. With practice, everyone can learn to do this, and everyone can eventually figure out what way works best for them.

Doggone!

Is your mind playing tricks on you when you try to communicate psychically with your animal? Try closing your eyes, relaxing, and opening your mind. If you look at your pet, you could be led astray by visual cues, especially if you suspect a physical problem.

Debbie remembers a woman who called her about her dog, Dot, who hadn't been acting right. Her person, Julie, couldn't quite pinpoint Dot's problem, but she just knew something was wrong. She had already taken Dot to two different vets who hadn't been able to find a problem. Yet Julie knew she didn't have the whole story.

When Debbie connected with Dot, Dot showed Debbie that she was having trouble breathing, something Debbie experienced by feeling her own breathing temporarily hindered. Debbie asked Julie about this, and Julie confirmed that Dot did seem to be having trouble breathing.

Next, Debbie did a body scan of Dot, and Dot kept showing Debbie a visual image of little fleshy lumps inside her. Debbie also felt a thyroid sensation, and asked Julie to have Dot's thyroid checked. Julie confirmed that Dot had been on thyroid medicine for a long time.

But Julie was concerned about the images Debbie relayed of the lumps, and took Dot to yet another vet. Because of the information Dot had relayed to Debbie, the vet found many fleshy tumors inside Dot's body. Some of these tumors were located around Dot's lungs, constricting her breathing. Had Dot not relayed this information, the lumps might have gone undetected and could have grown steadily worse.

Perhaps we humans once understood, in a simpler, less technological time, more of what went on inside us. Or perhaps humans have never (yet) been able to understand at an intuitive level what goes on inside their bodies in the way animals seem to understand it. In many cases, animals give animal communicators remarkably specific information about what is wrong, and even what they would prefer to be done about it, from radical surgery to nonintervention.

Horse Sense

How does a dog know what disease processes might be going on inside her? How does a dog know about, let alone relay, that she has a thyroid problem, or cancer, or a weak heart? We've become so estranged from our own mental and physical processes that we are no longer in touch with our bodies the way animals seem to be. While we may not know *how* they know, we do know that

Mental Postcards

Another client of Debbie's called to set up an appointment to inform her two kitties, Cecil and Samantha, that she was going on an extended vacation for three weeks. Jill was very concerned about her precious kitties while she was gone and wanted to know from the cats which pet sitter they preferred as well as what she could do to make this distance between them less unpleasant.

Debbie talked to the cats, asking Jill the first names and descriptions of the hair of each of two possible pet sitters, and the cats each showed her how they felt about each sitter. She received images of each sitter. One was bubbly and effusive and spent a lot of time with the cats; another, while nice, seemed to be rushed, and Samantha in particular wasn't comfortable with this pet sitter.

Debbie relayed this information to Jill, who said the cats confirmed her gut feelings about the two sitters. She hired the bubbly one, of course!

The cats also had a few particular requests. Cecil wanted to be put in charge in Jill's absence, and he wanted everyone to know it and acknowledge it. He also wanted to make sure he was fed on time because he hated waiting to eat.

Debbie advised her to telepathically connect with her cats while she was away, to help ease their stress. Because telepathy knows no time or space, Debbie assured Jill that her messages would be received no matter where she was, just as effectively as if she was talking and comforting her cats face to face. Jill agreed to try it. Debbie told her to picture what she was doing on vacation so that her animals would know that she was okay, and to also tell them how much longer it would be until she returned.

Samantha expressed gratitude and a feeling of comfort that Jill was going to connect with the cats while she was away, and looked forward to hearing from her beloved human.

CAUTION

Doggone! _____

> Pets can become confused and upset if you leave them without an explanation. The old "sneaking out with the suitcases" trick actually makes animals feel abandoned rather than fooling them into thinking you never left. It's better to explain to your pets exactly where you are going, what you will be doing, how much you will be thinking of them, and exactly when you will be coming home. (As soon as they see those suitcases, your pets probably know exactly what's going on anyway!)

When Jill returned, she booked another session with Debbie to find out if her cats had indeed got her messages. Samantha chimed excitedly, telling Debbie that she received every one of her messages. Debbie asked the cat to elaborate, and she sent Debbie a picture of her person with a pink winter coat on (it was the middle of summer at the time), and white all around her.

Debbie relayed the seemingly strange information to Jill, who laughed and explained that she had traveled to visit her son, and had gone skiing in the mountains. She said she communicated to her cats while on the chair lift, while wearing her favorite pink ski jacket. This was wonderful validation that the animals do indeed pick up our messages, and care about what we are doing.

Horse Sense

Making an effort to tune in to your animal is a very important first step to psychic communication. Try sitting quietly with your animal, eyes closed, for a short time each day. This is a wonderful way to help both of you relax, and to let your animal know you simply enjoy his company. You are not expecting anything, you just want to be with him.

Debbie's cat, Jimmy James, would run to the window everyday, about 10 minutes before Debbie arrived home from work. It wasn't the same time every day, but it was always 10 minutes before Debbie's time of arrival. Jimmy James was so in tune to Debbie that he knew when she was near. (He also knew exactly when Debbie had scheduled him to visit the vet—that was when he chose to hide! Your animals pay attention, so don't bring out that cat carrier until the last minute or you may find you have no cat in sight.)

Because telepathy can manifest in so many ways, as we talk to our pets, as they talk to us, and as we all seek to understand each other, you and your animal can find your own rhythm, your own mode of communication, and your own new level of communication.

Getting Started with Psychic Communication

Each person experiences telepathy in a unique way. This ultra-subtle form of communication is so easily obliterated by mental clutter, thoughts and worries, and distractions and noise.

In Debbie's animal communication workshops, she usually takes people through a variety of exercises to help them relax their minds and bodies, open their mind and hearts to the possibility of telepathic communication, and quiet the mental racket.

In this book, we will help you do the same thing with exercises in each chapter to help you discover and refine your own telepathic abilities. Here is the first one Debbie has designed for you.

The Imagination Game

Every day for the next week, try this preparatory exercise: Imagine you are having a conversation with your animal. It may sound strange, but this simple mind-expanding exercise will start to open the doors to your own telepathic abilities.

For example, you might reserve about five minutes after work each day. After you come home from your job or finish up your day's work at home, leave the stresses of work behind you and focus on your pet for a few moments. Sit back with them, relax, and in your mind, say (for instance), "Hi, Frieda!" Then, just imagine that in your mind, you "hear" your animal saying, "Hi! I'm so glad you're back!" (or whatever).

Then, imagine asking your animal about her day, and imagine what she says back to you. Maybe she says, "Oh, it was the same kind of day I usually have, except someone knocked on the door right in the middle of my nap! Don't worry, I scared them away for you. Oh, and I'm hungry. When's dinner?"

Let an entire conversation play out in your mind as you sit relaxing with your pet. Look at her and notice how she acts, or reacts, as you do this. Even just imagining a conversation means forming thoughts that your pet might already be able to understand or "hear" in some way.

Let each day's conversation be different. In your mind, ask your pet questions. Imagine the responses. Don't worry about really trying to "hear" or "read" your animal's thoughts for now. Just keep imagining what they might say to you.

This game is not only productive for enhancing your psychic abilities, but it is a lot of fun, and a great way to relax after a long day. Enjoy yourself, and enjoy this time with your pet. You've got many more delightful communication sessions to look forward to, and this is just the beginning!

The Least You Need to Know

- Your animals probably know and understand a lot more than you realize.

- Your words, actions, body language—even the psychic messages you send to your pet without realizing it—already serve as communication tools between you and your pet. Pet psychic communication simply helps you to use those tools more deliberately and with better control.

- Telepathy starts with developing intuition and keeping an open mind.

- Practicing communicating with your animals every day will help to refine and improve your skills.

Sacred Animals

In This Chapter

◆ The human/animal bond has many incarnat... ..s

◆ Animal communication: spirit-to-spirit, not brain-to-brain

◆ A look back at sacred, mythological, and historical representations of animals

◆ Finding your own power animal

◆ Creating a personal totem

Since humans first began to develop a consciousness that told them they were one species, and the birds, bears, tigers, horses, wolves, fish, and buffalo that lived around them were separate species, we have had an intimate relationship with animals. Humans have drawn animals on cave walls, painted them on canvases, and written songs and poems and stories about them. They populate our myths and stories, prayers, and sacred traditions.

Animals fascinate us because they are like us, yet unlike us. They have faces, bodies, brains, and yet they are mysterious. We try to understand them, and sometimes we think we've got it. Other times, we feel we don't have a clue what they are thinking. We love them, we keep them, and sometimes we mistreat them. Some of them we consider family members,

we think of them, however, we need to remember that
them.

Calling an Animal?

organized society, we tend to categorize animals: pets like dogs and cats, parakeets and hamsters; performance animals like horses and show dogs; livestock (food and dairy animals) like cattle, swine, and chickens; wild animals like wolves, bears, eagles, and deer. We have many other categories, too: insects, reptiles, amphibians, arachnids; mammals, birds, fish. Domesticated or not. We think some of them are smart, and others not so much. We wonder if dolphins equal us in intelligence, but we don't wonder if we are smarter than an ant or an earthworm. We have bigger, more developed brains than most animals, and in many ways, we can't help feeling that this somehow sets us apart.

Yet animals (all of us) are sentient beings, each with a unique energy. Just because one animal seems smarter or more evolved or more "humanlike" than another doesn't mean you can communicate psychically with your dog or horse but not with a snake or an ant.

Yet that spiritual energy we all share is the source of psychic communication. We have it, the elephant has it, even the cockroach has it. In psychic communication, energetic beings communicate on a level separate from the level of speech that we better understand. The pet psychic interprets this communication into language, and becomes adept at this interpretation, but just because your dog or your cat seems more human than your python or your bearded dragon, doesn't mean you can't communicate with all of them.

Debbie once communicated with an iguana named Ivan whose health was failing. His owner, Tony, wanted to find out what he could do to help Ivan. Ivan told Debbie that he was constipated, and needed his belly rubbed. Tony followed his iguana's suggestion, relieving the constipation and solving the problem. Ivan became "regular" again, and recovered fully!

Actually, animals that live with humans are easier to communicate with than wild animals, no matter how "smart" or "human-like" they are. A pet iguana is easier to talk to than a wolf, for example (although wild animals certainly can communicate) because nondomesticated animals operate on a much more instinctual level than domesticated animals and might not be interested in communicating with humans.

Cat's Meow

According to a 1999 Animal Hospital Association survey, pet owners have strong bonds with their pets:

♦ 84 percent of pet owners surveyed refer to themselves as the "mom" or "dad" of their pet.

♦ 72 percent of married pet owners surveyed said they greeted their pets first when returning home.

♦ 63 percent celebrate their pet's birthday.

♦ 80 percent cited "companionship" as the major reason they have a pet.

♦ 57 percent said if they could choose only one companion if deserted on an island, they would choose their pet.

Sacred Traditions

We certainly aren't the first culture or age to have relationships with or try to communicate with our animal friends. For thousands of years, every culture has incorporated animals into their mythologies. Native American culture honors and celebrates the spirits of different animals, and each person relates to certain animals as their personal totem animals. Ancient Asian, Egyptian, and African cultures include animal deities in their mythology, and throughout history, certain animals were honored, violence against them being punishable by death. From the good-luck appearance of a spider to the bad-luck crossing of a black cat across one's path, we infuse the animals around us with our hopes, our fears, and our belief systems.

Dogs and cats have, in different periods of history, been given royal titles, their own servants, and even fed by human wet nurses. Other, less lucky breeds or varieties, not so fashionable at any given time, were used for food or driven to work through extreme conditions. You and your dog or cat aren't just a human and a pet with a relationship. You are part of a long chain of historical and spiritual connectedness between humans and animals. The same goes for you and your horse, Burmese python, or scarlet macaw.

Horse Sense

The next time you look at your pet, see if you can see, deep within your pet's eyes or body movements, bark or meow or song, echoes of that animal's ancestry, the myths and legends that surround it, its history and evolution. This can help to add depth and understanding to your communications with your animal friend.

To help you appreciate the great tradition of human/animal connection, let's look back at some of the myths, legends, and stories from cultures all around the world that celebrate, narrate, and honor the human/animal bond.

The Horse

Horses and humans have an ancient history, but for thousands of years, humans hunted horses for food. Between 4000 B.C.E. and 3000 B.C.E., humans both hunted and domesticated horses. Stone-Age cave paintings in France and Spain show humans hunting horses, and a prehistoric artist carved a small horse figure out of the ivory from a mammoth's tusk about 30,000 years ago, according to the International Museum of the Horse in Lexington, Kentucky.

The earliest Cro-Magnon humans probably used horses as pack animals, but some archeological evidence suggests that nomadic humans in Eurasia were riding horses as long ago as 4000 B.C.E., much earlier than previously thought. As humans continued to refine their working relationship with horses, using them to herd, pull carts, hunt, and wage war, mythology also captured the spirit of the horse in its archetypal relationship to man.

The ancient Romans had many stories about the horse. The winged Pegasus, according to Greek myth, arose from the mingling of the sea foam of Poseidon and the blood of Medusa, the snake-haired Gorgon monster. Poseidon, god of the sea, often disguised himself as a stallion in order to seduce other goddesses and mortals, so his wife, Demeter, wouldn't know what he was up to. One affair produced a wild horse named Arion who could talk and who had human front feet. Clearly, the Greeks and Romans valued the horse for its virility.

The Greek writer, Homer, tells the story of the Trojan War in his epics, *The Iliad* and *The Odyssey*. The Trojan horse, that giant wooden trick, allowed the Greeks to finally penetrate the city of Troy during the Trojan War.

Ancient Indian mythology tells of horses drawing chariots across the sky that pulled the sun.

The Dog

Each individual breed of dog has myths in its history—so many, in fact, that they would make an entire book on their own. Here are a few dog myths we enjoy:

Stories of the Buddha say he traveled with a little Shih Tzu as his constant companion. If the Buddha was ever threatened or endangered, the little dog would shape-shift into a lion and protect the Buddha. Ancient "Foo Dogs" guarded Asian palaces and ancestors of the Pug, Pekinese, and Shih Tzu lived as royalty in the imperial palace. Ancestors of the Lhasa Apso guarded the Dalai Lama in Tibet. Many of the flat-faced, small Asian dogs were at some point in their history called "Lion Dogs" because the sacred lion was so essential to Buddhism. Buddhism first arose in India, but because lions were not native to Asia, dogs took over that sacred role when Buddhism flowered in China and Japan.

The ancient Aztecs considered the Chihuahua a sacred animal, but also used it for food. Montezuma II, the last Aztec rule, was said to keep hundreds of Chihuahuas. The Aztecs buried Chihuahuas with their owners, believing the Chihuahua would take on the sins of the human and lead him through the underworld. The Aztecs most prized the yellow or fawn-colored Chihuahuas because yellow was the color associated with death.

> **Cat's Meow**
>
> If you talk to the animals, they will talk with you, and you will know each other. If you do not talk to them, you will not know them, and what you do not know you will fear. What one fears, one destroys.
>
> —Chief Dan George, Sioux chief, actor, and activist

Another story says that on Noah's ark during the great flood related in the Old Testament, the ark sprung leaks during the storm. Noah was able to plug most of the holes, but couldn't stop them all. The two Afghan hounds he had on board the ark plugged the holes with their long noses, and ever since, the story goes, dogs have had wet noses.

The Basenji, that smooth-coated, barkless dog from Africa, was said to guard fire deep in the forest. When a man named Rukuba encountered the Basenji, he asked the dog for some of the fire. The Basenji said, "If I give you some fire, what will you give me in return?" Rukuba said he would take care of the Basenji forever. The Basenji gave fire to humans, and ever since, humans have vowed to care for the dog.

The Cat

The mysterious cat was among the last "pet" to be domesticated, but cats, large and small, have long been an enigmatic source of spiritual inspiration. Even today, humans who live with cats admit that the domesticated cat never quite seems entirely domesticated—or at least not entirely dependent on humans.

The cat was never as revered and worshipped as it was in ancient Egypt, and one of the most well known cat goddesses was Bast. Ancient Egyptian mythology told that the goddess, Isis, gave birth to the cat goddess, Bast. When Bast had a cat's head, she was a moon goddess, and when she had a lion's head, she was a sun goddess. Bast protected the great god, Ra (also her father) from the serpent, Apep. Bast also protected women, children, and families, and was so fierce in her protective duties that she ripped out the hearts of her enemies.

> ### Horse Sense
>
> Want to relate to your cat in a physical way? Try the yoga cat pose. On a mat or carpet, get down on all fours. Take a deep breath, then exhale. As you breathe out, arch your back up slowly, stretching into cat pose. Inhale, and return to a neutral position. Repeat three times slowly while visualizing a cat stretching.

Bast wasn't at first associated with the domestic cat, but eventually took that form as cats became more popular as pets in ancient Egypt. The ancient Egyptians also believed that the cat's eye contained the light of the sun.

The Egyptian Sphinx has the head of a king and the body of a lion. Other cat deities include the Egyptian lion goddess Sekhmet, the Egyptian snake fighter Mafdet, and the African panther god Agassou.

Many of the ancient cat deities were valued as protectors and snake fighters, perhaps reflecting one of the ways humans, long ago, most valued cats: for their ability to protect humans against dreaded serpents.

The Bird

From eagles to parakeets, falcons to chickadees, birds represent to humans the ability to transcend an earthbound existence. When we keep them as pets, we value their intelligence and their ability to mimic our language. Not everyone agrees how much birds actually understand about what they say, but because some of them can talk, and most of them can fly, humans have long been fascinated by our winged brothers.

Native American culture has many myths and legends about birds. The crow, raven, and blue jay appear as common trickster figures that outwit humans. The eagle was sometimes a hero, sometimes a healer, sometimes a messenger, and always a symbol of power and strength. The mythological thunderbird had eyes of fire and giant wings that stirred up thunderstorms. Thunderbirds often top totem poles that stand outside the dwelling places of Native American families.

In ancient Persia, the rooster scared off the demons of night, and the phoenix was an ancient Egyptian sign of immortality. The Phoenix, it was said, lived for 500 years, then became consumed by fire in its nest, after which it was reborn, rising out of the ashes to live again in an endless cycle.

Many of us keep birds for their song, their beauty, and their ability to talk. Just for fun, make up a myth about your own bird! A creation story? A joke on humans? Or maybe your bird brought the world some essential component of our culture, such as music. (Eve can hear her parakeets singing merrily in the living room at this very moment!)

The Goat

Some people keep goats as pets and/or use their milk, and appreciate the goat's curiosity and jolly sense of humor. The goat has served humans for centuries and is a primary source of milk and cheese in Europe, where limited grazing space makes goats more practical than cattle.

Perhaps the most famous example of the goat in myth is Pan, the god of the wood and flocks, and the patron deity of hunters and shepherds. Pan had horns and the lower half of a goat, and played the pan flute. Satyrs were also part goat, with the pointed ears and horns and lower halves of goats and the torsos and heads of humans. Satyrs were famous in Greek mythology for their great love of revelry. They liked to party! From long ago, humans have recognized the goat's ability to have fun.

The Rabbit

The prolific rabbit pops up in many mythological traditions. Manabozho, the Great Hare, was a trickster god in Native American mythology. African mythology has trickster Hare, and even our contemporary western culture has examples of the trickster rabbit, in the form of "Brer Rabbit" and the notorious and tardy white rabbit of *Alice in Wonderland*. The most familiar trickster rabbit in our culture today is certainly Bugs Bunny.

Those of us who have lived with rabbits have seen their clever merriment, and their ability to foil the expectations of their humans. Have you ever been outwitted by a rabbit? If so, you join a long line of humans in history.

> **Cat's Meow**
>
> Animals do not betray; they do not exploit; they do not oppress; they do not enslave; they do not sin. They have their being, and their being is honest, and who can say this of man?
> —Taylor Caldwell, from *Great Lion of God*

The Bull and the Cow

In ancient Mesopotamia, humans were already yoking oxen for use as draft animals, and humankind has relied so heavily on cattle for so many centuries that it is hard to imagine life without them. It is the cow's very capacity for sustenance, both in the form of milk and meat, that has glorified it to cultures throughout history. Several ancient Norse cow goddesses emerged in this icy climate to nourish the mythological giants of this region, an area where dairy cows help to sustain life.

The Egyptian bovine goddess Hathor, sometimes called the Celestial Cow, represented creativity and was sometimes pictured with a headdress holding a solar disk. Some archeological evidence suggests that Hathor existed even before Egyptian culture, as a pre-historical cow divinity. She was the original cow goddess whose influence spread to many other cultures including Greece and Rome, and she might have been absorbed into the Christian representation of the Virgin Mary.

In India, the cow is sacred and honored for the milk she gives, and the Hindu religion prohibits killing, eating, or even injuring a cow.

The bull is a symbol of virility and power. The Minotaur was a half-bull, half-human creature, son of a human and a bull who lived in a labyrinth in Greek mythology, and this human/bovine amalgamation could represent both human's fascination with and fear of our similarity to animals.

> **Cat's Meow**
>
> I don't like when other animals come into my home. Please keep them out. Oh, and I would like a cushion.
>
> —Iggy the pig

The Lizard and the Snake

No lizard is as deified as the basilisk, sometimes called the "Jesus Lizard," because it can run on water. Originally a Gnostic deity, myth tells that the basilisk freezes (or, in the *Harry Potter* movie, "petrifies") any who see it. The basilisk is sometimes represented with a snake's head and the body and wings of a dragon.

Of course, the serpent in the Garden of Eden in the first book of the New Testament was the instrument of the devil, coaxing Eve to take a bite of the fruit God had forbidden her to eat.

Yet not all reptile images are negative. The snake is often a sign of healing and rejuvenation, and still serves as a universal symbol of the physician in the form of two intertwined snakes, or the caduceus symbol. This ancient Sumerian symbol represented healing, and similar symbols can be found in ancient Greek, Indian, Aztec, and North American cultures.

Those of us who keep snakes as pets remain fascinated by their mysterious forms, their hypnotic eyes, their limbless, muscled, gorgeously mosaiced bodies. Few can deny the snake's mysterious beauty, even as they quake in fear at the very thought of the snake!

CAUTION **Doggone!**

You could learn from specific fears you have about an animal. Why do spiders, snakes, or large black dogs frighten you? Was it a past experience, or does a quality of that animal make you feel uncomfortable or vulnerable? What does it symbolize for you? Even if you can't conquer your fear, you could learn to understand it. One friend of ours feared spiders so much that he bought a pet tarantula. He is now a respected—and fearless—arachnid breeder.

The Fish

A fish tank filled with tropical fish and plants make a relaxing addition to any room, but in ancient Celtic mythology, the fish was associated with knowledge and secrets. It seems a secret knowledge indeed, to breathe water instead of air, and fish have fed, foiled, and fascinated humans for thousands of years.

The symbol of the fish is often associated with Jesus, that "fisher of men," but predates Christianity by many centuries. Many cultures worshipped fish deities, and the zodiac symbol of Pisces, a water sign, is characterized by intuitiveness and deep emotion.

The Biblical story of Jonah, in which Jonah is swallowed by a whale, is a Judeo-Christian myth about fish, and although few people have whales as personal friends, the fish in our own tanks might seem more familiar the more "fish stories" we know.

Cat's Meow

And God said, "Let us make man in our image, after our likeness: and let them have dominion over the fish of the sea, and over the fowl of the air, and over the cattle, and over all the earth and over every creeping thing that creepeth upon the earth."
—Genesis 1:26

Fish have also made great waves in classic western literature as worthy foes in the great struggle for life in the face of death, from Herman Melville's great and notorious whale, Moby Dick, to the mammoth, spirited, but ultimately defeated marlin in Hemingway's *Old Man and the Sea*.

The Arachnid and the Insect

Arachnids and insects serve many functions in the great food chain, but humans have in many ways feared arachnids and insects. Spiders, scorpions, bees, worms, roaches, and centipedes: Although many people keep each of these creatures as pets or breed and sell them, far more fear them. We keep some of them as pets while purging others from our homes.

In the past, many cultures have honored insects and arachnids, but arachnids in particular fascinate humans, perhaps because of their dramatic exoskeletons and sometimes-fatal venom.

Yet arachnids often represent protection and knowledge. The Ashanti people of Africa had a trickster deity called Ananse, also called the "Enormous Spider." The Ashanti people thought Ananse created the sun, moon, stars, day, and night, and was an intercessory between humans and the gods. Native Americans have a similar deity called Annancy, also a spider.

Spider Woman was an important holy figure in many Native American tribes, representing both a creation figure and a trickster figure.

The venomous scorpion also captures the human imagination. The Egyptian scorpion goddess, Serqet, lived in the underworld, protecting the mummies and guarding the jars containing their viscera. She also sent scorpions to protect Isis and to overcome an evil serpent who threatened the sun god, Ra.

The Nicaraguan creator and great mother goddess, Itoki, was a scorpion that lived at the end of the Milky Way and sent newly born souls to their bodies while receiving the souls of those who just died.

Finding Your Power Animal

What is your *power animal*? In some Native American cultures, adolescent boys traveled alone into the woods on vision quests and waited to meet their power (or totem) animal. The animal they would encounter would be the animal they would forever call their own, the animal that would offer them guidance throughout life. Sometimes, this animal would speak to them and give them their adult name.

Pet Speak

A **power animal** or totem animal is an animal that has particular significance to you, and whose qualities relate to yours or personally inspire you.

Everyone can have a power animal, and it needn't be the species of your favorite pet. Your power animal is the animal species whose energy, intention, and spirit speak to yours.

In Debbie's workshops, she teaches that we each have many power animals that come into our lives to help us with different stages, as well as a power animal that stays with us throughout our entire lives. Knowing your power animals can help you in your animal communication efforts.

When Debbie was a child, most of the pictures that portray her show her holding a statue of a deer. Her parents couldn't pry that deer away from her. She felt so drawn to deer that she was compelled to hold an image of a deer whenever she could, and she still has many of those deer statues to this day. Now, Debbie understands that the deer was one of her power animals, keeping her safe throughout childhood.

When Debbie first started doing animal communication as a profession, her power animal at that time was a white lion, which stood for courage, the kind of courage it takes to launch into your own business and admit to everyone around you, proudly, what you are doing. It took a lot of courage for Debbie to "come out of the closet" about being a pet psychic, because not everybody takes such a job seriously. The white lion helped Debbie to stay true to what she knew was her calling.

When Eve was younger, she was obsessed with otters. She loved their playfulness and their joy. Even the adult otters knew how to play, and to this day, Eve still feels a special kinship with the otter, a power animal that has helped her be a great playmate for her two young sons, as well as keep a sense of joy and wonder in the fun of daily life.

Debbie has a deck of Medicine cards that portray animals and what they mean. When she is going through a difficult situation in her life, or has hit a crossroads and seeks guidance, she pulls a card from the deck and reads about the animal she has drawn. It never fails—the advice contained within the card always helps her along her way.

Finding your power animal can be as simple as picking one, or as complex and mystical as setting out on your own vision quest and waiting for your power animal to find you. When you see animals, as they cross your path or bring themselves to your attention, they could be sending you messages. Pay attention to the animals that cross your path. If you are walking or driving and an animal goes out of its way to get your attention, pay attention!

For instance, if you suddenly see a little rabbit, this might mean you are holding back from facing a particular fear. Or maybe you see a hawk dip down from the sky. This could be a message to see a particular situation in your life from a higher perspective, to soar above or to warn you to be aware of various signals and signs coming your way. A hawk might also be a messenger that more is to come, so pay attention to the changes that happen in your life after you see a hawk.

Animals tend to bring other kinds of particular messages. Many of these you can figure out as you go, but just to get you started, here are some of the messages and emotions commonly associated with different power animals you may encounter along the way. While different books on this subject attribute different meanings to some of these animals, and while an animal's meaning may be unique to an individual, these are some of the meanings Debbie has discerned and intuitively discovered. For more information on the meanings of power animals, see Appendix A:

- Deer: You will encounter, or may need to display, more gentleness and kindness.

- Butterfly: You may be entering a new stage of life or a transformation. See the inner beauty in things.

- Wolf: You may soon encounter a teacher, or you need to be a teacher to someone else.

- Dragonfly: Things may not be as they seem. You may be under the influence of an illusion, or you may soon encounter travelers from different realms.

- Armadillo: You need or will find protection, or you need or will find a way to erect important boundaries in your relationships. An armadillo can also show you that you are afraid of being hurt.

- Ant: You need or will soon find patience, cooperation, and teamwork, or the ability to allow time to accomplish something important.

- Dolphin: You need to be reminded to breathe and to communicate. Dolphins also remind us to reunite our spirit with the feeling of joy.

- Hummingbird: You will be blessed with, or need to find, a more delicate balance of happiness and energy in your life.

- Black panther: You will learn to embrace the blind path that life may lead us on and to leap into your life purpose with trust and confidence.

> **Cat's Meow**
> I like to lie in the middle of the floor so people have to walk around me. It gives me great power!
> —Seamus, an orange tabby cat

Sometimes, you might not notice an animal for awhile, or you might live in a place where you seldom see animals, but there are other ways to seek your own power animals. Try some of these exercises.

Power Animal Meditation

In her workshops, Debbie teaches the following meditation to help people find their power animal. Have a friend read this out loud while you meditate, or record your own voice speaking the meditation in a slow, gentle voice, and use it whenever you need it:

Inhale deeply. Fill up your belly, chest, and throat with breath, then exhale deeply. Repeat five times. Let all the tension flow from your body with each exhalation.

Imagine you are walking outside in nature, in a place that you love or a place you imagine: your own backyard, on a favorite trail, near the water, or whatever natural place inspires you. As you walk down the path, you see a bridge in front of you. Take a minute to look at the bridge. What does it look like? What is it made of? What is its shape? Slowly walk across this bridge. As you walk, hear the sound of the birds singing, and the smell of wildflowers in the air. Feel the bridge under your feet. Does it creak, or sway, or stand solid and silent?

As you reach the other side of the bridge, you see a path and decide to follow it. Notice the scenery along the path. What is the sky like? The trees, the plants? Spend some time envisioning the world around you.

At last, you arrive at a clearing where you see a bench surrounded by beautiful flowers. The sun is shining, but the air is crisp, cool, and clean, with a gentle breeze. You sit on the bench and close your eyes. You offer gratitude for finding such a beautiful place, and you know in your heart you can come here any time.

Today, you decide that you would like to meet your power animal, and you speak this intention. You close your eyes and say: "I want to meet my power animal, to help me better communicate with animals." Suddenly, you hear something coming toward you, and you await the appearance of your power animal with eagerness and anticipation. You slowly open your eyes and there is your power animal, approaching you. Take some time to appreciate the qualities of this being. What does it look like? What is it here to offer you?

[Take a few moments here to observe and meditate about your power animal]

Now you know it is time to bid farewell. You can return whenever you like. Thank the animal or animals you met and stand up from the bench. Slowly walk back down the path to the bridge. Notice the animals, birds, and insects you see along the way. Smile and inhale deeply and exhale deeply and cross over the bridge. Feel the earth below your feet and the sky above, and the way you move as an integral part of the natural world around you.

Take a few deep breaths until you feel grounded and centered in your body. When you feel you have fully returned, open your eyes, rest for a moment, and then if you wish, immediately write down the experience you just had so you don't forget.

Nature Walk

Another way to find your power animal is to take an actual walk in nature. Spend some leisure time in a park, a forest, or a nearby wood or field. Find a place to sit and relax. Breathe deeply and open yourself to the natural world around you. Observe everything you can: the birds that fly overhead, the squirrels that run along the branches, the butterflies floating past, the ants making their way through the grass. As you watch the animal life around you, concentrate on which animal seems to speak to you, which you are drawn to, what you notice most.

Maybe you will encounter an animal you wouldn't normally see on your average walk: a deer, a bobcat, or a bald eagle. Or maybe you will see wildlife you normally see but never really noticed before. Either way, keep yourself open. The animal that comes forward in your consciousness is your power animal.

Is Your Power Animal All Around You?

If you have a special relationship with an animal already, this could be your power animal. If you and your dog have an unusual connection, or if you have loved horses for as long as you can remember, of if you are perpetually fascinated by tarantulas or finches or can't imagine having any pet other than a rabbit, you might already know your power animal. Maybe, like Debbie, you've always collected pictures and figurines of a certain animal, or felt a special camaraderie with one, the way Eve did. Think about how the animal you love relates to you, and what you have in common. What about this animal empowers you to be a more complete person? What inspires you about the animal? How does your relationship with this animal enrich you? What characteristics do you share?

Horse Sense

The more time you spend in nature, the more you will feel connected to the natural world. Make a daily effort to step outside and breathe the fresh air, feel the sun or rain or breeze, and see nature around you: a tree, flowers, squirrels, the first robin, a cardinal in a snowy tree. These natural connections will help you tune in more effectively to your pet.

Creating Your Totem Pole

Although you probably don't have the opportunity to hire an authentic *totem pole* carver to create a personal totem pole for you, you can envision or even draw or build one for yourself. A traditional totem pole is a carved wooden pole displaying family crests and power or totem animals or other symbols or figures that represent a family or an individual. You can create your own personal totem pole, or a representation of one, in a less traditional but equally meaningful way.

One easy way to do this is to find pictures or symbols of the animals or other natural objects (trees, mountains, stones, lakes) you relate to and create a *totem* collage to keep in a special place, either displayed or hidden for your eyes only. Glue the pictures, one below the other, starting with your power animal. Or you can just "collect" your totems in your mind and envision what your totem pole or collection of totems would include.

Cat's Meow

A **totem** is an animal, or even a plant or other natural object such as a stone or a mountain, that serves as an emblem of an individual or of a family or clan that is thought to represent that person or group and serve as protector and sometimes as originator or creator of the family line. A **totem pole** contains a series of symbolic representations of animals, plants, and/or natural objects and is typically erected outside a dwelling.

What else should you include in your personal collection of totem animals and objects? Even though you have fixed on a personal power animal, you probably relate to many other kinds of animals as well. Does your zodiac sign represent an animal? Pisces is the fish; Aries is the bull; Capricorn is the ram; Leo is the lion; Cancer is the crab. Maybe one of these animals speaks to you.

Maybe you admire the beauty of the horse, even though you've never ridden one. Include one in your totem. Maybe you cherish the loyalty of the dog or the independence of the wolf, the autonomy of the cat or the speed of the cheetah. Collect favorite animals, special animals, the animals that speak to your spirit, and include them in your totem.

Your totem can change over time. You can revise it or completely redo it. The point is to keep it in your mind and in your heart so that you always feel a special, spiritual connection to the animals in the natural world, and the earth itself, of which we all are an integral and connected part.

The Least You Need to Know

◆ Pet owners consider their pets to be more "family member" than "animal."

◆ You can communicate with any kind of animal, not just dogs, cats, and horses.

- Many sacred and mythological traditions use animals as symbols and deities.

- Your power animal is the animal you relate to or that inspires you.

- Create your own personal totem pole by drawing or making a collage of the different kinds of animals that have meaning for or "speak" to you.

Chapter 3

Animals Communicate with Us Psychically All the Time

In This Chapter

- ◆ How Debbie discovered she could "talk" to animals
- ◆ What it's like to communicate telepathically with an animal
- ◆ Finding and choosing a professional pet psychic
- ◆ Getting the most out of your communication session

Just how does somebody become a pet psychic? As a kid, Debbie's greatest wish was to be able to talk to the animals, just like Dr. Doolittle. She used to spend lots of her spare time working for people at various barns, just so she would have the opportunity to be close to the horses and other animals that lived there.

Debbie distinctly remembers sitting in a little Shetland pony's stall for hours, thinking that if she was stubborn enough and waited long enough, he would say something to her. Little did she know that he was speaking to her all along. It just wasn't in the form of verbal words. Debbie wishes she would have known then what she knows now!

Debbie's Story

Debbie remembers hearing about animal communication, and thinking it sounded too good to be true. Was her lifelong dream, her greatest fantasy, a real possibility? She knew Dr. Doolittle was just a fictional character and that no horse was going to start chattering away to her like Mr. Ed.

When Debbie heard that animal communicators held workshops that taught people how to "talk" to animals, she scoffed at the whole idea. One day, however, a few of Debbie's friends decided to take one of these animal communication seminars, so she grudgingly agreed to join them. That day changed her life forever, providing Debbie with a life purpose and a whole new view of the world she always thought she knew.

Debbie will never forget her first validated conversation with an animal, at an animal communication workshop at Spring Farm Cares Animal Sanctuary in Clinton, New York. The class took a break, during which the students were to go off and attempt to communicate with the animals on the farm. The class had been inspirational, and Debbie was excited to try her first animal communication. With pen and paper in hand, she marched out to the barn.

As she entered the barn, she heard a lot of things, but felt pulled over in the direction of a little goat who had his front feet up on his gate. As Debbie approached him, she heard, from inside, a voice that said, "Don't ya think I'm handsome?"

"Well, yes!" she responded. She chuckled to herself, thinking she must surely be making this up in her own mind, or losing her mind … or both! Debbie wondered if she should even tell her husband about what she had heard. "He'd have me locked up!" she thought to herself.

Then the goat kept talking.

"Your pants are funny," he said.

"Excuse me?" Debbie looked down at her pants. She had to admit they were probably justification for an arrest by the fashion police. Flowered stretch pants? Debbie wondered what she could have been thinking, to make a fashion choice that a goat would criticize!

Then the goat continued. "So what do you think of my ornament?"

Huh? Ornaments? Debbie wasn't sure where that came from. Then the goat graced her with his final thought. "Move along now, other people want to talk to me, you know."

Well! Debbie figured she'd move along then. Feeling slightly baffled by the experience, Debbie moved on and had "conversations" with some of the other animals—conversations she enjoyed, but wasn't entirely sure weren't products of her imagination.

When the time for animal communicating was over, the class reconvened to share what had happened in their attempts to talk to the animals. Debbie was nervous, but finally summoned the courage to tell the class what she had heard. The teacher laughed and told Debbie that this goat always has hay or grass hanging from his horns, and that the barn staff always remarks that he has nice ornaments hanging from his horns.

Ornaments!

Debbie's jaw dropped. Had she really done it? She hadn't heard that anywhere. Suddenly she knew, at that moment, that animal communication was indeed real. She hadn't been making it up in her mind. She had been hearing those animals talking to her. She had been talking to the animals!

From that day forward, Debbie practiced daily with the enthusiasm of a child. She formed practice groups, read every book she could on the subject, and began to strengthen her telepathic "muscle" to the point where she felt she could actually help people with their own animals. And that's just what she does!

Cat's Meow

I am a star. I just have to convince everybody else.

—Alabaster Moon, a horse considering a show career

Some people feel that one must be born a gifted psychic to communicate with animals, but as Debbie realized, everyone has this innate ability. Some people do tend to pick it up faster or take to the process more easily. Some might get pictures and not words, or words and not pictures. However, believing that you can do it helps to dissolve the barriers your consciousness erects in your mind, the barriers that keep you from realizing your own psychic abilities. Continue to believe in yourself, and your psychic abilities will continue to develop.

Debbie worked hard to develop her abilities. She didn't just wake up one day and "hear the animals." She wishes it was that easy! However, because Debbie has gone through the process, from skeptic to practicing pet psychic, she knows what learning it takes and what practice it requires, and she can help you learn how to do it, too.

What Pet Psychic Communication Feels Like

What does it feel like to have a psychic communication with an animal? This is one of the first questions people ask Debbie during her seminars, but the answer isn't easy. Psychic communication "feels" different for different people, but in all cases, the communication is a subtle one, which can come in the form of words, pictures, moving pictures, emotions, feelings, tastes, and smells.

For instance, maybe you ask your animal a question, and in reply, you will "hear" an answer in your head that sounds a lot like an answer a person would give you. Something like, "Hey, how's it going?" or "That dinner was really disgusting. Can we have something else next time?"

Or maybe you will see an image of a special place your pet loves, or hear a sound familiar to him. If he is in pain, you may feel the pain in your own body.

CAUTION

Doggone!

Sometimes animal communication involves pain—from just a tickle to intense pain—when an animal transmits a particular feeling to you. However, don't be afraid of this pain, or you could block the communication. Open yourself to what the animal is feeling. Any sensation probably won't be as severe as what the animal feels, but it will be in a corresponding place on your body. Also, the pain is short-lived, only transmitted to give you the information.

For example, Debbie was called as a last ditch effort to save a stallion named Winger. Winger had been classified as violent. He had already seriously injured one person and had badly hurt his trainer. When Winger's owner, Sheila, called Debbie to communicate with this stallion, what Debbie witnessed was not a violent horse, but a horse with a sane mind and gentle demeanor who was in extraordinary pain.

When Debbie connected with Winger, he immediately began to show her, through images, that he had been beaten in his stall and hit over the head. The person who was now training him was so scared of him that he handled him roughly and with great fear. Winger told Debbie that his body hurt badly. Then he sent Debbie the pain he was feeling so she could understand.

Debbie was immediately struck with an intense headache and her body started to ache. Winger showed her how he would get blinding headaches that felt as if a black wall were rising up in front of his eyes. When these headaches descended, Winger would panic and strike out at anything in his path. Debbie saw how his aggression rose up out of fear and pain.

Debbie suggested Sheila move Winger out of the trainer's facility immediately. She explained that Winger was only being aggressive due to pain and abuse, but that once these two factors left his life, he could change.

She then suggested that Sheila seek the help of a veterinary chiropractor specializing in horses because she felt that Winger's head was badly out of alignment, causing the severe headaches and loss of vision. His pelvis also felt out of alignment, crooked and misplaced. In addition, Winger had a cut on his left front leg that needed attention.

Of course, Debbie isn't a vet! She can't diagnose illness, and would never claim to do so. Yet because of the pain Winger sent to her, she was able to alert Winger's owner to exactly those issues that needed attention.

After a few months, Debbie received a wonderful follow-up from Winger and his owner. Sheila had moved Winger out of the trainer's facility that weekend, taken him to a chiropractor, and confirmed that Winger's head was indeed badly in need of an adjustment, along with his pelvis and back. Sheila told Debbie that Winger's temperament had changed immediately, and she now trusts Winger enough to let her 13-year-old daughter, Pam, safely into the paddock with him for stroking and attention. Since this time, Winger has gone on to sire several beautiful foals.

Horse Sense

In many animals (and in humans!), pain engenders aggression. Consider pain as a factor when trying to communicate with an aggressive animal. Are you receiving any pain sensations?

Then there was Sophie. A client named Karen called Debbie, at her wit's end about her Labrador Retriever, Sophie. Karen had to crate Sophie every time she left the house or Sophie would literally destroy the house. She had chewed on speaker wires, couches, chairs, and many more of Karen's possessions.

When Debbie connected with Sophie, she told Debbie that the reason for her destructive behavior was because she was very anxious when her person left and she didn't know what to do with all this nervous energy, so she began to chew anything in sight. Debbie explained to Sophie that she had a very important job to do while her person was away. She was to watch over the inside of the house and make sure everything was in order. Debbie explained to Sophie that when her people came home at night and saw the great job she did, she would get rewarded.

Debbie chatted with Sophie a little bit more and made sure she understood the behavior involved in doing her job. Debbie did her best to fill Sophie with pride regarding her new job. (When trying to change an undesirable behavior, it's important to explain to the animals what type of behavior is acceptable, rather than what type of behavior you don't want them to do. We will go into more detail about this in Chapter 14.) Sure enough, Sophie never chewed anything in the house again, and eventually learned how to spend increasingly longer periods outside her kennel when Karen was away. Karen also sensed a new calmness in Sophie's demeanor and behavior.

Doggone!

Of all the species Debbie has communicated with, she has found more tragedies and misunderstandings between horses and humans than any other kind of animal. Nevertheless, plenty of dogs, cats, birds, and other animals often live with suffering because their humans simply don't get what's wrong. The better people can learn to communicate with animals, the less frustration, pain, and abuse animals will have to endure.

A regular client of Debbie's asked her to talk to his new filly. She was wonderful in every way, but he was hoping Debbie could convince her to learn how to go the bathroom in one place in her stall. She tended to be a very messy stall keeper. Even Debbie was unsure if she would comply, but the client has since told Debbie that since their talk, the filly has indeed used only one corner of her stall as her "bathroom." Debbie has since had this talk with her horses, thinking they, too, could improve their habits. They just laughed at her. Oh well. She tried!

Experiences like these keep Debbie inspired to continue her work as an animal communicator, but they also show the many ways animals can communicate with us, even in a single session: They can send us words, pictures, images, and even very specific pain.

How to Find a Professional Animal Communicator

As you develop and refine your own animal communication skills, you might want to experience a session with a seasoned pet psychic, to see how it works and to get some insight into your pet's behavior, personality, and health status.

Believe it or not, it's easy to find a professional animal communicator. So many seminars and courses teach the skill that people practice animal communication in many cities. Also, because animal communicators often do readings over the phone (so they can tell you what your pet has to say), anyone can have a reading done easily.

Penelope Smith, one of the leading pioneers of this field, has a website (www.animaltalk.net) that lists communicators by state along with their contact information. Many of these communicators follow the code of ethics that she developed (we'll talk more about this in a moment). Often communicators have websites where you can find out about fees, how they work, testimonial statements, and so on. You may feel particularly drawn to a particular communicator this way.

However, one of the best ways to find a "good" pet psychic is through word of mouth or referrals from friends. Many established animal communicators don't advertise and some are booked weeks in advance. One of the greatest compliments an animal communicator can receive is a referral from a former client and repeat customers.

So how do you know you are hiring a "good" pet psychic? How do you know you aren't getting ripped off, or thrown into the hands of someone who only *thinks* they are a pet psychic? These are common fears, but there are ways to tell the authentic animal communicators from the inevitable charlatans who pop up in any business to take advantage of people and give those with more noble intentions a bad name. Consider the following before making your choice:

♦ Beware of anyone who *insists* that you agree to a pre-set number of sessions in order to solve a problem. Each case is different, and an authentic pet psychic will handle each client and situation on its own merit. A good communicator will be able to uncover why undesirable behavior occurs by asking the animal what will help correct this behavior, or by communicating a mutual compromise between human and animal. A good communicator will get the person involved with the communication session, empowering the person and animal to come together to mutually resolve the issue.

> **Horse Sense**
>
> Remember that communicators can be wrong. Just as with any type of communication, sometimes one or both parties misinterpret the feelings and thoughts of the other. Communication is an extraordinary tool but should not be relied upon solely if you feel in your heart the information you are getting does not add up.

♦ Most communicators do not have a degree in veterinary medicine, and therefore, clients should always use their information in conjunction with a qualified vet. Many vets have become more open to animal communication. Debbie has had many vets and chiropractors confirm her health readings on animals, but she is careful never to overstep boundaries when it comes to a health diagnosis. Debbie always follows up with whatever information the animal gives her by specifically stating that she is not a vet, and that she recommends the person speak to their vet or animal chiropractor. Communicators can describe to you where the pain is, or where the affected organs are. They can tell you how an injury happened, and sometimes why. The animal might even have some advice as to what helps the problem and what hinders it.

♦ Beware of anyone charging outrageous rates. Most communicators charge between $30 and $100 dollars, depending on the amount of time a session lasts.

◆ All communicators work a little differently. Some require pictures, some like to communicate with the animal in person, some don't want to know too much background information, and others prefer to know the animal's history. Some communicators do the consultation while you are on the telephone with them, as if it is a 3-way conversation. Others will get your questions in advance, connect with your animal, and then contact you to discuss. One is not necessarily better than the other, it is just the preferred method that the communicator uses. Any communicator should be happy to share his or her methods with you beforehand. You may be more comfortable working with some methods than others.

Horse Sense

A good communicator will, to the best of his or her ability, communicate with you and your animals with truth and compassion. Pet communicators won't just tell you what you want to hear, but they will communicate the truth in a sensitive and empathetic fashion.

◆ A good communicator will not judge you or your animal or have any preconceived notions about what you "should" be doing. Pet communicators are there to bridge the gap of understanding so that problems can be resolved, harmony is achieved, and healing is accomplished.

◆ Some communicators specialize in certain areas, such as lost animals, birds, or behavioral issues, and some communicators do all of the above. It is important to feel comfortable with the person you choose, and to choose someone whose specialty matches your concerns.

In addition, a good communicator should abide by a code of ethics that animal communicators widely accept. Debbie and many other animal communicators believe in and agree to abide by the following code of ethics, developed by animal communicator guru Penelope Smith, and reprinted here with her kind permission:

CODE OF ETHICS for INTERSPECIES TELEPATHIC COMMUNICATORS
Formulated in 1990 by Penelope Smith, www.animaltalk.net

Our motivation is compassion for all beings and a desire to help all species understand each other better, particularly to help restore the lost human ability to freely and directly communicate with other species.

We honor those that come to us for help, not judging, condemning, or invalidating them for their mistakes or misunderstanding but honoring their desire for change and harmony.

We know that to keep this work as pure and harmonious as possible requires that we continually grow spiritually. We realize that telepathic communication can be clouded or overlaid by our own unfulfilled emotions, critical judgments, or lack of love for self and others. We walk in humility, willing to recognize and clear up our own errors in understanding others' communication (human and non-human alike).

We cultivate knowledge and understanding of the dynamics of human, non-human, and interspecies behavior and relationships, to increase the good results of our work. We get whatever education and/or personal help we need to do our work effectively, with compassion, respect, joy, and harmony.

We seek to draw out the best in everyone and increase understanding toward mutual resolution of problems. We go only where we are asked to help, so that others are receptive and we truly can help. We respect the feelings and ideas of others and work for interspecies understanding, not pitting one side against another but walking with compassion for all. We acknowledge the things that we cannot change and continue where our work can be most effective.

We respect the privacy of people and animal companions we work with, and honor their desire for confidentiality.

While doing our best to help, we allow others their own dignity and help them to help their animal companions. We cultivate understanding and ability in others, rather than dependence on our ability. We offer people ways to be involved in understanding and growth with their fellow beings of other species.

We acknowledge our limitations, seeking help from other professionals as needed. It is not our job to name and treat diseases, and we refer people to veterinarians for diagnosis of physical illness. We may relay animals' ideas, feelings, pains, symptoms, as they describe them or as we feel or perceive them, and this may be helpful to veterinary health professionals. We may also assist through handling of stresses, counseling, and other gentle healing methods. We let clients decide for themselves how to work with healing their animal companions' distress, disease, or injury, given all the information available.

Cat's Meow

Why do you watch TV that makes you cry?

—Jerri the cat, when asked if she had any advice for her person

The goal of any consultation, lecture, workshop, or interspecies experience is more communication, balance, compassion, understanding, and communion among all beings. We follow our heart, honoring the spirit and life of all beings as one.

Getting the Most Out of Your Communication Session

Once you've selected the animal communicator you feel comfortable with, prepare for your communication session to make it the most productive experience possible for both you and your pet. Here are some tips to get you in the right frame of mind:

◆ Keep an open mind. If you spend your communication thinking that the whole business is surely a hoax, then you are closing off your own mind and blocking your pet's desire and willingness to speak freely. Animals are incredibly intuitive and can sense your hesitation, doubt, or other barriers. When people put up energetic walls, it slows down the exchange of information and inhibits the communication. We're not saying you shouldn't be a skeptic! Being skeptical is healthy, and Debbie admits to being one of the biggest skeptics of all. However, there is a time and place for skepticism, and smack in the middle of your animal communication session is neither the time nor the place. Let yourself analyze the experience later, but stay open and positive as it happens if you want to get the most out of your session. You owe it to your animal to remain open during the process. When you project a positive, enthusiastic energy about the conversation, your animal will feel this and join in your enthusiasm. This makes the connection for the communicator much stronger and results in a clearer telepathic exchange.

◆ Don't give out too much information in the beginning. People sometimes call or e-mail Debbie with their animal's full history or every ache and pain and diagnosis, then ask her to do a body scan. Debbie prefers not to know too many details in the beginning, so that she can see what surfaces without any preconceived notions. She likes the animal to have first dibs on telling or showing her what is bothering him or her. After Debbie gets the animal's side of things, she might ask the person what areas they were worried about, in case she missed something. Then, she can go back and zoom in on specific areas. Feedback from the person is very important, of course, to keep the connection strong and the animal focused. However, sometimes first impressions are the most powerful and accurate.

Horse Sense

Listen to what your animals are saying during the consult. Some people don't want to accept or listen to what their animal is trying to say. They only see their side and refuse to compromise. This erects an immediate and powerful barrier to the relationship.

◆ Don't be afraid to validate what your animal communicator says to you. Validation helps the session flow better and adds valuable positive energy to the situation. Being too emotional over an issue or situation inhibits the communication. The very next day after an animal passes, for example, people often ask Debbie to communicate with their animal to see if they are okay. Debbie usually asks people to wait at least a week, so that the animal can take time to transition, but even more so, so that the people can have time to grieve and handle the strong emotions that could interfere with a clear communication.

◆ Don't expect a communicator to "fix" the problem. Having an animal means being in a relationship. Both parties need to listen and work toward a mutually beneficial compromise. A communicator can counsel the animal, voice the animal's concerns, and try to mediate a solution. A communicator can't just "fix" the problem with some magic wand. Many undesirable behaviors can be corrected after a communication session, but others take time and patience.

The Least You Need to Know

◆ Debbie used to be a skeptic, but discovered that she could actually communicate with animals. You can do it, too!

◆ Psychic communications from animals can come in the form of words, pictures, moving pictures, smells, tastes, or tactile sensations, such as pain in a particular part of your body.

◆ Many practicing pet psychics are available, but good ones won't judge you, won't overcharge, and will judge each situation on its own merits.

◆ To get the most out of your communication session, stay positive and keep an open mind. You can always critique the conversation later.

4

A Psychic Conversation with Your Pet

In This Chapter

◆ The different modes of psychic communication

◆ The many ways in which animals are in tune with the world around them

◆ Exercises to test the way you receive psychic information

◆ Exercises to help you begin to access the different modes of psychic communication for yourself

The world is an amazing place, filled with images, visions, sounds, smells, tastes, and textures, not to mention the emotions such a sensory festival inspires in the creatures who live within it.

In psychic communication, those senses, which we so often take for granted or even ignore, become of the utmost importance. As we've mentioned before, psychic communication is incredibly subtle, compared to the more obvious spoken or written word. Are we so caught up in what we tell each other and see right there in front of us that we have lost touch with those quieter, softer, more nuanced forms of communication?

Just because you've developed a habit of relying on only some of the forms of communication available to you doesn't mean you can't retrain your mind and body to get back in touch with a wider range of communication. Such work is essential for refining and developing your psychic "muscle." In this chapter, we will consider the many ways communication happens, to help you tune in to *all* the channels available on the psychic satellite dish that is *you*.

The Many Modes of Psychic Communication

Because humans are so centered on verbal and written communication, we forget how many other modes exist and are so easily accessible. But the animals haven't forgotten. They often send messages using many different modes, and if we don't learn how to read those messages, we won't "hear" the message.

This concept is difficult for some people to understand. We get all kinds of questions like, "How can you get messages from animals in complex human English?" or "How does an animal know how to send a smell or an image?" or "Animals wouldn't really know how to describe that!"

When Debbie asks an animal a specific question, she gets an answer that is like a ball of energy. She receives that energy and then tries to interpret it.

Every individual has different telepathic strengths. Some people see images, some people hear words, some people feel, and many have combinations of different sensory skills they possess. The animal sends the message, but the way you receive the message has to do more with *you*, and not necessarily the way the animal sent it.

In other words, two different people could speak with the same animal and get two slightly different answers to a question, even if the animal sent them the same message, because the way each person receives and interprets that message could vary.

Horse Sense

Interpreting a psychic message is like going to a foreign film with subtitles. Eve saw a movie in Chinese once with a friend who spoke fluent Mandarin. Her friend kept telling her when the subtitles, in her opinion, didn't exactly capture what was being said. These were the interpretations of two different people, because when one language changes into another, or one mode of communication (energy) changes into another (words or pictures or feelings), no exact translation guide exists. The translation depends on the sender's and receiver's feelings, biases, strengths, and weaknesses.

For example, say you and Debbie both ask Bingo the dog what his favorite game was. You might see an image of a ball, or a moving picture of a ball sailing through the air. Debbie might hear the words, "playing fetch!" but not know what the object used to play fetch would be. You might describe the experience by saying, "Bingo loves to play ball," and Debbie might say, "Bingo loves to fetch things." Each of you described the message you received in different ways, even though both are equally valid interpretations of the message Bingo sent out to you. (Animals aren't always entirely objective in what they send out, either!)

To better understand the different ways of receiving telepathic information from your pet, let's look a little more closely at each, and why tuning via a particular mode can help you better relate to and receive messages from your pet.

Clairvoyance

Clairvoyance is seeing pictures or scenes in your mind. This can be an effective way to understand a message from your animal because animals often have a highly developed clairvoyant sense. Many animals also have keener or differently oriented vision than humans. For example, some animals may not see colors as vividly, but they can see movement from very far away. Others have intense perceptions of colors.

Animals also both feel and see the energy people emit. Some animals have described to Debbie the color of a person's energy. It seems some animals, like some people, actually perceive the auras of the people (and probably the other animals) they encounter. Sick animals have sometimes told Debbie what color of energy would help them heal.

> **Horse Sense**
>
> I guard him in dreamtime, to make sure all his dreams are happy ones.
>
> —Samwise, a Golden Retriever, when asked why he always slept in the little boy's bedroom

Ferrus, a beautiful orange tabby cat, was very ill with kidney disease and old age. His person, Melanie, contacted Debbie to see what she could do to help him during this difficult time. When Debbie connected with Ferrus, he told her that Melanie was using her hands to help heal him, and that the violet energy she was sending felt wonderful. Debbie told Melanie what Ferrus had related, and Debbie could almost hear Melanie smiling across the phone line.

Melanie explained that she had just started taking *Reiki* classes and was practicing on Ferrus. The color she felt inclined to send Ferrus for healing was indeed violet. This beautiful conformation of her efforts showed Melanie that Ferrus was indeed receiving and enjoying the healing she sent him.

Pet Speak

Reiki is a form of energy healing in which the Reiki practitioner moves his or her hands just over the body to manipulate, free, and channel universal healing energy. Although traditionally a human healing modality, Reiki also works on pets, and many Reiki practitioners willingly treat pets as well as humans.

Animals can also see things humans can't usually see. Many times, animals have shown Debbie images of apparitions (spirits/ghosts) they see in their homes. They show Debbie where the apparition appears and what it looks like. Although people occasionally do see apparitions, this kind of vision is common for animals.

A woman named Beverly called Debbie to talk to her dog, Tucker, a Husky/Lab mix. Tucker seemed depressed and refused to leave the woman's bedroom. Whenever he did, he acted frightened and nervous. Beverly didn't know what was wrong, and feared Tucker might be ill.

When Debbie connected with Tucker, he showed her that a ghost was wandering the home. He sensed the change in the air in the home when the ghost was near, and it frightened him. Debbie asked Tucker to show her what the ghost looked like, and Tucker sent Debbie an image of a teenaged girl with long hair.

Debbie is always a little apprehensive about telling people they have a spirit in their home! However, when she explained the image Tucker had showed her to Beverly, the woman shouted, "I knew it!" Beverly explained to Debbie that the previous family that owned the house had lost their daughter in a drunk-driving accident. She then related many strange things that were happening in the home that she couldn't explain. Beverly had sensed that there was a spirit in the house, and this was just the confirmation she needed.

Horse Sense

Because animals have such highly developed sensory perception, they can be incredibly helpful to humans in assessing threats, including people with good intentions and people with less-than-noble intentions. Many a hopeful suitor has been shown the door when the resident dog or cat didn't approve ... and probably with good reason!

Beverly also mentioned that Tucker had lost his original owners to a drunk-driving accident as well! This odd connection gave Debbie goose bumps, and also helped to explain Tucker's unusual apprehension about the presence. Debbie quickly reconnected to Tucker, to help him deal with both his past and this current situation. She explained to him that this spirit needed help finding her way home, and that all he needed to do when he saw her was to tell her to go towards the light and others would be there to greet her.

Tucker still expressed feelings of fear, but agreed to do his part. Debbie also acknowledged the grief Tucker still felt over the loss of his original family.

Debbie also instructed Beverly to encourage the spirit, when she sensed her presence, to move toward the light and find her way home, and provided her with the name of a psychic practitioner who performs house clearings. A house clearing many times involves clearing a house of unwanted energies. In Beverly's case, a house clearing would help this lost spirit find her way to the light and help restore harmony to the home from an energetic standpoint. Some people will also burn sage in their home to clear a home of negative, or uninvited, energies.

Clairaudience

Clairaudience is the psychic ability to hear sounds. You might hear words, which will probably sound like your inner voice talking in the way you "talk to yourself." It sounds like your own voice because this is you, interpreting the energetic message from your animal. Sometimes, you might also hear sounds the animal sends to you, sounds he or she hears that are important for the message.

Refining your clairaudience can also help to make messages from animals particularly clear. Some animals have highly developed hearing and can hear things we can't, particularly sounds in a higher range than the human ear can perceive. These sounds, inaudible to us, can be incredibly intense to other species. For example, sonic testing, which we can't hear, is piercing and disorienting to whales and dolphins, and can even make them ill. Learning to listen can help you to "hear" messages from your hearing-sensitive animal.

Debbie was cleaning her barn one day, and one of her horses, Max, was in the barn. He was a big dark bay Hanoverian/Thoroughbred cross with soulful eyes, and a fairly new addition to the family. As Debbie was sweeping the floor, she heard a voice in her head saying, "Do you think *now* you can take down that sign?"

The voice caught Debbie off guard because she hadn't been thinking about the horse, or anything else in particular. She turned around, and noticed Max staring at her. Puzzled, she looked around the barn, and then she noticed that hanging right across the stall from Max was a huge sign that said, "Finnegan's Home."

Debbie's husband had made the sign the year before, when Finnegan was the only horse in the family. Debbie suddenly realized that Max was offended by the sign! She promptly took it down.

Debbie reassured Max that he was a member of the family now, and that this was his home, too. After Debbie removed the sign, Max stopped staring at Debbie and proceeded to eat his hay. If Debbie hadn't been able to "hear" Max's voice in her head, she never would have recognized his feelings of insecurity about that sign proclaiming his barn the property of another horse.

Because animals themselves are so sensitive to sound, they often develop fears related to sounds. People often call Debbie because their animals become jumpy in reaction to noise. Some animals are even more sensitive to sounds than others. One dog Debbie spoke with was a rather large Samoyed who explained to Debbie that when he was younger, he had an awful ear infection that made his ears very sensitive to noise and wind. When he traveled in the car with the windows open and the radio blaring, he often whined. The noise and air pressure were too painful for him, and his person had no idea how much a "pleasant" drive in the car was hurting her animal! Many animals exhibit similar behavior with thunderstorms, fireworks, guns, lawn mowers, and vacuum cleaners, simply because the sounds, which may be loud to us, are incredibly intense to them. It's no wonder animals so easily "hear" the psychic communications of humans and other animals.

> **Cat's Meow**
>
> He's okay, but he can get very loud and it interferes with my nap!
>
> —Shadow, a black cat, when asked what he thought about the family's pet parrot

Kinesthetic Sense

Feeling sensations in your own body that the animal sends is another important and useful way to receive psychic messages. Animals have a highly developed kinesthetic sense in some ways, even if they behave more stoically about pain than your average human. To receive a message kinesthetically means you might feel sensations in your own body that the animal sends to you, such as physical pain or a strong emotion.

Animals often feel things people miss because people have lost touch with their kinesthetic sense. Animals have told Debbie that they will sometimes sit or lean against their person in a certain spot, to help the person heal. Often, this is the very area in which the human is having pain or trouble. They really *can* "feel your pain."

A woman named Kara once called Debbie about her horse, Taylor. Kara wanted to know what Taylor thought about each of his trainers. Debbie asked Kara to tell her only the trainers' first names and hair colors. Then Debbie went through each trainer with Taylor and asked what he thought. Taylor had some interesting remarks about each trainer, but when he got to the final trainer, he said that this man was extremely ill and held a lot of emotional and physical pain inside of him. Kara gasped in amazement. How could Taylor know? She told Debbie that this particular trainer had a painful form of cancer. He was a quiet man who kept to himself, but anyone paying attention could see the deep pain in his eyes when they talked with him. To Taylor, the man's pain and suffering was obvious.

Horse Sense

When an animal sends a message of pain, you might feel the sensation of a feather brushing across your knee, or a quick ache or twinge. Sometimes, however, you might feel intense pain, depending on what the animal communicates. Although you can block this pain, feeling it can be a valuable tool. After disconnecting with the animal, the pain typically disappears, but if you notice the pain lingering, dispel the negative energy by visualizing cleansing white light around you. Also try "shaking it off" by shaking your hands or stomping your feet lightly.

In a similar way, animals feel atmospheric changes. Dogs, birds, and horses get nervous when a storm approaches. Animals also sense our emotions, sometimes before we do! Debbie's cat, Jimmy James Junior, can sense when he has a vet appointment and has learned to hide so thoroughly that sometimes Debbie has to cancel the appointment! (Smart cat.) Animals can also sense the feelings of the people in the household. Our development editor Lynn's cat Bill lies on her chest whenever she is feeling upset, but never at any other time. Another cat slept on Lynn's bed with her for one week following the passing of the other cat in the house, comforting her in her grief—something the cat had never done before, and never did again.

To an animal, sensing feelings and changes is a normal part of life; there's nothing unusual about it. You can't lie to an animal because they know. They can read *you*, they don't rely on your words. Some animals get very angry when their humans lie to them or don't keep them informed or prepared about what's going on.

Cat's Meow

I make her laugh. That's one of my best achievements!

—Bill, a brown tabby cat, when asked about his person

Humans sometimes believe that if they "sneak out" on vacation when the animal doesn't see, the animal won't notice they're gone. On the contrary, such behavior often makes animals feel hurt at best, and betrayed, tricked, and abandoned at worst. Animals much prefer being told exactly what's going on, where you're going, and when you'll be back. They want to "be prepared" as much as any boy scout!

Olfactory/Gustatory Sense

Sometimes, you might interpret energetic messages as smells or tastes the animal wants you to understand. These two very basic sensory mechanisms are often lost on humans. Sure, we like to taste food and smell flowers. Bad smells and tastes warn us away at an instinctual level, while good smells and tastes attract us.

Yet we no longer need to rely on our sense of smell and taste for survival in the way we once did. Animals still retain an intense ability to smell, and some dogs can detect a few molecules of a scent, far beyond what any human could ever detect. To a Bloodhound, for example, a scent trail no human could detect is as obvious as a four-lane highway.

This is the sense that allows some dogs to work as seizure-alert or heart-attack-alert dogs. They can actually smell the chemical changes in the human body before we can, allowing their owners to prepare for the seizure by getting into a safe place, and/or taking medicine or calling for help. Even mild illnesses smell differently, clueing animals in to when you are sick (they can also feel your emotions and pain). Some dogs have even been trained to smell skin cancer cells, alerting their owners (or patients in the clinics where they actually work!) to malignant skin changes and saving their lives.

Animals often "show" Debbie the smells they dislike on their people. These smells often turn out to be cigarette smoke or alcohol! Animals also may react negatively to a pet who has just come from the vet's office because they recognize the smell and associate it with an unpleasant experience. Some animals even reject their young if they have a strange smell!

> **Cat's Meow**
>
> Have you lost weight?
> —Quarter Horse gelding, when asked if he had any questions for his person

Your pet might send you the taste of that awful new pet food, or the smell of something delicious. Or in some cases, you might receive a taste or smell that helps to solve a problem.

Molly was a sensitive Greyhound Debbie had consulted with because her person, Greta, was concerned with her health. She just didn't seem right. When Debbie connected with Molly, she sensed that she had an allergy to something because she felt an irritation in her throat and her eyes burned. Debbie asked Molly to describe the allergies, and although Debbie was expecting a picture or a word, instead she received an incredibly strong smell of bleach.

Debbie asked Greta about the bleach smell, and Greta admitted that she had recently washed down the entire room where Molly eats with bleach. She had thought that she had rinsed it well enough, but Molly was proof that she hadn't. Once Greta moved Molly's food dish and rinsed the floor again thoroughly, Molly's condition improved.

Clairsentience

Clairsentience is a type of psychic perception that doesn't seem to come necessarily through any sensory channel. Somehow, you just *know* something. This knowing is a direct transmission of the energy message from an animal into your consciousness.

Clairsentience is a common form of communication that people experience with their own animals all the time. It is a very powerful form of communication, but often the one that also gets overlooked, because we don't know *how* we know something. "I just know" hardly seems like hard evidence!

Clairsentience is a hard sensation to trust, but if we learn to trust our intuition, we can open ourselves up to a world of information. This wonderful tool, which is something like a direct connection to intuition unfiltered through the senses, can be useful in all aspects of your life: buying a house, deciding whether or not to take that new job, whether or not someone is the right person to marry, and so on.

In some consultations, Debbie will find herself intuitively knowing what herb, food, or supplement an animal might need. Although Debbie can't explain where this knowing comes from—the animal, or a higher source—she is usually right on target.

Laura called Debbie about her horse, Magic. Magic was on the road to recovery after a long illness, and Laura was interested in connecting with Magic to see if she could do anything further to improve his health and comfort. Magic told Debbie he needed a second water trough in the paddock, because the other horses bullied him and kept him from using it, and that he would like more massages. However, Debbie also received a distinct feeling of knowing about adding kelp to Magic's diet. Debbie wasn't even sure if horses were supposed to eat kelp! As always, Debbie explained to Laura that, while she thought Magic needed kelp, Laura should first speak to her veterinarian about this—preferably a holistic vet with specific knowledge about nutritional supplements like kelp—and whether such a substance would benefit, and not harm, a horse.

Laura's vet confirmed that giving kelp to Magic was a good idea, considering it was a natural form of the very ingredients in which Magic was deficient, due to a sluggish thyroid. If Debbie had ignored that inner knowing, Magic wouldn't be receiving the benefits he enjoys today!

Cat's Meow

I like to help people see themselves differently. I help them see their faults.
—Vernon, a German Shepherd

Assessing Your Sensory Strengths

Everyone has certain tendencies when it comes to psychic communication. Debbie tends to receive messages predominantly in the form of pictures. You may think of yourself as particularly verbal, but you could receive your messages as feelings in your body, or as a sudden knowing.

In most cases, messages come through in several ways. However, you can tap into your strengths when first practicing psychic communication by concentrating on those areas that feel most comfortable to you. Here's an exercise to help you assess whether you tend to relate to the world through sight, sound, feel, smell, taste, or a general knowing.

Stop what you are doing and sit very still for one minute. What is the first or most prevalent thing you notice?

A. The sounds: traffic, the white noise of a computer screen, birds singing.

B. Whatever object happens to be in front of me.

C. The smell of the air.

D. Physical sensations: a slight headache, an achy back, an empty stomach.

E. The feel of your tongue in your mouth. The taste of whatever you were recently drinking or eating.

F. Myself sitting quietly.

Horse Sense

Making a particular effort to pay attention to the sensory ways you relate to the world can help to tune you in to more subtle energies in your environment. Try paying attention to sensory modes you wouldn't normally notice, and exercise that psychic muscle.

You may be surprised that you noticed sounds when you thought you would notice sights, or that you felt inner stillness when you expected to hear thoughts racing through your head.

What You Send To and Receive From Your Pet

Consider how you predominantly communicate with your pet. Most people probably think of themselves communicating verbally with their pets: "Watch the house, I'll be back soon." "Dinner time!" "Lie down. Good dog!" "Here kitty kitty kitty …"

However, you communicate to your pet in many ways. When you talk to your animal, you are unconsciously sending to them pictures, feelings, and emotions behind the words you speak, in addition to the body language you display and the tone of your voice. Animals rely heavily on this, much more than on the words themselves. Debbie has found that by consciously wording things to an animal in such a way that you send a positive picture, he or she understands more quickly and readily. (We'll go into more detail about this in Chapter 5.)

Sending a telepathic message is the easy part, but now consider how you *receive* telepathic messages from your pet. This is the part that takes practice, but never fear.

Your animals communicate psychically to you all the time, and you have plenty of opportunities to practice.

One way to start defining and tuning in to your own sensory tendencies as they apply to receiving psychic messages is by considering the many alternatives. Remember our example about asking a dog about his favorite activity? Let's say you asked your cat how she is feeling. Here are more ways different people might receive the same message:

♦ A still picture of your cat's ear surrounded by an aura.

♦ A moving picture of your cat shaking her head.

♦ Hearing the words, "My ear hurts."

♦ Feeling an itching sensation in your own ear.

♦ Suddenly knowing your cat has an ear infection.

Each of these messages is the same message filtered through different peoples' consciousness, and each is ready for interpretation. When the message is more complicated than an ear infection or a happy game of fetch, you can see how different people might slightly misinterpret the message. That's why successful animal communication takes so much practice! The more you do it, the better you develop your sense about the true and exact meaning behind a message.

Cat's Meow

As long as I am putting in requests, rolling grassy hills would be nice, with lots of trees on the perimeter. Yes, soft rolling hills would be ideal, and certainly worthy of me.

—Mumm, an American Saddlebred horse

Exercise Your Personal Telepathic Tendencies

Debbie teaches this fun exercise in her workshops to help people determine their own tendencies. Debbie always starts with this exercise because it is somewhat difficult, and she can then tell her students that talking to animals is much easier than this exercise! To do this exercise, you will need a willing friend and a piece of paper and pen.

Sit facing each other. Decide who will be the sender and who will be the receiver.

Receiver: Close your eyes and relax your body by breathing deeply and exhaling through your mouth.

Sender: Write down the name of a color on your piece of paper. Write down if this color is hot or cold. Write down a simple object that is this color.

Sender: Quiet your mind so all you are thinking about is your color. Tell the receiver that you are going to send them the color, and then imagine it going over to the person. See the color all around the receiver like a thick mist. Then send the feeling of whether the object is hot or cool to the person. Let him or her feel the heat or the coolness. Then picture the object you wrote down and send this object right to the person's forehead. Focus.

For example, if you chose the color blue, you would choose the feeling of coolness and you might choose a blueberry or the sky as your object.

Doggone!

Human-to-human telepathic communication is much harder than human-to-animal telepathic communication because in the latter case, at least one of the participants is already highly skilled in this form

This exercise should only take a few minutes. Try to stay focused and clear.

When the sender is done, ask the receiver what they perceived.

Receiver: As the sender is sending, try to remain quiet, relaxed, and open to whatever images might come into your mind.

Finally, switch roles so that the receiver gets to send, and the sender gets to receive.

People typically react to this exercise in different ways. Some people might only get a feeling associated with the color. They might not know the color but they might feel the coolness. Others might get an emotion. Yellow feels happy, while blue feels sad to some.

Some people will see the color quickly at first, and then their minds will take over and start guessing what color it is, getting in the way of the pure message they first received. When the mind takes over, intuition is overruled. The mind will always fight with your intuition, and this is perfectly normal. Acknowledge this is going on, and try to allow your mind to become quiet and open again.

Some receivers find it helpful to ask their inner intuitive sense about what color it perceives, almost as if one's intuition were a separate being. Also, if a color keeps coming back persistently, chances are that is the color the person is sending.

Some people might hear the name of the color in their minds: "Blue" or "Red" or "Yellow." Some people will not see the color but will see an object that is that color. Sometimes it will be a different object than the sender was sending, but will be the right color!

Others might get the whole package at once or in succession. The way you receive the color message in this exercise can help clue you in on the way you may be likely to receive messages from animals.

Again, remember that this is a very hard exercise, so try not to feel frustrated if you can't get the message. The point is to begin to get an idea of what telepathy feels like for you.

The Least You Need to Know

- ◆ Psychic messages come as energy. How you perceive them depends on your personal sensory tendencies.

- ◆ Animals tend to have much more highly developed senses than humans, who rely largely on verbal and written communication.

- ◆ Psychic communication can happen in the form of clairvoyance (seeing images or moving pictures), clairaudience (hearing words or sounds), kinesthesia (feeling pain, emotions, or other tactile sensations), olfactory sensations (smelling), gustatory sensations (tasting), or clairsentience, a general "knowing" the substance of the message.

- ◆ Knowing your own sensory tendencies will help you to refine and develop your communication with animals.

Part 2

Sending and Receiving Psychic Messages

Even if you believe in animal communication, you might have difficulty understanding exactly how to go about it. Actually, it's easy, but like anything else, the more you do it, the more skilled you will become. This section will teach you, step-by-step, how to relax and send messages in the most direct and clear way possible. Next, we'll show you how to open your mind, banish your judgment, and receive messages from your animal. We'll give you exercises for strengthening and growing your own natural intuition, and we'll help you build a closer relationship with your animal, because the closer you are, the better you will communicate. (Sounds like any other relationship, doesn't it?) The section ends with a chapter on how to communicate with your animal wherever you might be, whether held up at the office or on vacation half way around the world.

Sending Psychic Messages to Your Pet

In This Chapter

- ◆ Sending messages might be easier than receiving them, but first you have to tune up your intuition

- ◆ How to send telepathic messages your animal will actually understand

- ◆ The importance of sending unbiased, positive, clear, simple messages

- ◆ An exercise to help you practice sending a telepathic message to your animal

Psychic communication with animals may seem complicated, impossible, or at best, confusing. Even professional pet psychics don't always understand how it works. However, whether or not you know how it works, anyone can do it. Sending a telepathic message is actually simple, and the best way to learn is simply to start practicing.

As we mentioned in Chapter 4, sending messages is easier than receiving them, so let's start there. But, before we do, you can benefit immensely from some basic exercises that will help you get in touch with your psychic intuition.

Intuition Tune-Up

Everyone has intuition, but many of us have forgotten how to listen to that "still, small voice" inside—the one that tells us to avoid that particular side of the street, skip that flight, or that your mother is definitely on the other end of the line when the phone is ringing.

To help fine-tune your intuition, all you have to do is some daily "target practice." Target your intuitive side with some dedicated focusing and you'll feel your intuition blossoming into something incredibly useful in your daily life.

The first and perhaps the most important thing you can do to help your intuitive side to mature is to *listen*. Stop talking, stop the mental babble within, be quiet, and listen. Listen to your body—how does your gut feel when you meet someone new, or you enter a building? Listen to that voice in your head that tells you someone is worth getting to know, or that you shouldn't take that job. Are you sometimes drawn to certain places or people, or do you sometimes feel compelled to take a different route home but you don't know why? Pay attention! That's your intuition talking.

 **Horse Sense**

Although we can't prove it, we believe there are no accidents, and everything happens for a reason. The more effectively we utilize our intuition, the better chance we have of grasping the big picture and seeing how things fit into the larger scope of life. What seems like a defeat might be a nudge over to a better path. What seems like bad luck might actually be an opportunity. Intuition can be like a compass for the journey of life.

Intuition plays a major role, not only in our everyday lives, but also in the effect our lives and actions have on others. Intuition is something we can all tap into, a fantastic and indispensable resource waiting, largely dormant and ignored, within us. Just imagine what you could do in life if you finally learned how to use that power! It's amazing more of us don't take the time to develop this skill, especially because that development takes little more than just sitting quietly and listening to our inner voices. Compared to developing your biceps, triceps, and quadriceps with daily workouts at the gym, that's pretty easy!

Let's practice.

Chill Out!

The first step to opening your mind to make room for your intuition is to learn how to calm, quiet, and relax your mind. Most of us tend to have an ongoing internal chatter that pipes up the loudest when we try to sit quietly. Here are some tips to help you ease your overactive brain into a more relaxed state:

♦ Sit quietly, meditating or just relaxing, in the company of your animals. Your animals will enjoy spending this kind of easy, relaxing time with you, and you can help each other bask in calmness.

♦ Sit quietly outside in nature. Focus on the natural world around you, not on your distracted thoughts about the past or the future. See how much you can notice with your five senses about your immediate surroundings. This is good practice for training and focusing your mind.

♦ Listen to relaxing music. Music has an incredible power to energize, calm, inspire, or stir the passions. To help you relax, choose music that feeds your soul and relaxes your body. For some people, this might be classical, jazz, inspirational, or New Age music. Experiment with different kinds of music to find your most relaxing favorites.

♦ Practice healthy habits. Eat healthy, natural foods; get some moderate exercise on most days; get seven or eight hours of sleep every night; and keep a mostly regular schedule. These habits are most conducive to a calm, centered, focused mind, and they keep your body in good health and free of aches, pains, and other physical distractions that could interfere with a total focus on intuition. The healthier your body, the more space and energy you have to expand other aspects of your consciousness.

Horse Sense

Meditation practice is an excellent way to help calm, relax, and "cross-train" your brain for more effective pet psychic communication. Take a class, join a meditation group, or read a book. We like *The Complete Idiot's Guide to Meditation, Second Edition*, by Joan Budilovsky and Eve Adamson; or *The Complete Idiot's Guide to Zen Living, Second Edition*, by Gary McClain, Ph.D., and Eve Adamson. Of course, being a co-author of both, Eve is biased.

Intuition-Expanding Exercise #1

Debbie teaches several exercises in her seminars to help people relax their minds and expand their intuitive sense. Try them on your own, or with a friend. This one quiets the minds and body:

1. Find a comfortable position, either sitting or lying down.

2. Close your eyes and breathe deeply.

3. Inhale through your nose, filling up your belly and then your chest with air.

4. Exhale deeply and as completely as you can, out of your mouth.

5. Wiggle your fingers and toes, then breathe deeply again.

6. Imagine all your stress draining out of your feet and trickling away from you.

7. Now, visualize yourself barefoot in the grass or in the sand.

8. Keep breathing. Wiggle your toes. Imagine roots growing out of your feet and deep into the earth below, finding their way home in the grass or the sand.

9. Imagine energy flowing back up the roots from deep in the heart of Mother Earth. The energy encircles your body and flows from your feet all the way to the top of your head.

10. Now imagine you begin to feel a tingle above your head.

11. Visualize white light collecting overhead, then streaming down from the sky, into the top of your head, through your body, and out of your feet—the power of Earth and the power of heaven conjoining inside you!

12. Relax and bask in this ultimate union with your world. Keep breathing, slowly and deeply. Feel how relaxed and calm you are.

> **Cat's Meow** ___
>
> He is not very graceful. He walks really hard on the floor, and I run for cover!
>
> —Buttercup, a white Persian, when asked what she thought of her person's husband

Intuition-Expanding Exercise #2

This exercise will help you to get in touch with your own, very personal intuitive sense.

1. Write down a question for which you seek an answer, a decision with which you are struggling, or describe a situation you wish could be clarified or solved.

2. Sit quietly where you won't be interrupted: a bedroom with the door closed, a study, even in your car or the bathroom if that's what it takes to get privacy. Bring your notebook.

3. Verbalize your exact intention. Don't just think it. Figure out exactly how you would say it, then say it out loud. It might be something like, "My intention is to let my intuition help me to discover the answer to

_____."

4. After you've spoken your intention, sit quietly. You'll surely hear thoughts racing through your mind. Don't try to stop this flow. Just observe it. Let it happen.

5. As you refuse to engage the mental chatter, you may find that what runs through your mind begins to change. You may start to get pictures, words, or feelings. Don't try to direct your thoughts. Just continue to observe them.

6. As your mind slows down (be patient, it will), you might keep coming back to certain images, sounds, or words. Keep watching, keep observing. What sticks with you, or makes a more distinct impression? Write down whatever seems significant or persistent.

7. If you feel you are getting nothing, write that down as well. Don't analyze what you are getting, or critique it. Don't worry about how well you write it, either. Just accept what comes, and write it down as honestly as you can.

8. Repeat this entire process, using the same stated intention, five different times on different days. However, each time, use a new page in your notebook. Do _not_ look back at the previous pages until the five sessions are finished.

9. After the five sessions, go back and in one sitting, read all your notes. What themes continue to surface? Think about what your intuitive mind is trying to tell you about your problem, issue, or situation. Spend some time meditating on your summary of written reactions. See if you can find the answer pushing its way out from between all that written text. We're betting it's in there somewhere!

This exercise helps you to seek out your intuitive side in a proactive manner. By writing down the information that pours forth from your mind after stating your intention, you acknowledge your own intuition, opening the door for that intuition to grow and increase in strength. The more you practice, the more easily the answers will emerge.

Horse Sense _____

Keeping a journal of your growth and progress in pet psychic communication can serve as a tool to help you recall and learn from mistakes, remember and celebrate successes, and record, for posterity, the amazing growth and development of one person's intuition (yours!).

Intuition-Expanding Exercise #3

This third exercise can be an ongoing project. Start and keep your own personal dream journal. Keeping a dream journal is fun, and it gets you actively thinking about what goes on in your subconscious mind: how you process the events of your day, what your inner concerns and worries are, and where your intuition is telling you to go … or not to go!

Horse Sense

Sometimes dreams provide us with important messages from our own subconscious minds. If a dream seems particularly memorable, write it down, then go back to it several days later. Consider what messages you might be sending yourself.

To start a dream journal, keep a notebook beside your bed. Each night before you go to bed, write down the words, "My intention is to remember my dreams tonight." Some people have a harder time remembering their dreams than others, but rest assured (no pun intended), everybody dreams. Even if you wake up and don't remember anything, keep repeating your intention each night before you go to bed. Eventually, you will begin to remember bits and pieces, and eventually, longer parts and even entire, long, complicated dream sequences.

Every morning, as soon as you wake up, before you get out of bed, write down everything you can remember about your dreams: images, plot lines, characters, sounds, smells, colors, anything at all, even if it doesn't make any sense to your logical, waking-up brain. The more you wake up, the less likely you are to remember the details, so get in the habit of writing first thing. Some people even start to write before they open their eyes, while the dream images still float freshly in their mind's eye.

How to Send a Psychic Communication

Sending information to an animal might seem straightforward: Think it and imagine sending it. However, knowing how to frame your messages, what to avoid, and how to send them so the animal can most clearly understand you will help you to accomplish faster, more direct communication.

One of the most important tips Debbie gives to all her students is this: "Animals want to know what to do, not what *not* to do." In other words, accentuate the positive.

Clarity is crucial in animal communication, and because we "speak" different languages, animals often read the psychically transmitted images behind our words (you send them, whether you know it or not).

For example, Sassy, a bulldog cross, loved to chew on the sofa when her person, Stacey, went to work. As a result, Sassy was often "in the doghouse" (so to speak), and eventually had to be crated or locked in the kitchen while Stacey worked.

Debbie asked Stacey what she told her dog before she left for work every day, and Stacey said that every day she told Sassy not to chew the sofa!

Debbie asked Stacey to say that slowly to herself, paying attention to the images that arise when she says, "Sassy, don't chew the sofa." Stacey was silent on the other end of the line for a moment. Then, she said, "Well … I know what I am saying, but I guess I am picturing her actually chewing the sofa."

> **Doggone!**
>
> Sending a message of a behavior we desire is easier to understand than sending a message of a behavior we *don't* desire. What are you going to do, put a red circle with a line through the behavior? Follow it with an image of your angry face? This is much harder to understand than a clear picture of the animal doing the *right* thing.

Debbie explained that many times, animals pay attention to the pictures behind the words, rather than the words themselves. Without realizing it, Stacey was sending Sassy an image of her chewing the sofa. Did Sassy fully comprehend that's what Stacey *didn't* want her to do? Who knows? (Only Sassy!)

For clarity and as a way to channel Sassy's energy and boredom, Debbie told Stacey that she needed to give Sassy a job to do while she was away at work. Furthermore, Stacey needed to explain to Sassy the details of the job, and the rules of the house.

Debbie chatted with Sassy about her very important job of watching over the house and keeping everything in order. Debbie asked Stacey to reinforce this message to Sassy every day. Now, every day before work, Stacey was sending Sassy images of her patrolling the house and making sure everything was in order, in good condition, safe and sound, then getting rewarded for a job well done at the end of the day. This new focus channeled Sassy's excess energy, made her feel important, and gave her much more interesting things to think about than gnawing on a sofa. After all, she now had a house to keep, and that is a big responsibility!

> **Cat's Meow**
>
> The ladies love me. They can't help it!
>
> —Ernie, a gray tabby cat

Leave Your Bias at the (Mental) Door

One of the most important things to remember in sending a message is to be impartial and unbiased in the way you frame your message. Animals, like people, are subject to innuendo and prejudice in the way you present something, and a biased question is likely to engender a biased answer.

When people call Debbie about a problem with their animal, the first thing Debbie does is to survey the situation in an unbiased manner, as much as possible. Without framing her questions in a way that assumes anything about what the human is doing or the animal is thinking, Debbie asks the animal what is going on from their point of view. This allows the animal to express his or her own perspective, free of the human's influence.

Doggone!

If your animal is having a problem such as refusing to use the litter box or chewing on furniture, finding out the cause of the problem and addressing that first is a more effective approach than simply sending a message to stop the undesirable behavior. Listen! You might be surprised at the cause. (A bladder infection? Feelings of neglect or loneliness? No readily available chew toys?)

Instead, Debbie likes to find out first exactly what is going on, then give the animal some choices about a solution. This provides the animal with an active role in the problem-solving process. This approach also helps the animals see that they are responsible for their own behavior.

For instance, Debbie's cat, Jimmy James Junior, loved being outside. Debbie would get nervous when he stayed out after dark, and she used to call and call. Jimmy James liked to crouch in the bushes and laugh at Debbie, then stay out all night, just as he pleased. Debbie lost a lot of sleep worrying about what could happen to her cat!

Finally, Debbie decided she had to do something about this problem. She sat down with Jimmy James and communicated to him exactly how she was feeling, the rules of the house, and his choices in the matter. She didn't say, "You can't stay outside all night!" or "Stop laughing at me and disobeying me!" Instead, she showed him, by sending him images, of the possible dangers he could encounter during the night, and she also sent him her feelings of worry. Debbie explained to Jimmy James that she loved knowing he was safe in the house at night. Then, she offered him a choice: He could go out all day, and come in before dark when she called him, or if he didn't honor this deal, she would have to keep him inside until he felt he could keep his end of the bargain. She also showed him that when he came running at her call to come inside for the night, he would get a special treat.

This deal put the responsibility on Jimmy James, and he knew it! After that day, without fail, Jimmy James came running to Debbie when she called him. Debbie used to chuckle as she saw Jimmy James come flying out of the woods at the sound of his name.

Sure, nobody is perfect, and sometimes Debbie had to call a few times or give Jimmy James a chance to get within hearing range. However, he had honored his side of the bargain, and Debbie has honored hers (by keeping those treats coming!).

Animals aren't robots. They are individuals with needs, desires, aversions, preferences, and sometimes, a pretty stubborn nature! You can't just tell an animal to do something and expect them to do it without question. Just like you, they want to understand why you want them to do something. We try to initiate compromise and allow the animal to understand our view, just as we understand and acknowledge their view. That kind of attitude shows mutual respect, and honors each being's individuality.

Horse Sense

We've seen a bumper sticker we think is funny. It says "Animals are people, too!" Obviously, animals are not people, but the gist of the joke is, of course, that animals have many of the same traits, complexities, and characteristics that people have.

The Importance of Clarity

The second thing to remember when sending a message to an animal is to be clear and organized in the images or words you send. Have you ever received a phone message on the answering machine or an e-mail message that just didn't make sense? Maybe the person hadn't organized their thoughts, maybe the reception wasn't clear, maybe typos or grammar errors made the meaning of the message ambiguous. An unclear, disorganized telepathic message is no different.

Before you send a message to an animal, think about the best, most clear, most direct, and most positive way to orient the message. Relax, organize your thoughts, and only then, send the message. Consider it akin to proofreading your e-mails before you hit the "send" button!

Cat's Meow

I put my ears back and warned him first. He makes remarks about me under his breath and I hear them. I was getting him back for what he was thinking. But I did warn him first!

—Samson the horse, when asked why he kicked his person's teenaged son

Barbara called Debbie about her horse, Merlin. Merlin was a beautiful gray Arabian with a lot of spunk. He was very animated in the way he communicated, and Debbie really enjoyed chatting with him. Except for a few minor body aches and pains, Merlin was a healthy and happy horse.

However, Barbara had one complaint about Merlin. She loved to ride him on the trails, but she said Merlin seemed to be afraid of the rocks along the trail, making the ride difficult and, for Barbara, dangerous.

Rather than sending Merlin a message not to be scared of the rocks, Debbie asked Merlin, simply and directly, why he was having trouble with the rocks on the trail. Merlin explained to Debbie that he had to be on guard because things pop out from behind the rocks, and sometimes the rocks themselves move. He thought that the rocks were sneaky and that he had to keep his eye on them.

Again, without judging and with full respect and understanding for Merlin's explanation, Debbie explained to Merlin exactly what rocks were, and, because of what they were, why they couldn't move. She sent him clear, simple images of rocks from all sides, inside and out: big inanimate solid blocks of mineral, incapable of movement.

However, Debbie was sure to let Merlin know that she understood his fears. She also explained that his obsession with the rocks was a problem, keeping him from enjoying his outings and making it difficult for Barbara to ride him. Debbie showed Merlin that the obsession about the rocks was of his own making. Yes, sometimes small animals live behind rocks, but they aren't worth the obsessive energy and attention of a big, strong, proud horse. Nothing in or around the rocks, Debbie explained, posed a threat to Merlin and if he just ignored the rocks, he could have a much more enjoyable time with Barbara.

Then, to further clarify what Barbara wanted Merlin to do (instead of what she *didn't* want him to do), Debbie sent Merlin images of how to walk past the rocks, confident with a relaxed frame, looking forward and being bold.

Since their talk, Barbara reports that Merlin doesn't think twice about going past the rocks now, and that he even acts a little bit cocky about the whole business!

Cat's Meow

I really would like to see more people. I'm a people dog! How about more walks? I love to parade in front of people and meet them all.

—Gregor the Rottweiler

Such immediate results don't happen with every horse, or every animal. Some animals are easier to convince than others, and some have deep-seated fears that take longer to resolve and release. (We will go into how to help animals overcome fears and emotional scars in Chapter 11.) However, simple, clear questions and positive images always work best in communicating with animals, and are most likely to help the animal understand what you want to know, or what you need the animal to do.

The Power of Positive Thinking

You've heard the cliché: "Never underestimate the power of positive thinking." In the case of animal communication, that cliché is a sacred truth! Positive visualization can be one of your most valuable tools in communicating with your animal friends.

People tend to draw the things they fear nearer to them by worrying and engaging those fears. Knowing this is true, however, you would think we would spend more time concentrating our energy on the things we want, the things we desire, and the things to which we aspire!

Debbie has learned this lesson many times the hard way, but one of her greatest teachers and guides along the way has been her horse, Finnegan.

Finnegan is a dark bay Thoroughbred with a vivid memory and amazing intelligence. He also holds his fears close, and reacts quickly, getting easily spooked.

When Debbie first brought him into her family, they struggled for years. She was lucky if the two of them could go for a full 15 minutes without a major spooking episode. Debbie would tense up whenever they approached an object she thought might alarm the horse. She would picture how the spook would play out, in dramatic detail, preparing herself for the worst. Of course, with images like that surrounding him, Finnegan spooked every time!

Despite Debbie's comforting words to her horse, each time they encountered a potentially startling object or situation, Finnegan could feel Debbie's body tense and see the pictures of him getting spooked. Instead of listening to her words (which were much less in his "language" than her emanating emotions and images), he reacted to her body and psychic language. Without even realizing it, Debbie was exacerbating an already troubling problem.

Now, Debbie has discovered that she has to ride Finnegan with her mind, and that isn't always easy. The experience did teach Debbie the importance of positive visualization, however. Now, when she approaches an object she knows will frighten him, she pictures him relaxing and walking calmly by. She tells him, "I have your back," or "I have this side covered," so that he doesn't feel like he has to be on guard from all sides. She tries to relax her body and loosen the reins, fighting her own natural instincts to clutch on for safety. This, Debbie has found, is the most effective way to ensure a positive outcome.

Before Debbie rides a *dressage* test or a jump course, she always pictures in her head exactly how she wants to ride the maneuvers, and then she goes over them with the horse. This way, she prepares both herself and the horse for the upcoming event.

This practice has become incredibly valuable before a cross-country course or stadium jumping, where the rider is the only one who sees the jumps beforehand. You can use your telepathy to picture each jump in your mind's eye and send that picture to your horse. You can even go one step further and actually picture for your horse how you want him or her to jump it, how many strides in between, as much detail as you think will help. Just remember to be clear and straightforward in the pictures you send.

Another important concern is to avoid overexaggerating. For example, Faye called Debbie about her dressage horse, Arrow. Faye was having a terrible time trying to get Arrow to cooperate during dressage. Arrow fought with her the whole time.

When Debbie asked Arrow what was wrong, why all the fuss and fighting, Arrow stated that there was no way he could possibly do what his person was asking of him. Debbie explained to him and pictured for him what she was asking. Arrow answered, "Well, I can do _that_, but she is picturing something entirely different!"

Then, Arrow sent Debbie images of what Faye was picturing: an overly exaggerated head set, a cramped-up, collected body, everything she really needed taken to the extreme. It looked pretty painful to Debbie, and she could see why Arrow had protested!

Debbie asked Faye to soften and modify her picture of how she wanted Arrow's body to look during dressage, and Arrow began to be more cooperative right away. If we picture something for our animals to do that they feel they can't achieve, we are setting them up for failure and resentment toward the job.

Many times horse show and dog show competitors will call Debbie before or during a big competition, if they are having trouble with a particular obstacle or maneuver. Nancy called Debbie about her dog Gibson. Gibson loved doing _agility_, but when it came time for him to do the weave poles, he would do the first pole and then dash off to the next obstacle before finishing the maneuver. Nancy was concerned that Gibson disliked agility competition.

When Debbie asked Gibson why he was avoiding the poles, he explained that it hurt his right hip when he rushed through the poles and that he couldn't make the tight turns. He also told her that he hurt his hip slipping on the wet grass doing the poles during practice.

Debbie explained to Nancy what Gibson said, and she confirmed that he did indeed slip during practice but she didn't think he had hurt himself. She agreed to call a veterinary chiropractor to look at his hip. A few weeks later, Nancy called to let Debbie know that Gibson had won his first agility class and that the chiropractor had found a definite weakness in Gibson's right hind leg. Once they removed his source of pain, he was back to his old self, mastering the weave poles.

> **CAUTION**
>
> **Doggone!**
>
> Whenever we think about something, we give it energy. If you constantly worry about things, you give them energy. When you give something enough energy, you can actually make it happen! (Isn't that a scary—and also inspiring—thought!)

Exercise for Sending Telepathic Messages

Sending a message to an animal can be as simple as visualizing an image and mentally projecting it to your animal—a sort of talking to your animal without talking. However, the more you do it and the more you refine your skills, the more easily your pet will receive and understand your message. Try this exercise to help you perfect your ability to send telepathic messages to your pet.

This exercise is a good one to help you get started because it involves something your pet has strong positive feelings about: treats!

1. Think of a food or toy your animal likes—something you have on hand. Don't picture a treat you don't have or a toy you have lost. Make sure you have the object immediately available. For example, you might picture a delicious peanut butter dog treat, a small piece of chicken, or that favorite stuffed toy.

2. Picture the object of your animal's desire in your mind's eye. Try to picture it in as much details as you can, using all your senses. Imagine the object's texture, color, smell, shape, weight, volume, and anything else you can think of.

3. Next, say your animal's name in your mind a few times.

4. Now, send a picture of the treat to your animal. Imagine them eating the treat or playing with the toy.

5. When you are done, give your animal the treat or toy. You may or may not get any kind of reaction from your pet that tells you he or she got the message, but that doesn't mean it wasn't received!

6. Repeat the exercise daily until you feel comfortable with the process. Keep watching your pet for a reaction. You'll get one sooner or later!

7. The more you do this exercise, the more you can expand it, using different treats, toys, or even activities which you picture, then do with your animal (such as a game of fetch).

This exercise is designed to help you send information to your animal in a clear, simple manner, immediately followed by an actual participation in the image you pictured and sent. In addition to giving you something simple and positive to send, this exercise will encourage your animal to tune in to your messages because of the positive association. "Listen to my person, then get a treat? What a deal!"

Horse Sense

Our animals are used to connecting with us telepathically all the time. They are also used to us missing the messages they send because our minds are too busy or we aren't listening. As a result, our animals often resort to other behaviors—both desirable and undesirable—to get our attention.

This exercise helps you to take an active step that tells your animal, "Hey, I can do this, too. I'm tuned in. I'm paying attention." This kind of new communication might seem too good to be true to your animal, who may have believed this kind of communication with you was a hopeless endeavor. The animal might not quite believe it at first, but keep practicing, stay true to your word when delivering messages (a broken promise is a broken promise, whether spoken or telepathically transmitted), and eventually your pet will understand that you really are listening. Be patient and soon you will discover the wonders of a whole new level of communication.

The Least You Need to Know

◆ Prepare to send messages to your pet by developing your intuition.

◆ Telepathic messages to animals should send positive, unbiased images of what you desire, not negative images of what you don't want your animal to do or judgments about what the animal does.

◆ Clear, simple images and messages are best for beginners. Animals are more likely to receive and understand them.

◆ Begin practicing by sending simple, positive images of something your animal enjoys—a treat, a favorite toy—then immediately giving the animal that same thing.

◆ Once your animal gets used to the idea that you really are able to communicate in the way animals are accustomed, he or she will become more receptive and responsive to your telepathic messages.

Chapter 6

Becoming Receptive to Psychic Messages from Your Pet

In This Chapter

- The state of mind most essential for receiving psychic messages

- How to get and keep an open mind

- A visualization to increase mental receptiveness

- The best tips for receiving psychic communications from animals

Sending messages and receiving messages go hand in hand, because "communication" implies a dialogue, not a monologue. However, receiving messages is more difficult than sending them, not because we don't have the skill but because we erect so many barriers, blocking our minds from becoming receptive to the psychic messages our animals send us—messages they send out all the time!

Receiving psychic messages means making yourself open enough to absorb the psychic energy from another being and then letting it rise up into your consciousness for interpretation. If you think you already know what your animal will say, or if your mind is too busy, rushed, and noisy for a subtle message to penetrate, you'll never "hear" anything.

Shhhhh ...

Quieting your mind sounds nice and relaxing, doesn't it? Actually doing it is quite another matter. If you don't quiet your mind, your animal's telepathic messages can't come through, or you won't hear them. If you don't open your heart, your animal's love for you won't be able to penetrate, accessing your inner spiritual energy, where psychic messages first make contact.

> **CAUTION**
>
> **Doggone!** _____
>
> Without a quiet mind, you probably won't hear psychic messages. Who would notice a drop of rain in a raging, storm-thrashed lake? Yet on a still, calm, quiet lake, a drop of rain ripples the surface, its rings of influence widening far beyond the tiny space where water first made contact with water.

The first step in becoming more open to psychic communication is obvious: It's all in your head! You have to *believe* in your own intuitive abilities. Otherwise, that pesky conscious mind will keep rearing up in protest, questioning and analyzing and getting in the way. Even if you think of it as a sort of temporary, willing suspension of disbelief, when working on opening yourself to your animal, you must get your rational, skeptical mind out of the way. That's not where psychic communication happens! No, we're not saying you should stop being rational, or even skeptical. But tell your brain to put a lid on it, just for the time being.

As for the quietness we so often crave, the best way to teach your brain to settle down is simple: practice. Taking some time to sit quietly, with or without your animals, in meditation or not, teaches you how to turn off all those mental switches, just for a few minutes, and remember how to relax, open up, listen, and just *be* for awhile.

To communicate with animals, you certainly don't need to be an expert in meditation, or even be able to quiet your mind for very long (if you can make it to 5 or 10 minutes without incessant mental chatter in the background, that's really pretty good!). You will need to learn how to quiet your mind just long enough to be able to receive, perceive, and acknowledge the messages your animals send to you.

In the last chapter, we gave you some tips on ways to practice quieting your mind. What works for one person might not necessarily be the best approach for you. Figure out what you need by trying different things:

◆ Meditation takes many forms, but its purpose is twofold: (1) learning to focus on a single thing, to concentrate mental power into one river instead of lots of tiny streams flowing every which way; and (2) finally becoming so focused that mind merges with object and they become one, opening into a new space where you are in direct spiritual connection with everything around you. Because of its ultimate goals, meditation is an excellent preparation for psychic communication. The more your spirit merges with the world around you, the more obvious psychic messages will become.

You might meditate by focusing on an image, such as a candle flame, a flower, or a picture of your animal. Some people like to meditate by counting to 10 slowly and focusing on the numbers. When you get to 10, start back at 1. See how long you can keep counting before your mind wanders, and when it does, gently guide it back to counting.

Horse Sense

Some people like to meditate by humming, chanting, or repeating a favorite mantra (a word or phrase used for focus during meditation), focusing their minds on the sound and repeating the mantra slowly and softly, either out loud or in the mind. Here are some mantras we like: "om" (the sound of the universe), "love," "one," and "open."

◆ Remember in the last chapter when we suggested listening to music? Music is an excellent way to relax, and because music is pleasant to hear, it helps your brain learn to focus on a single thing rather than scattering itself in every direction.

◆ Changing your diet can change your life. Substances like caffeine and alcohol can help to keep you from focusing well. Also, eating more organic, whole foods rather than processed, preserved foods will make you feel more centered, balanced, and able to concentrate, focus, and relax. For some people, gradually phasing out meat helps them feel more in touch with the animals in their lives, but for others, this isn't necessary. It all depends on you.

◆ Exercise is an excellent way to relax, counter-intuitive as that may seem. Rather than sitting still, some people relax much better on the move because working muscles help to focus the mind. Maybe a quiet, meditative walk works for you. Or maybe a run through the park or on the treadmill is more your speed. Some people might prefer a yoga class, or an intensive session on the elliptical trainer at the gym. Whatever your preference, exercise can help get that distracting body nice and tired so that it doesn't interfere so much with your mind. Also, when you exercise, your brain, out of necessity, concentrates on what your body is doing and that's good mental exercise, too.

Horse Sense

All that mental relaxation, meditation, focusing work, exercise, and eating right are bound to help you in other areas of your life—you'll concentrate better at work, pay more attention to people when they talk to you, be in better shape, even sleep better!—so relaxation in all its forms is actually a very efficient way to spend your time.

Visualization for Mental Receptiveness

When Debbie teaches workshops on animal communication, before anybody actually starts communicating, she likes to lead the group through a visualization exercise. Everyone closes his or her eyes and listens to Debbie, following her words and visualizing the images she directs them to imagine. This helps everyone to relax and feel less nervous.

Visualizations also help people become more receptive to external images. If you focus on the images someone else suggests with their voice, you also learn to be more open to images sent psychically.

For this visualization exercise, either have a friend read you the following meditation, or tape it yourself so that you can play it at any time. Although you don't need to do a meditation before every animal communication, Debbie does find that for beginners, this preparatory exercise really helps.

This simple visualization helps to open up each of your intuitive senses for clearer reception. It will also help you to relax in preparation for an animal communication session.

1. Lie down on a firm surface (a mat or blanket on the floor works well). Close your eyes.

2. Take a deep breath, inhaling through your nose. Allow the air to fill your abdomen, chest, and back.

3. Exhale slowly through your mouth. Repeat this inhalation and exhalation three times, breathing slowly and deeply.

4. Imagine your body slowly relaxing, beginning at your toes. Imagine your feet gently melting into the ground under you.

5. Feel your calves relaxing and let the tension flow out of your knee and hips joints. Imagine your thighs gently relaxing into the earth.

6. Let your abdomen, chest, ribs, and shoulders melt gently into the earth. Feel your elbows releasing tension, your arms and hands gently sinking deep into the earth.

7. Let the tension flow out of your neck and release your head, letting the earth cradle the full weight of your head and your body. You feel safe, relaxed, warm, protected by the earth.

8. Now, imagine that beautiful, golden roots begin to grow from your feet, finding their way into the earth below.

9. Feel the way the earth accepts you and holds you, the golden roots binding you together.

10. Feel the mutual communication of energy between your spirit and the spirit of the earth. See how the energy flows back and forth, in a wide-open pathway of communication. You are earth: earth is you.

11. Continue breathing, basking in this union, exhaling every last bit of tension from your body, inhaling love, light, and openness to the natural world.

12. Slowly bring your consciousness back, drawing the roots back out of the earth and into you, knowing that at any time, you can reach this union with any other being.

13. Gently wiggle your fingers and your toes, stretch your muscles, and turn over on your side.

14. When you are ready, open your eyes.

Tips for Receiving Messages from Animals

Because receiving psychic messages from animals is a process that can take some practice, we've got some great tips to help reorient your mind before you actually launch into a full-scale communication session (we'll walk you through one of those in the next chapter).

When receiving messages, and also when engaging in a psychic dialogue, preparing yourself in just the right way can make the conversation flow more easily and make more sense. Keep in mind the following suggestions during your psychic communication practice.

Attitude Adjustment

The way you view animals—in general, as well as your own pet in particular—influences your communication receptivity and the willingness of the animals you are connecting with to talk to you. If you approach animals with respect and appreciation for who they are, they will be more likely to be receptive. If you view them as substandard or inferior in any way, you will limit your ability and awareness, as well as the animal's openness to you (how open are *you* to others who obviously think you are "beneath" them?).

> **Cat's Meow**
>
> Cats don't belong on the floor. They belong up high where I don't have to see them!
>
> —Buddy, a Terrier mix, when asked why he bothers the family cats

To truly experience the spiritual essence of another being, you must leave any preconceived notions, as well as doubts and fears, behind you. Open your heart and allow the animal's true self and energy to come through to you. This works best when your attitude is one of humility and receptivity, which will help the animal feel comfortable opening up to you.

If you feel you are having trouble feeling truly receptive to the animal with whom you would like to communicate, you can try specifically focusing on several things:

- Admire the animal's spiritual qualities, rather than focusing on a shiny coat, pretty eyes, perfect form, etc. Focusing on qualities such as honesty, loyalty, patience, joy, integrity, wisdom, and kindness encourages mutual respect and builds the relationship into one of deeper understanding, ultimately strengthening the two-way communication between both of you.

- Remember and reflect on past positive interactions between you and your animal, and what that time together meant to you. How has your animal enriched your life? Let a feeling of gratitude extend from your being to your animal's being.

- Consider the animal as a potential teacher, rather than in a more servile role. This will enable you to observe your animal with more objectivity, encouraging the free flow of information from animal to person.

Animals can indeed be our teachers, in many different and fascinating ways. Expecting animals to send us messages related to our mastery over them can limit what you will learn from your animal, who may be far wiser than you know.

At one of the first animal communication workshops Debbie attended, the class had to go into the barn and pick an animal to communicate with. Debbie opened one of the stall doors and entered a small barn that had a few goats, sheep, and a llama.

Debbie had never seen a llama up close, and she was intrigued by this one. As he approached Debbie, with his intense eyes and rather large body, she immediately became tense and nervous. Her body went rigid and she backed up, just a little closer to the door.

The llama came closer, looked at Debbie with what she can only describe as disdain, and said, "You are not advanced enough to talk to me." Then the llama turned away in disgust and walked off. Debbie admits to being just a little relieved, but also upset with herself and her attitude, which clearly erected barriers between them: barriers of fear, hesitation, difference. Debbie's attitude projected the thought: You are different than I am and I fear you. The llama was right. She wasn't ready to talk to him yet.

> **Doggone!**
>
> Stereotyping an animal as a member of a certain breed or species can inhibit the subtle nuances of communication. Instead, view each being as an individual. Give the animal the respect and love you would give to a family member or friend of your own species. See the animal as another being, not as something different from you.

The experience strengthened Debbie's resolve to work on her attitude and learn from the llama. A few months later, Debbie attended a second workshop at the same place, and by that time, she was feeling more confident with her ability to communicate with animals on a level of mutual understanding and respect.

When the time came to scatter and find an animal for communication, Debbie headed straight for that llama. This time, she was ready.

The llama sauntered over to Debbie and told her that he remembered her. Then he sent Debbie a message that still amazes her today:

> *Dwell within your inner peace. In that place, you will find truth. This place is not a place of imagination or fleeting fancies. Realize that herein lies your higher self, ready to teach you. Listen. I can't tell you enough to listen. Absorb and listen.*
>
> *Herein, you will begin a process of growth. You will see answers to questions you have long asked unraveling before you. Don't get caught up in the pondering. Don't feel confused, or try to understand. Just accept what is. Know that what is, is what is supposed to be. Listen to the why and grow from it.*
>
> *The key is this very growth. Move at a pace that makes you comfortable. When you begin to feel confused or overwhelmed, return to that place of peace deep inside yourself. There, the confusion disappears and the answers wait. Just listen.*

No path is straight and flat. If it were, what would you learn? Life is a journey. See it as a journey and every day will be a new experience, a new lesson, and a new appreciation of the present, the "right now."

Thank the gentle wind for the delicate balance it brings. Acknowledging the simple elements will open doors to miracles. Miracles exist everywhere, but most people don't see them. Energy flows everywhere, but most people never know it. Absorb. Be a student, and then be a teacher. Experience the world in its purest form, and then tell others.

That is all. Now, go and practice.

And some people call animals dumb! Debbie felt like she'd just visited a Tibetan monk on a mountaintop! (The Dalai … Llama?) She also felt an overwhelming sense of rightness and truth in the llama's words. She would continue to learn, absorbing the teachings of the earth and its energy. And then, she would teach.

If Debbie hadn't been open to the wisdom of that animal, she never would have received this message, the message that so inspired her to direct her life's path. With the wrong attitude, she would have missed out on the experience. Keep your attitude similarly open, and you might be amazed and inspired by what the animals you encounter along the way have to tell you.

Open Your Heart

Learning how to communicate with the animals can be a very emotional experience. Humans naturally tend to protect themselves emotionally, some more than others, but a closed-off heart will also stand in the way of successful and open receptivity.

Whenever Debbie teaches a workshop, her own animals become the teachers. In every workshop she has conducted, at least one person will be moved to tears by a communication experience. Animal communication involves an intense opening of the heart, and Debbie witnesses it firsthand, all the time.

CAUTION

Doggone!

Fear of feeling too strongly can close off your heart. Yet animals can teach us how to open our hearts again, allowing the pain to drain away so our hearts can fill with love.

When Debbie holds a workshop, she has her students pick one of her own animals that they would like to communicate with. One of Debbie's cats, Mamma Kitty, has an amazing gift. In every class, she would share the pain of her past with one of the students. Many of Debbie's students still write to her about how much Mamma Kitty helped them and how they still think of her.

When Debbie first moved to her home in Massachusetts, Mamma Kitty was a skinny stray with broken teeth and worms that Debbie discovered living on the property. Frightened of people, she used to hide in one of the old barns. Debbie would leave food out for her and encourage her to trust, so that Debbie could help her. Mamma Kitty was pregnant at the time, and Debbie was hoping to be able to catch her and her kittens so that she could bring them inside and give them all a fair chance at survival.

Mamma Kitty was elusive, and had her litter of kittens underneath the floor of the barn, so that Debbie couldn't reach them. Eventually, she moved them into the hay and Debbie promised her she would not hurt them. Mamma Kitty even allowed Debbie to touch them, but then again became insecure about Debbie's presence— who knows what experiences had led her to be so fearful of humans—and Mamma Kitty moved her kittens again, out of reach. When Debbie went to find them one day, they were gone.

Debbie searched everywhere for the missing kittens with no luck. A few days later, Mamma Kitty appeared again in the barn. She was crying. Debbie went over to where she was, and Mamma Kitty showed Debbie the head of one of her kittens. Debbie burst into tears, deeply disturbed by the sight, but then, she realized how Mamma Kitty must feel, and she put her own feelings aside to sit with the grieving mother and try to comfort her in her pain. (Debbie later found out the entire litter had been eaten by a coyote.)

After this incident, Debbie continued to help Mamma Kitty grieve over the loss of her kittens. She finally allowed Debbie to take her in, and Debbie had her spayed. Mamma Kitty still lives with Debbie at her home in Florida.

In each of Debbie's workshops, Mamma Kitty picks one person in the class to talk about this great tragedy in her life and her grief over the loss of her kittens. Mamma Kitty still wonders if she was a good mother, but years after the experience, she has pulled out of her pain and now uses the experience to help those people she thinks can benefit from hearing about it and feeling some of what she felt.

How open this cat's heart must be, to be able to bring that experience back to the surface again and again! Mamma Kitty also seems to pick those students whose hearts are also particularly open, because these are the humans who can best understand and accept the message she has to send them: that grief, loss, and suffering are part of life, but that when we experience these things, we needn't do so alone. We can share them with others, alleviating our suffering by the bond of friendship and love.

By Mamma Kitty sharing her pain with others, she was in fact healing herself. The moving messages and distinct communication of her past pain helped many students experience animal communication in its purest form. By being a teacher Mamma

Kitty was also able to heal the hole in her own heart and at the same time open the hearts of others. Some of the students Mamma Kitty has shared her story with have experienced a similar loss in their own lives and were able to relate to the pain she felt.

Exercise to Open Your Heart

To help you get better in touch with your own heart and help you to open it, try this visualization. This exercise is particularly helpful right before a communication session, especially when the questions you want to ask your animal might be of an emotional nature.

1. Imagine that there are two large doors that lead to your heart. Imagine what they look like. Are they glass or wood or steel? Take some time to design them in your mind so they are yours.

2. Inhale deeply, holding for a count of two. Exhale deeply to the count of four.

3. Imagine yourself opening these doors into your heart. Continue to breathe deeply, two counts in, four counts out. Open the doors as wide as you can.

4. As the doors of your heart stand wide open, feel the tension pouring out and melting away. Imagine filling that space before you with a huge wave of love, a wave that consumes you and floods your heart with light and courage.

5. Let yourself stay here for another minute or so, continuing to breathe deeply. When you are ready, open your eyes.

Horse Sense

For some people, believing in their abilities is the hardest part of animal communication. We want to judge, we want to analyze, we want to doubt, both the very nature of animal communication and especially our own ability, even our own worthiness to participate in it.

Believe in Yourself

We've already mentioned several times that belief in your own intuitive ability is crucial for successful animal communication. However, we're going to keep saying it because it is so very important for successful communication.

We might not know you personally, but we do know one thing about you, and we know it with all our hearts: You can do this. You have this ability, even if you haven't yet unearthed it. It is there, and all you need to do is the work involved in accessing it.

Sometimes, this work is easy. It's just a matter of jumping right in with both feet and trying it, and trying it again, and again. Others might need to overcome greater barriers, but with persistence and hope, anyone can reclaim this ability.

Part of believing in yourself is refusing to judge what comes through to you. Maybe you won't like or believe what you hear, but it is very important to accept whatever you get, and thank the animal for sending it to you, no matter what the message. Pay attention to everything you feel, see, hear, and smell. Don't discount anything.

Horse Sense

To remove the blocks that inhibit a successful two-way communication, you must believe valid communication is possible and believe in your intuition. We guarantee that at first you will think, "It feels like I am talking to myself." This is exactly what it feels like in the beginning, but the more you practice and the more you trust in what you receive, the more your confidence grows, the more real and clear and solid the experience will become.

Yes, some things you think you hear may sound odd, and your mind might try to convince you that you are making it up or that what you are receiving can't be right. If you experience this, just call out the animal's name in your mind, and ask the question again. Your logic and rationality *will* try to diminish your intuition and "argue" with what comes in, so it is very important that you not give in to it during a communication session. Be open to surprises. Accept anything you get, no matter how strange it may seem.

It took Debbie many years before she became confident and comfortable enough with her abilities to begin using them in a serious manner to help other people. Animal communication is a continual growth process, but if you can let yourself go with the flow of it, and don't forget to have fun and enjoy the ride, then you are in store for a life-changing experience that can quickly become an integral part of your life and your relationship to both the animals that you meet, and the entire community of life on Earth.

Don't Overwhelm the Animal

During a communication session, remember that communication goes both ways, and that sometimes, animals must be protected from *our* strong emotions, especially when we are talking to animals with whom we have a very emotional attachment.

Be careful not to project your own strong emotions toward the animal. If you approach an animal with too much emotion, you could frighten the animal or make him or her shut down to you. Whether your emotions are positive ones, like overwhelming love, or negative ones like fear and sadness, you risk blocking this two-way process, or having your own emotions bounced back to you.

Doggone!

What if a friend walked up to you and suddenly broke into tears, pouring out how wonderful you are and how much they love you? You *might* like it, but you might also feel very uncomfortable, or even be tempted to run away. Be sure to respect your animal's boundaries by ending "conversations" that make your animal uncomfortable and by not forcing physical contact when your animal doesn't want it. Stay attuned to your animal's physical and psychic feedback so you know when enough is enough.

Don't Try Too Hard

Over-trying is a common mistake among people just starting out in pet psychic communication. If you try too hard, you might miss the subtle communication that animal communication is all about, and you could block the subtle exchange of energy. Rather than forcing the process, just try to be in a receptive mode. Relax, open your hands, sit back, open your chest, breathe slowly and deeply, and close your eyes if you like. Relax and let the communication flow.

When Debbie teaches workshops, usually at least one person sits hunched over his or her notebook, gripping a pen, with squinting eyes and obvious tension in the neck and shoulders. Debbie immediately asks such people to lean back and think of something funny. This lightens things up and gets the energy flowing again. When you focus too much on "getting the right answer," you immediately stunt the flow of intuition and communication, because now your brain is taking over. Once the rational mind kicks in, you've probably lost the connection. It's like using a bulldozer to sweep the kitchen floor!

If you feel yourself trying too hard, go back to the beginning: Quiet your mind and open your heart. Or think of something funny to make you laugh. Even Debbie gets stuck sometimes! When she does, it helps her to get up and walk around, maybe take a walk outside. Then she can come back and try again, starting fresh. Different strategies work for different people, but the point is to let the communication be easy, soft, open, and quiet. Otherwise, you'll miss it.

When Debbie first started communicating with the animals, it took her a long time to quiet her mind. The room had to be perfectly quiet, too, and after the communication,

Debbie felt exhausted. After years of practice, Debbie's mind can still get chaotic (just like anyone else), but Debbie has found personalized ways of sifting through the clutter to hear and understand an animal's message.

Debbie has also had to do consultations with extensive noise in the background, such as during construction on her house—something she never could have done at the beginning. She has connected with animals in front of cameras, crowds, and skeptics, all of which was possible by simply tuning out distractions and focusing inward.

Horse Sense

The more you practice, the more your abilities will grow. Life will continue to challenge you in different ways, and every challenge represents a new opportunity to learn and help your skills evolve.

Accept What Comes

Accepting what comes to you—whether feelings, pictures, impressions, thoughts, words, sounds, bodily sensations, or just a knowing—is vitally important in effective receiving. The more you become familiar with what and how you receive information, the less you will analyze and criticize the information that comes through.

A nonjudgmental attitude is equally important, especially when speaking with someone else's animal. Your job is not to judge the animal or another person. Your job is to listen to the animal and convey his or her message as accurately as you can. If you color your interpretation with your own emotions, ideas, and judgments, you run the risk of altering the message and possibly damaging the sacred bond between human and animal. Being open, accepting, and nonjudgmental will keep you from being responsible for a misunderstanding between two friends.

Openly acknowledging whatever communication you receive without fear or hesitation will open intuitive doors for you in many ways. That also means acknowledging when your animal is done talking, or simply has nothing to say. (You don't always want to talk either, right?) Accept and acknowledge what you receive and let the meaning or story appear by itself. Everyone's animal communication experience is different, so rather than comparing yourself or your experiences to anyone else's, accept what you get and let yourself be a conduit. Doubt inhibits the flow. Acceptance releases the flow.

Horse Sense

Always acknowledge what you receive and express your gratitude by thanking the animal. Animals appreciate manners as much as people! Expressing your appreciation will keep the animal receptive to you and willing to continue. Animals deserve thanks when they open themselves up to us!

Practice

The key to building the telepathic muscle (just like learning to do *anything* really well) is practice, practice, practice. When Debbie first started communicating with animals, she was so hungry for it that she wanted to practice all the time. She and a few of the other classmates kept in touch and used to practice with each other's animals, animals within their families, any animals they could. The more you practice, the more validation you will receive, which will in turn boost your confidence and help you to understand the way you are receiving information from the animal.

Have Fun!

Finally, animal communication should be lighthearted and fun. This can be easy to forget, but it's an essential ingredient for success. Who wants to talk with somebody who is all stressed out? Don't get frustrated. If you feel you are not receiving anything, review the previous steps again. We all have bad days and many things can inhibit telepathy, but in the long run, your skills will grow. Enjoy the process! It really *is* fun.

The Least You Need to Know

- Receiving psychic messages becomes easier with a quiet, listening mind.

- Believe you can receive psychic messages and you will dissolve your mental barriers to psychic communication.

- As you practice receiving telepathic messages, remember to have a positive attitude, believe in yourself, open your heart, don't overwhelm the animal, don't try too hard, and accept what comes to you without judgment.

- Practice every day, to develop and refine your skill. Above all, don't forget to enjoy yourself!

Chapter 7

Building the Intuitive Bond with Your Pet

In This Chapter

- ◆ Getting ready to communicate
- ◆ Telepathic communication with your pet, step by step
- ◆ Building a bond with Maggie
- ◆ Telepathy blockers and telepathy enhancers
- ◆ Exercises for telepathic communication practice

In the past two chapters, we've talked about preparations for asking and receiving questions. Now it's time to start practicing in earnest, time to start actually communicating telepathically with your animal! Don't be nervous, we'll walk you through the process, step-by-step.

Communication is not only fun, but a great way to get to know your pet better. The more you communicate, the more you will build the bond between you and your pet. It's the best way for friends to get to know each other better. So are you ready to have fun and become a little more enlightened about the nature of the animals in your life? Then let's get started!

Getting Ready

Before any communication session, it pays to get ready. Find a quiet spot where you won't be distracted. Relax and sit comfortably. While some people like to have their pets in the room with them, it isn't necessary. You can even communicate with an animal from miles away! Now, follow the steps outlined in the next sections.

Concentrate on Your Breathing

Breathe deeply for a minute or so. Then, take a long inhale through your nose. As you breathe in, feel the breath fill your abdomen, then feel it rise into your chest and back so it fills your entire body.

Exhale slowly and steadily through your mouth. As you exhale, imagine all the negative energy and stress leaving your body.

Keep breathing, and with every inhale imagine inhaling invigorating energy full of love and possibilities. Keep exhaling all stress and negativity.

After a few minutes of deep breathing, when you feel very relaxed, calm, and cleared, filled with love and empty of negative energy, visualize the doors to your heart slowly opening wide.

CAUTION

Doggone! _____

Many of us get in the habit of shallow breathing, never really letting the breath reach deep down into the depths of our lungs. This kind of breathing impedes our access to the life energy all around us. Practice deep breathing on a regular basis and infuse your body with a more vibrant healthful energy as well as a greater access to intuition.

State Your Intention

Now that you feel open and relaxed, the next important step is to state your intention. You aren't stating this to the animal, necessarily, but to your own consciousness.

You might state your intention in any of several ways, either general or specific, depending on what you want to accomplish. As you first begin your practice, you might want to stick with a general intention. The more experienced you get, the more you can zero in on individual issues. Some examples:

- My intention is to communicate with Sally.

- My intention is to communicate with Sally, to be able to hear her messages with clarity and accuracy.

◆ My intention is to communicate with Sally, and I ask that none of my fears, personal blocks, or barriers stand in the way of receiving her messages.

Let your intention sink into your mind and stay there throughout your communication session.

Get the Animal's Attention

Now it's time to "dial the phone." Get your animal's attention by calling the animal's name in your head. As you call the animal's name, picture the animal in your mind's eye, if you can.

> **Horse Sense**
>
> Stating your intention helps clarify your goals in communicating with animals, but it can also be a valuable tool you can use in all areas of your life. Stating your intention before you go to work, have an important conversation, give a performance, embark on a new adventure, or attend an important meeting will help to direct your energy productively.

Because Debbie does many consultations with people who live far away, she might never see the animal and must picture him or her based on a description from the owner. However, as you begin your practice, you might want to communicate with an animal via a picture if you have trouble "seeing" him or her in your mind's eye.

Even if your animal is in the same room with you, close your eyes and picture the animal anyway. This will help to tune your spirit in to your animal's spirit.

Introduce Yourself

If you communicate with an animal you've never met (like Debbie so often does), you can introduce yourself by telling the animal (in your mind) your name and why you are contacting him or her. If you are communicating with your own animal, simply say (in your mind) something along the lines of, "Hello, Sally. It's me, Eve."

Ask Permission

An important step in the process is asking permission. Even though your animal will probably be happy to talk with you, asking permission shows the animal respect and honors the boundaries between you. If you just start "talking" without asking if the animal will allow it, you send a message that you are the master and the animal has to do what you say. This is not conducive to open communication!

> **Cat's Meow**
>
> If he wants to shoe me, he should talk to me first ... I want it all explained to me first. They are my feet, after all.
>
> —Annabelle, a Tennessee Walker mare, talking about her farrier

Instead, say something like, "Sally, I would like to talk with you for awhile. Would you like to talk with me?" or "Sally, may I have permission to talk with you?" or whatever wording seems natural to you. The point is to ask, not to force the communication on the animal or assume the animal feels like chatting. Then, stay open and listen for words, images, or a feeling of acceptance that your animal has agreed to have a conversation.

You're Actually Doing It!

Once you're in, you can start your conversation! You may be eager to start firing questions at your animal, anxious to learn the answers to all those things you always wondered. "How did you get in the animal shelter?" "Who were your previous owners?" "What do you think about the cat?" "Why do you chase your tail?" "Do you really love me?"

Think how an immediate barrage of personal questions feels to you! Talk about an unpleasant conversation. Instead, we'll show you how to ease into the conversation in a pleasant, polite, and ultimately more rewarding way. Just follow this next set of steps.

Understand the Essence

The first thing Debbie always does when making contact with an animal is to take a few minutes to allow the animal to show its essence. When you first begin a psychic communication with an animal, a moment of quiet focus will help you to see and feel the animal's essential being.

This will clue you in to some basic characteristics of the animal: personality, sense of self, inner knowing, life purpose, etc. Give this step some time. Feel this spiritual connection as the animal shows you who he or she is at the spiritual level.

Send Questions

Once you have a sense of your animal's spirit, you can begin presenting your questions. Focus on one question at a time, and ask it in a clear, simple way in your head, as we explained in Chapter 5.

To get you started, here are some questions you might want to ask:

- How are you feeling?

- What are your favorite activities?

- What can you tell me about your previous home?

- Is there anything you would like to change about your life?

- Is there anything I can do to make your life more enjoyable?

- What do you think of [another pet, another person in the family]?

- Who is your favorite person? (Don't ask this one if you don't really want to know the truth!)

- Do you have any advice for me?

> **Cat's Meow**
>
> Yes, I *would* enjoy showing. Especially the pampering. I know just how to look and how to enhance my gait to make people gasp with delight. I would enjoy being treated like a star. Maybe we should start right now!
>
> —Lola, a Thoroughbred horse, when asked if she would like to participate in showing events

The more you speak to your animal, the more you will get a sense of what is appropriate or relevant to ask. Remember to start with the basics and express your questions in a simple way.

Tune in to Answers

As we explained in Chapter 6, after each question, keep your mind and heart open for whatever answers might arise. You might not always like what you hear, or you might be completely surprised by the answers that come to you, but try not to judge and stay tuned in to everything that comes to you, no matter how insignificant it may seem. This is the key to really learning how to listen telepathically.

Give Thanks

You might feel like you could talk to your pet all day! However, like any other conversation, eventually you need to move on with your day, and so does your pet! After you are finished asking questions and receiving answers (your pet might even tell you he or she has had enough for now), be sure to thank your animal for taking the time to open up to you and communicate with you.

Giving thanks and expressing your deep appreciation for the animal is very important for maintaining a healthy, positive relationship and effective future communications, so don't forget this essential and final step! Let your animal know you appreciate not only the conversation, but your animal companion, and everything he or she does for your life. Who wouldn't want to hear how loved and important they are?

> **Horse Sense**
>
> To remind you of the basic steps involved in an animal communication, remember this acronym: BOSSCATT (Think of it like "Boss Cat"). BOSSCATT stands for:
>
> **B** reathe
>
> **O** pen your heart
>
> **S** mile to relieve tension
>
> **S** tate your intention
>
> **C** all the animal's name
>
> **A** sk for permission
>
> **T** une in
>
> **T** hank the animal when you are finished

Maggie's Story

Building a bond with an animal struck close to home for Lynn, our development editor. At the time she was editing this book, she was dealing with a challenging situation involving a stray kitty she later named Maggie. A beautiful gray-spotted tabby with a distinctive white bib and white-tipped paws, Maggie was feral, or wild—she had most likely been born to a stray—and Lynn had been leaving food out for her all summer. She appeared to be about five months old. With the cold weather coming on, and to prevent the kitty from either fathering or producing a litter of more unwanted kittens, Lynn decided to trap the cat using a *Have A Heart* humane trap and get her some help.

The trapping, while not pleasant, went off without a hitch, and Lynn took the cat to the vet. After getting a clean bill of health, Maggie was spayed and given her shots, and Lynn took her home.

Then came the decision. Originally Lynn had planned to release Maggie outside and continue to feed her, because feral cats (especially past a certain age) often do not make good pets. But Lynn was soon smitten with Maggie's feisty personality and decided she would try and keep her. Also affecting that decision was the fact that Maggie got along well with Lynn's other two male cats, and they with her.

Because Maggie had spent five months looking out for herself—and doing an admirable job of it—she was stubborn and resisted the efforts Lynn made to befriend her. She soon settled into a routine but remained fearful of any human contact and often looked for places to hide (one morning Lynn found her squashed behind the refrigerator!). Finally Lynn asked Debbie for help in connecting with Maggie. Debbie was able to do so, reporting back to Lynn that Maggie was a very smart little girl with a determined attitude and survivor instincts. Debbie explained to Maggie what had happened, and assured her that Lynn loved her very much and wanted to help her feel more secure in her new home. She then asked Maggie what Lynn could do to help her feel more comfortable, and ended the reading by sending Maggie lots of love and light and assuring her she was in a safe place with people who loved her. Debbie also later connected with Lynn's other two cats, Bill and Willie, to enlist their help in making Maggie feel a part of the family.

As of this writing, Maggie is adjusting to life as a pampered housecat—Lynn has made sure she has every comfort under the sun—and is becoming more used to human contact. In the several months she has been with Lynn, Maggie has grown quite close to the other two cats in the family, while the bond between her and humans is growing slowly but surely. Her favorite activities are playing with Bill (as she gets in touch with her "inner kitten" for the first time) and taking naps under the bed.

> **Cat's Meow**
>
> I enjoy dark closed-in spaces. I feel more secure. Big spaces are overwhelming to me ... I enjoy the toys that make noise and ones that are soft so that I can sink my teeth into them. I am quite fast, you know! I can catch anything!
>
> —Maggie, a feral gray tabby cat

Telepathic Blockers and Clarifiers

Some days, a telepathic communication may seem almost effortless. Other days, it may seem virtually impossible! What's the difference? In her years of experience, Debbie has observed that certain factors tend to block the free flow of telepathic information, while others seem to enhance it. Here's what Debbie has observed:

Telepathy blockers include the following:

- *Carbohydrates, like bread, rice, potatoes, and pasta.* This is a hard realization for us carb junkies, but a meal of whole vegetables and some lean protein helps ground and center the mind more effectively. Don't eat a large heavy meal prior to trying psychic communication.

- *Sweets.* Cake, cookies, candy? They might taste great, but they could dull your psychic abilities.

- *Caffeine.* Don't try to communicate telepathically just after you've finished that full pot of coffee!

◆ *Alcohol and drugs.* A mind altered by psychotropic substances can't clearly perceive the subtle nuances of telepathic communication.

◆ *Internal clutter.* If you have too much on your mind, feel emotionally vulnerable or upset, or stress has got you bogged down mentally, you could have trouble tuning in.

◆ *External clutter.* Noise and distractions all around you will make centering and quieting your mind difficult. How will you hear your animal with all that racket?

◆ *Negativity.* Sometimes, we are our own worst enemies, and a negative attitude can halt a psychic communication in its tracks. Believe you can do this, be gentle with yourself, and be patient. Stay open and you'll get through.

◆ *Prejudgments and assumptions.* By judging another person or animal, you are blocking your intuition. Remain calm and unbiased so you can receive what the animal is trying to relay to you.

Telepathy enhancers include the following:

◆ Exercise

◆ Spending time in nature

◆ Relaxing music

◆ Meditation

◆ Eating a healthy diet of whole foods

◆ Being thankful

◆ Letting yourself feel love, and using love to heal and help

◆ Getting enough sleep

Communication Exercises

Once you've accomplished a telepathic connection, you deserve to feel proud of yourself! However, that doesn't mean you should rest on your laurels. Practice, practice, practice!

Fortunately, this kind of practice is fun. You can continue to practice in the way we explained earlier, but you can also try different kinds of questions or tuning in to different things to help refine your skills. Ask your animal's help in this during the communication. See if your animal is willing to help you get better at communicating. It can only benefit both of you!

Of course, any practice should also stay focused on the ultimate goal of communication—furthering the relationship. If you waste too much time focusing on silly telepathic tricks, your animal could get bored and your conversations will stop being productive. Or maybe your animal will enjoy helping you to test yourself. It all depends on the animal's personality and your relationship.

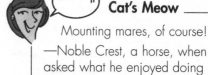

Cat's Meow

Mounting mares, of course! —Noble Crest, a horse, when asked what he enjoyed doing the most

Staying open to what comes will help you to determine your animal's willingness to help you practice in different ways, whether that means testing your ability to receive certain pieces of information you can later validate, or simply spending more time chatting about whatever comes up.

Debbie remembers when she first started communicating with animals and a client named Nancy who owned eight black Poodles wanted Debbie to do a reading. Debbie thought to herself, goodness, this is going to be a challenge! Eight black Poodles!

Debbie knew that by strongly stating her intention to speak with a specific dog each time, she would be able to differentiate between all eight dogs, but Nancy (like many of us) was a skeptic. She asked Debbie to ask each Poodle the color of his or her collar.

Nancy admitted her skepticism, and kept laughing at herself for calling an animal communicator. She wanted hard evidence that Debbie was a psychic and could "see" the collars of each dog. It was a test, and Debbie knew it.

Debbie explained to the woman that the poodles might not really care what color their collar is, or even really know. Could they even see their own collars? Plus, a dog's sense of color is different than ours, so it would be easy to misinterpret the information they might send.

Also, Debbie explained that the dogs might have more important things to discuss or convey to her, and that the two of them should give each dog the respect of allowing each personality or essence to emerge first. Just imagine if you finally heard from someone you'd wanted to talk to for years, and the first thing they asked you was a cynical and challenging, "So what color is your shirt?"

She agreed that nailing each collar color wasn't what this was about. Her prejudgments had been hindering her openness to the situation. Instead of letting the dogs talk, she wanted her own proof. Nancy finally agreed to defer to Debbie's judgment, and Debbie let each dog come through in his or her own distinct way. Nancy left the consultation knowing much more about each of her dear Poodles than she had ever imagined she could.

By the way, the only Poodle who cared about her collar was a beautiful female called Belle, who expressed to Debbie her excitement about a new black collar with sparkles that none of the others had. As for the rest of them, they couldn't have cared less.

The purpose of this story is that when you are communicating with your animal and you "test" yourself by asking your pet to communicate something red he sees in the other room and you get nothing, or if you are communicating with someone else's animal and the client asks you what color their animal's food dish is and you get it wrong, that doesn't mean that you are not getting through. Color, in itself, is difficult anyway, for the reasons we've already told you about—dogs don't necessarily see it the way we do, or care much about it at all. Although dogs and cats sometimes express color to Debbie, especially lost animals who might show Debbie they are, for example, in front of a yellow house with a red car, color isn't necessarily something animals choose to bring up as important.

Horse Sense

You may or may not feel compelled to test your own abilities. Practice without the pressure of tests can help communication to flow more freely, and validation will come to you soon enough. You'll see.

The point is to make sure you have the personality first, a far more important part of connecting and communicating than validation tests. And, if your animal does enjoy practicing validation tests with you, let the tests come from the animal first, to see what the animal is motivated to work on with you.

Exercise #1

This first exercise will help you to connect with a pet you don't know, or don't know very well. This kind of connecting is good practice because you might be able to be more objective and keep from infusing the communication with your own personal knowledge about your pet.

For this exercise, enlist an interested friend with a pet. Ask your friend to give you a picture of one of his or her animals, preferably a picture showing the animal's eyes (which are, as we well know, truly windows to the soul). Get a pen and paper, or do the communication at your computer, where you can type the answers (for some people, this is much faster and more natural).

Set aside a time when you will not be disturbed, and attempt to connect with this animal via the picture. Go through the steps as stated earlier in the chapter to connect, and don't forget to introduce yourself and ask permission!

When you feel you have a connection and have given the animal a moment to show you his or her spirit, ask the animal the following questions, and write down the answers:

- Tell me about your personality. Are you outgoing or shy?

- Do you tend to be more nervous or more relaxed?

- When you meet someone you don't know, or don't know very well, are you more affectionate or more aloof?

- How would *you* describe your personality?

- What do you enjoy doing?

- What do you dislike?

- Where do you like to sleep?

As you ask each question, allow the images, words, feelings, and impressions to surface. Write down anything and everything that comes through to you.

If an answer seems unclear or you aren't getting anything, ask the question again. Remember that the answers will be subtle and might feel like they are coming out of your imagination. You might feel unsure about whether you are just making up the answers, but rest assured, this is part of the process, especially for beginners. Just acknowledge whatever you get, write it all down, and don't forget to thank the animal for taking the time to communicate with you.

Sometimes, new communicators truly feel like they get nothing at all from the animal with which they are trying to communicate. Think about whether or not you are blocking your openness to the messages with skepticism, doubt, or negativity. Breathe and try to release these feelings, just for the time being.

If you still feel that you are getting nothing but dead space, another trick that can help to jump-start the process is to imagine that animal is answering you. You know how animals in cartoons always talk? Just imagine the animal you are trying to talk to is answering you. Write down your imagined answers.

This exercise utilizes a process to help you open up your intuitive side, so that the energy of the conversation can flow through you more easily. Most psychic information comes through the imagination, and by jumpstarting it, you might be amazed at the information you receive!

Most of all, don't get frustrated, and don't give up until you have answered each of the questions, *even if you had to imagine the answers.*

Horse Sense

An active imagination ties directly into your intuition, and activating one can activate the other.

To wrap up the exercise, set aside a time to speak with your friend about the answers you received, and ask for feedback. Maybe some of your answers will be right on target, according to your friend. Some may seem surprising, or downright wrong. That's fine, too. The point is to practice, and practice, and practice, and this is just one more way to practice. The more you do it, the more your abilities will evolve.

Exercise #2

This exercise is one of Debbie's favorites in her workshop. People often comment on how effective and enlightening it can be. This exercise requires a deck of animal cards, which you can buy in New Age bookstores, catalogues, or on the Internet. Try browsing Internet bookstores like Amazon.com for keywords like "animal cards," "medicine cards," or "animal tarot" to see what's out there. Some feature North American animals only, and a Native American slant. Some feature animals from other countries like Australia, or might have a shamanistic, druid, or tarot slant. Look around for what you like, and a deck that speaks to you and attracts you. Debbie uses a book and deck combination called *Medicine Cards* by Jamie Sams and David Carson (St. Martin's Press, 1999).

Animal cards can help people to relate to animals they wouldn't normally consider. This exercise can be fun to do as a group because Debbie has noticed that inevitably, the one person most afraid of, for example, snakes or spiders, will end up getting that card! This forces them to experience what it is like to be in the body of a being they thought they feared.

Horse Sense

Each animal represents a certain strength and energy, and many animal decks come with books that detail the lore and symbolism behind each animal. You can buy a book separately to go with your homemade deck, or just use your intuition to discover the message each ani-

If you don't want to buy or can't find a deck of animal cards, you can make your own animal cards. Just take a stack of index cards. At the top of each one, write down an animal. Do 30 to 50 cards, however many you feel you need. Some animal species you might use include: Bear, Deer, Skunk, Salmon, Dolphin, Whale, Butterfly, Dragonfly, Armadillo, Alligator, Horse, Eagle, Hawk, Crow, Peacock, Rabbit, Bat, Coyote, Wolf, Turtle, Swan, Frog, Otter, Mountain Lion, Black Panther, Dog, Hummingbird, Squirrel, and of course, Snake and Spider! A book

Debbie recommends to help you create your own deck is *Animal Speak* by Ted Andrews (Llewelyn Publications, 1993).

You can use the cards as they are, or you can draw or cut out and paste pictures of each animal on its card, to help make your visualizations more vivid.

When you have your animal deck, try this exercise:

1. Shuffle the cards so you can't see the names of the animals. Pick a card.

2. Look at the card you picked, then close your eyes. Breathe deeply. Relax, and try to imagine yourself as this being. Go into the animal's body and slowly become that being.

3. Feel the animal's (your) body. What do your feet feel like? What about your legs, back, neck, mouth, eyes, ears, tail, wings? What does your hair (or fur) and skin feel like? Is your body large or small? Spend as much time as you can feeling all the different parts of yourself as the animal.

4. Picture your habitat. Where do you live, and who do you live with? Are there other beings around you? What do you do? What do you eat? How do you sleep?

5. Imagine yourself moving as your animal. How does your body feel as it moves? How do you see, hear, smell, taste, feel? Do you run? Fly? Swim? Creep? What does it feel like?

6. Think about yourself as an individual of this species. Are you male or female? Young or old? What is your personality like? What are you known for among the other animals? What are your strengths, your weaknesses, your fears, your joys?

7. Spend as much time as you need to visualizing yourself in this animal's skin.

8. When you are ready, let go of the animal with which you've had this communion, and bring yourself back to yourself. Feel yourself flowing back in, rooting to your inner body, centering. You are you again. Open your eyes.

This is a wonderful exercise to refer to when you are working with lost animals, and need to "go into their bodies" to help you get clues as to where they are and what they are near. (You'll read more about connecting with lost pets in Chapter 16.) This is also a wonderful exercise to use if you feel you are just getting stuck and need to recharge your senses. The animal card you pick may hold some message or direction for you as to how to strengthen your present situation.

You may design other exercises for yourself, but we can't encourage you enough to practice communicating with animals every day. You and your own pets can gain a whole new level of understanding, but you'll also be amazed at the changes that will happen in every aspect of your life.

You'll be more in tune to the world around you. You will gain a new reverence for the natural world. Best of all, you will discover the true, complex, beautiful, miraculous nature of the animals that have always lived all around you, the animals you never thought to really know.

The Least You Need to Know

♦ Prepare for an actual animal communication session by engaging in concentrated breathing, stating your intention, getting the animal's attention, introducing yourself if you don't know the animal, and asking permission to have a communication.

♦ During the communication, first allow the animal's essence to emerge, then ask questions, tune in to answers, and always remember to thank the animal for "speaking" with you.

♦ Certain states, habits, and behaviors can hinder telepathic communication, such as having just eaten too many carbohydrates, including sweets, caffeine, alcohol, drugs, having too much on your mind, being upset or stressed, communicating in a noisy or distracting environment, negativity, and prejudgments or assumptions.

♦ Certain states, habits, and behaviors can enhance telepathic communication, such as exercise; spending time in nature, music, meditation; eating a healthy diet of whole foods; being thankful; using love to help and heal; and getting enough sleep.

♦ Specific communication exercises can facilitate your practice, such as asking a list of pre-set questions to animals you don't know or using a deck of animal cards to experience the being of other species.

Chapter 8

When You're Not There: Long-Distance Communication with Your Pet

In This Chapter

♦ Psychic communication and geographical distance

♦ The benefits of long-distance communication

♦ How to connect with your animals when you are away

♦ A fun exercise for long-distance communication and validation

It's vacation time! You're off for two weeks in the sunny tropics ... but what about your pet? You may have hired a professional pet sitter or made reservations for your pet at your favorite boarding kennel, but pet psychic communication can add a further dimension of preparedness to your vacation plan: You can actually tell your pets what's going on!

One of the aspects of pet psychic communication that some people find hard to grasp is the notion that geography is irrelevant to telepathic communication. When spirits interact, communicating words, images, and feelings, it doesn't matter if the two beings sit next to each other, or span the globe. Psychic communication with your pets not only enables you to understand how they feel and what they think, but also allows you to connect with them if you can't be physically with them.

Why Communicate Long-Distance?

Debbie has had some of the most interesting conversations with her animals while on a plane, traveling in her car, or on vacation in another state. Because this type of communication can take place anywhere and over any distance, it can be a wonderful tool to keep yourself connected to your pets while you are on vacation ... or even when you are at work during the day!

Say you are running late, or have some unexpected errands after work. Animals thrive on routine and get used to your return at a certain time. Some animals wait at the door before our cars even come down the street, and when we are late, they worry. By communicating with your animals that you will be late, you keep them from worrying unnecessarily.

Cat's Meow

I wish you would talk to me like you talk to everyone else and not like you are talking to a baby. I understand what you are saying and I get bored when you treat me like I don't. I also understand why you talk to me that way, but just know that I really do understand you!

—Velvet, a long-haired, white-chested black cat, when asked how she would like her person to talk to her

This kind of communication can be particularly valuable during vacations, short or long. When you leave your animals for an extended period, they definitely notice! Don't think you can sneak out with the suitcase and pull the proverbial wool over their eyes. Your absence without explanation can trouble them, and so can the change in schedule inevitable when your animal moves to a boarding kennel, or even has a pet sitter.

Debbie's horses tend to be quite punctual, and they have grown accustomed to being fed at 5 P.M. Once, Debbie had to leave town for a week, so she asked a close friend to stay at the house and take care of her animals while she was away.

The third night of Debbie's trip, the friend called Debbie in a panic because Finnegan wouldn't come into the barn for his dinner. He stood at the furthest end of the field and wouldn't budge, and Debbie's friend couldn't figure out what was wrong. Was he sick? Hurt? The friend told Debbie it was raining and cold, but yet, Finnegan refused to come inside.

Debbie connected with Finnegan and gently asked him why he wouldn't go in for dinner. He replied in a very annoyed manner, "She has been late in feeding us dinner, and I am very upset about it!" Debbie told her friend what Finnegan had said, and the friend admitted that she had been kept late at work and had not been able to feed them until at least 7 P.M. on all three nights of Debbie's absence.

Debbie reconnected with Finnegan and explained to him why he was being fed late, and that it was not intentional. She asked him to please come in from the rain and eat his dinner. She also told him that she understood that he felt upset and was used to being fed earlier, but if he could just cut the friend a break this week while Debbie was gone, she would really appreciate it.

Doggone!

If you know you will be late getting home from work, avoid upsetting your animals by communicating the fact of and reason for your tardiness from wherever you are. Tell animals why you will be late, when you will be home, and thank them for being so patient and understanding with you. (A little flattery goes a long way!)

Finnegan grudgingly accepted, and trotted in for dinner. Debbie's friend felt so relieved that the horse wasn't hurt! And Finnegan had got his point across, too. He came in each night for dinner for the rest of the week, but remained aloof to Debbie's friend, apparently still disgusted at the change in his schedule.

Before Debbie learned how to communicate with her animals, she used to come home from vacation and Finnegan would turn around in his stall, rear-end facing Debbie, and completely ignore her. Debbie also noticed that her cats would give her the cold shoulder, running and hiding at her approach.

This would go on for days, until the animals felt Debbie had suffered enough for her transgression. Now that Debbie understands how much animals want to know exactly what is happening in their lives, especially when things change, she always prepares them for her absence, and communicates with them while she is away. Now she comes home to happy animals.

Many people describe the way their animals shunned them when returning home from a vacation. Clearly, animals feel hurt or angry when they don't know where

Doggone!

Moving to a new location can be very traumatic for pets. The more they know, the sooner they know it, and the more often you remind them and explain to them what is going on, the better they will handle the transition.

we've been. How would you feel if your spouse or child or even a very close friend disappeared for two weeks without telling you why, then suddenly reappeared and acted like nothing had happened, or even expected you to be just as happy and worry-free as you usually are? We know we wouldn't like it!

Communicating with your animals before a long trip is just as important as communicating with them while you are away. This allows the animals to prepare mentally for your absence, as well as for a change in schedule.

When Debbie moved from Massachusetts to Florida, she communicated to her animals how long the trip was going to be. She didn't sugar-coat it by saying "just for a day or so," but explained to them exactly what the trip would involve: Driving $2\frac{1}{2}$ days in a cramped environment and staying in unfamiliar places overnight. Debbie, her husband, the animals (three cats and a dog), and all the luggage in a medium-sized car didn't exactly make for spacious quarters!

During the trip, Debbie's cats remained remarkably calm, and her dog, who usually whined and danced around in the car, behaved perfectly. Debbie also communicated

Cat's Meow

Don't you know a pregnant mare shouldn't ride in a trailer? It will rumble my stomach!

—Genevieve the (pregnant) horse

to them pictures of their new home, so they could share in her excitement about the move, rather than leaving the animals in fear and confusion. Any long trip, not to mention a move to a new home, will be difficult for animals, but with proper communication and preparation, you can alleviate a lot of the misery.

Debbie also used flower essences to help her animals with the high emotion of the traveling and moving. We will go into using flower essences in Chapter 11.

Sometimes, our animals must also travel without us. When our producer, Lee Ann, moved to the Pacific Northwest, she sent her cat, Ruthie, to Seattle by plane. She explained to Ruthie in advance exactly what was going to happen and what to expect. Lee Ann sent along Ruthie's favorite items and some of her own clothing, and also let Ruthie listen, over the phone, to the voice of the friend who would be picking her up at the airport. Communication before, during, and after an animal travels alone can make a big difference in how well your animal weathers the trip. And yes, Ruthie did fine—and comforted Lee Ann, letting her know she'd be waiting for her when Lee Ann arrived in Seattle a week later!

When Debbie's horses and goats were moved from Massachusetts to Florida, she hired a professional shipper. Debbie explained to the animals beforehand what the trip entailed, the importance of drinking water whenever it was offered to them, and who would meet them at the other end. It is also necessary to communicate with your animals telepathically after they have arrived to make sure they are okay, and to let them know when you will be arriving.

How to Communicate Long-Distance

In Chapter 7, we walked you through the step-by-step process of an animal communication session. When you are at work, on vacation, or anywhere else away from your animals, the process is exactly the same. You relax, breathe, and connect with the animal.

The only difference is that, because humans are so accustomed to noticing distance, and because typical human communication must be altered according to distance (something the Internet is gradually changing), you might erect mental barriers to long-distance communication. Rest assured, you manufacture these barriers, and they have nothing to do with the distance. Communicating with your animals is the same, no matter where each of you might be.

Simply set your intention to connect with your animal while you are away, then go ahead and start chatting. You might choose to bring your animal's picture with you when you are gone to help you connect, but it isn't necessary.

Just remember the formula: BOSSCATT (breathe, open your heart, smile, state your intention, call your animal's name, ask permission to speak, tune in, and thank the animal when you are finished).

If you are going on any kind of trip, even if it is only a weekend, you can also do some specific extra things to help ease the process for your animals. Practice these steps before any vacation, and you'll find your animals handling the change better than ever before:

- ◆ Two weeks before the trip (if possible), tell your animals that you will be going away for awhile.

- ◆ Explain to your animals exactly who will be watching over them while you are gone.

> **Horse Sense** _____
>
> Practice communicating long-distance by talking to your animals when you are at work or running errands. Then, when you have to leave them for an extended period, continue "talking" just as you've been practicing. They will get the message.

◆ Give each animal an important job to do while you are away, such as watch over the house, watch over the other animals, make sure everything stays in its rightful place, catch up on their rest, or whatever else seems relevant to your individual pet.

◆ Explain to your animals that you will be connecting with them while you are away, so you can keep in touch with how they are doing.

◆ The day you leave, remind your animals how long you will be gone, and that you will connect with them each day. Also remind them of their important jobs.

◆ While you are away, set aside a time when you will be least distracted and most able to remember to connect with your animals. Or put a picture of your animal on your nightstand, in the bathroom, etc., to help you remember.

◆ Connect and say hello!

Exercise for Long-Distance Psychic Communication

Animals love to hear about what you are doing on vacation. Debbie likes to send her animals "mental postcards" each day on her trips, so they can see what she is doing and what she is seeing.

Don't neglect the part of this exercise involving the receiving and writing down of what you get. This can be a fun way to validate your long-distance telepathic experience. The more you write about what you receive, the better chance you have of having your pet sitter help you to validate the experience.

Cat's Meow

Debbie: You've been eating plants a lot. Why do you do this?

Pandora the Cat: They give me the roughage I need, and it's something to do. I have a lot of energy and this releases some of it. I also like the way the leaves crunch in my mouth.

Debbie: Do you think you could refrain from eating the plants?

Pandora the Cat: Oh, I don't think so. They are right there, you know?

Debbie: But you are killing them by eating them.

Pandora the Cat: They don't mind.

Here's how to do it:

- When you find yourself in an interesting or picturesque spot, take a moment to breathe deeply and connect with your animal.

- Look at the scene you would like to send your animal.

- Tell your animal you are sending him or her an image.

- Concentrate and imagine projecting that picture to your animal.

- Explain where you are and what you are doing.

- Take some time to stay open and receive an answer back from your animal. He or she might react to the image, or have other things in mind to tell you. Stay open to whatever comes through.

- Write down the messages your pet sends back to you, and the time of day.

- Do it again the next day!

- When you get home, check with the person who was watching your animal to see if he or she noticed anything relevant that confirms the message you received back from your pet.

> **Cat's Meow**
>
> Take time to listen. Use all of your senses, don't turn them off. They will add to the message you are getting. Use your heart, emotions, touch, visions. All these things work to give you the complete message. Don't rush through it. Take your time.
>
> —Llama, when Debbie asked what she could do to improve her animal communication

The Least You Need to Know

- Near or far from your animal, psychic communication works exactly the same way.

- Use long-distance psychic communication to tell your animals if you will be late coming home from work, why, and when you will be back.

- Use long-distance psychic communication to explain to your animals ahead of time when you will be away for an extended period. Tell them where you are going, how long you will be gone, who will take care of them in your absence, and what their important jobs will be while you are away.

- When away for an extended period, connect with your animals each day, sending them "mental postcards" of where you are and asking them how they are doing.

Part 3

How Much Do You Know Intuitively About *Your* Pet?

Your pet is an individual with a unique personality all his own. Your animal has her own likes and dislikes, needs and wants, hopes, dreams, and desires. If you think of your animal as just a "Golden Retriever" or "Persian" or "Scarlet Macaw" or "Thoroughbred" or "Hamster" or whatever your animal might happen to be, you are missing out on a lot! This section will help you get to know your animal as an individual. We'll talk about the importance of your animal's name and you'll learn how to ask just what your animal thinks of the name you bestowed! You'll also learn how to explore and uncover your animal's emotional injuries and fears, and how to begin to work together to help resolve these issues. Finally, we devote a chapter to the importance of letting your animal know exactly what is going on in your life and home.

Chapter 9

Every Pet Is an Individual

In This Chapter

- How your animal's personality transcends species, and even breed
- Using psychic communication to really get acquainted
- Animal-animal communication and other family relationships
- Conflict resolution for pets

Sometimes it seems all Labrador Retrievers are hearty, good-natured fellows who love everyone and live to jump in the water to retrieve a stick. Sometimes it seems all Thoroughbred horses have an aristocratic attitude and mild disdain for any species "beneath" them. Sometimes it seems all Siamese cats slip enigmatically into the shadows, gracing us with their attentions exclusively on their own terms.

In many ways, species and individual breeds *do* have common characteristics, but every animal, like every human, is also an individual, and psychic communication can help you discover your pet's true individuality and unique spirit.

Are You Species-Prejudiced?

One of the reasons humans continue to maintain purebred animals is because they like knowing what an animal will look like and, to a large extent, act like. A Rottweiler bonds closely with his family but has a strong inner drive to guard the property. A Shih Tzu won't grow very big and enjoys lots of lap time. These animals were bred for centuries to encourage certain characteristics.

One could say the same thing about humans, but if you carry the analogy too far, you will surely be accused of prejudice. Animals are no different, in that although some stereotypes are based on certain trends due to the environment and conditions in which a species has been bred for many years and the selection of certain traits, like humans, every animal is indeed an individual. Some preconceived notions have nothing to do with the individual, or even the breed!

Anyone with two Labrador Retrievers, one black and one yellow, will tell you that people tend to be more afraid of the black Lab than the yellow Lab. People assume big black dogs are more likely to be mean. (Have we all watched the movie *The Exorcist* too many times?) People also assume yellow dogs are mellow and friendly. In truth, color in Labrador Retrievers (as in humans) has nothing at all to do with any kind of inbred temperament or behavioral difference.

Horse Sense

Some animals are high achievers and eager to please, while others don't like to be told what to do. Some have a complex agenda, while others aspire simply to be loved. Some want everyone to notice them and some would prefer to deflect the attention elsewhere. Some animals come here to teach, others to learn and grow. Some animals project the energy of old souls, and just being in their presence is truly a treasure.

Where Did That Personality Come From?

Just as two animals that look different can be equally friendly, two individuals of one breed or species, even those that look almost identical, can have very different personalities. One tabby cat craves constant affection, while another shies away from too much physical contact. One Chow Chow is aloof or suspicious of strangers, while another loves every walking creature that comes her way. One Scarlet Macaw loves to talk, while another prefers to climb around the cage all day without uttering a sound.

Clearly, many of these differences hearken back to upbringing, socialization, and the way an individual animal has been treated since birth. Just as with humans, life experience largely shapes personality. How you treat your dog, cat, or horse, or how others treated, cared for, and communicated with him or her can drastically shape who your animal is today.

The point is that, just because you have a Golden Retriever, doesn't mean he will be the "perfect dog for kids." He might! But maybe he just isn't the type who cares much for those fast-moving, erratic little humans. Maybe he never met a child until he was an adult, and now they scare him or irritate him. Or maybe he has been playing with kids since his whelping-box days and couldn't imagine any creature more delightful.

The same goes for any animal. Just because you have a Persian cat with a reputation for vanity and aloofness doesn't mean she will spend her days posed on the windowsill looking pretty for you. *Your* Persian might much prefer nudging you to pet her and hold her as much as she can. Maybe as a kitten, she was handled a lot and grew so fond of people that she can't get enough of the ones who treat her nicely. Or maybe she is just the kind of cat who would rather not have humans constantly invading her personal space. It all depends on the individual, no matter the cause of the traits, whether *nature or nurture*.

> **Pet Speak**
>
> **Nature or nurture** is a phrase coined by psychologists to describe the ever-present argument about whether personality and behavioral traits stem from genetics or experience. Most agree that any human or animal is a complex combination of the effects of both nature (genetics) and nurture (life experience).

Furthermore, because every pet is an individual, training, schedules, and even modes of psychic communication that work well for one pet might not work as well with another. The more you communicate with and tune in to your animal, free of prejudice and assumptions, the better you will understand exactly what your individual pet wants, needs, and best understands.

Debbie once spoke with a horse that reminded her of the cowardly lion from the Wizard of Oz. When she spoke with him, the horse puffed himself up and told Debbie how tough and fearless he was, but as the truth came out, he confessed that he was afraid of a lot of things, but he often put on a big show so that no one knew the truth. Sound like anyone you know?

With animals, as with humans, first impressions are *not* everything, and what you see is *not* necessarily what you get. Getting to know an animal leaves no room for judgment or preconceived notions. Leave your stereotypes behind

> **Horse Sense**
>
> Debbie used to play a fun game when she was younger: trying to figure out what profession her horses, dogs, and cats would be if they were human. What would your animals choose as professions if they were humans? Ponder your animals' various personality traits and strengths. Would your dog be a pediatrician? Your cat a temperamental painter? Your horse a CEO?

when communicating with your animals, and you'll open up a space for understanding your animal as the unique individual he or she really is.

Getting to Know You Exercise

This contemplative exercise can help you to learn even more about your pets. It might even dispel some ideas you already have about the personalities of your pets.

Using a pen and paper or a computer, take a minute to list each animal in your family using a chart like the one we have here. Each animal in your family gets one row (if you only have one animal, the chart can look more like a list with two columns):

Animal's Name	How I See the Pet	How the Pet Sees Herself	How the Pet Sees Other Family Members

Now, jot down a few words to describe each animal's personality, as you understand or perceive it: shy, outgoing, eager to please, confident, submissive, dominant, pushover, couch potato, cautious, athletic, smart, funny, serious, aloof, suspicious, friendly, persistent, hesitant, impulsive, joyful, happy, annoyed, impatient, etc.

Now, take a minute to prepare yourself to connect with each animal, one at a time. Remember BOSS-CATT: breathe, open your heart, smile, state your intention, call out your animal's name, ask for permission, tune in, and thank the animal when you are finished.

When you connect with each individual animal in turn, ask each animal how *he or she* would describe *him or herself*. Write down anything you receive, and be prepared for anything that comes, no matter how

Cat's Meow

Just because I'm a horse does not mean I necessarily have to be ridden, does it? Can't I just be a pet?

—Charlie, a rescued horse living in an animal sanctuary

different it sounds from what you had listed in your column. Debbie once had a horse tell her that he was the playboy type! (He thought he was a stallion!)

Now to make it even more interesting, ask each animal what he or she thinks of the other animals in the family, and the other humans, too. Again, be prepared for anything. You might be amazed at exactly who thinks what about whom!

Animal-Animal Bonds, and Other Family Matters

As you learn more and more about pet psychic communication, you will learn more and more about the unique personalities of your animals and the relationship you have with each of them. However, human-to-animal isn't the only relationship in a multi-human and/or multi-animal household.

Animals in the same family, whether or not they are the same species, are more than just aware of each other. They have relationships with each other, just like they have relationships with us. Sometimes, those relationships run deep and can even give animals a reason to live, or when the relationship ends for any reason, cause animals to become depressed and even launch them into an extended grieving period.

A married couple named Phil and Marisa called Debbie about their dog, Roscoe. Roscoe was a medium-size Lab-mix they adopted six months earlier from a local animal shelter. Phil and Marisa loved Roscoe dearly, and his tendency to escape concerned them. He would often get loose and run away, although he always returned.

> **Cat's Meow**
>
> Oh, Maxine. Maxine is the visitor. She likes to make her rounds. She is good, and very excitable. She actually brings out the silly in me sometimes, and I can be very serious. She has a way about her. She glows, you know.
>
> —Miss Frannie Mae, an orange tabby cat, when asked about the dog, Maxy, across the street

Debbie connected with Roscoe to ask why he kept escaping the property and running away. Roscoe told Debbie that he was looking for his friend, and he showed her a picture of a little black dog. Roscoe then communicated a great feeling of sadness about his absent friend, and Debbie's heart went out to the dog.

Roscoe also told Debbie that his people shouldn't worry that he escaped and that he would always come back. It was just that he felt compelled to continue looking for his little friend. He felt unable to give up hope that he could find her.

Debbie explained to Roscoe the dangers involved for a dog wandering around loose. She asked him to please try to stay within his yard, and that she would tell his people about his friend to see if they could help him. When Debbie relayed the information to Phil and Marisa, they couldn't think of any black dog in the neighborhood that Roscoe would have been friends with or looking for, but they would look into the matter further.

Two days after the consultation, Debbie got a phone message from Marisa saying that they had contacted the shelter where they had adopted Roscoe, and found out that Roscoe had indeed been brought into the shelter with a little black dog they believed was his sister.

Horse Sense

Often, an animal with a fear, shyness, or anxiety problem has that problem because of a traumatic past experience. Animal communication can reveal that experience, so that you can help your pet learn to heal and trust again.

Moved by the poignancy of Roscoe's faithful search, Phil and Marisa felt compelled to find Roscoe's sister, to see if they could reunite them for a visit. The shelter workers were similarly moved by the story, and to-date, Phil and Marisa continue to work with the shelter in their search for the little black dog.

Animal relationships can be complex. Each animal is an individual, with a history and a life purpose that makes each unique. Some animals have vivid memories and hold the abuse from their past very close to them, refusing to let it go or forget it for fear that it will only happen again.

In many ways, holding on to these memories affects the way animals react both to humans and to each other. Other animals tend to live one day at a time, letting their past problems float away like soap bubbles. These animals tend to be more open, friendly, and accepting of other humans and animals because they approach life with a fresh, uncomplicated view. Still others hold fear that might not necessarily come from any discernible situation, fear that might even have arisen from a past life experience. The more we talk to and know the animals, the more we will understand what motivates and drives each individual.

Cat's Meow

We respect each other, and we grow. It's the inside that matters. Tell her that.

—Skat, a gray Appaloosa, when asked if he wanted to teach his person anything

In your own home, you may notice that you love all your animals equally, but there could be one animal where the bond is inexplicably strong. You might not be able to define the depth of your relationship with this certain animal. Debbie often notices this bond in certain communication sessions because it always arises as intense.

But this kind of deep bond isn't limited to human-animal connections. Sometimes two animals can have such a soul-deep bond, making the loss of one animal a deeply painful experience for the other.

Debbie had the wonderful opportunity of communicating with a Great Dane named Zeus. Zeus seemed to Debbie to be quite obviously an old soul. No one could deny his wisdom and compassion. Zeus battled months of illness that left him weak, but his determination to fight kept his people searching for ways to get him healthy. Sadly, Zeus lost the battle and passed over into spirit.

Zeus's person, Vicky, had one of those deep, special bonds with her animal. Mourning over his loss, she felt (as do many humans who have recently lost their animal friends) the need to connect with dear Zeus in spirit, to find out if he was okay. Vicky also felt the need to connect with her two other living dogs, to determine how they were each handling Zeus's passing.

When Debbie connected with Zeus in spirit, he assured Vicky that it was his time to go and that he was fine. Then he asked Debbie to ask Vicky if she had received the flower. Debbie relayed the information, and Vicky fell silent.

Then she told Debbie that a few days earlier, she had found a single rose on her doorstep. She asked her husband and the neighbors if they had left it, but no one seemed to know who had left the flower.
Debbie told her, "It was from Zeus."

Then Vicky noticed that the bush in their backyard where Zeus was buried had just begun to bloom. When love governs a relationship, miracles really can happen at any time, across any distance, even across the line between life and death. Zeus's and Vicky's bond continues to be as strong as ever, and even though she misses his physical body greatly, Zeus's spirit and gifts remain with her daily.

CAUTION

Doggone! _____

When you lose a pet, you may be so busy dealing with your own grief that you neglect to notice the grief your other animals experience. Be with them during this time. You can support and comfort each other. (Isn't that what family is for?)

As for Vicky's two other dogs, Debbie found that each dog had a very different way of handling her grief. Sunflower admitted that she was in denial, and she was having a very hard time coming to terms with the loss of Zeus. Sunflower and Zeus had shared an interesting relationship; they didn't always get along, but now that Zeus was no longer in physical form, she missed him terribly. Sunflower was stuck in the grieving state. When Vicky asked her how she could help her to heal, Sunflower said that she would heal in her own time, and that when she went off on her own, it was out of sadness and the need to grieve alone. Vicky felt helpless, wishing she could do something but knowing Sunflower would handle her grief in her own way.

Vicky's other dog, Lacey, seemed better able to cope with and understand Zeus's passing. She confirmed that Zeus himself had prepared her for his passing—they had that sort of communicative relationship—and that Zeus visited her often, in spirit. Lacey felt at peace with his passing and carried on with her daily routine as if nothing had changed, while Sunflower's refusal to accept Zeus's death kept her in a prolonged state of grief, perhaps unable to cope with the loss of the physical Zeus.

> **Cat's Meow**
>
> I like the music my human plays. I would like to get out more and dance around and scare the cat.
>
> —Oliver, a yellow-naped Amazon parrot

Yes, animals do grieve, each in their own way. When you know an animal is sad or grieving, acknowledge the pain they are feeling. This helps the animals enormously, not only to heal but also to let them know we understand what they are going through, so they feel less alone, and assured that grief is normal.

Conflict Resolution for Animals

When Debbie lived in Massachusetts, she had a stray male cat that would come into her barn and terrorize her female cats. Ernie would sleep up in the hayloft and pee on the hay bales. Things were getting out of hand, so Debbie communicated to him that he could live in her barn, but that would require Debbie taking him to be neutered, and he would also have to agree to be nice to the other cats.

Debbie rented a *Have A Heart*-brand humane live trap and finally captured this feral kitty. She brought him to the vet to be neutered, and got him all his shots. When she brought him home, she opened his cage, fully expecting him to run off. Instead, Ernie walked out of his cage and rolled on his back in front of Debbie. Then he walked over to Debbie's dog, Champ, who always used to chase him, and rubbed up against him! Ernie had been craving somewhere to belong and a family to belong to.

Debbie patted him for a while, and couldn't help but fall in love with him. Ernie never left the property again, and became Debbie's little shadow. He did continue to have a trouble-making streak, of course. It was part of his personality! The female cats continued to dislike him, and he continued to stalk them and frighten them.

When Debbie communicated to Ernie about this continuing problem, Ernie said he wasn't hurting them, he was just playing. Debbie explained to him that he was playing too roughly, and that he needed to be more gentle. Debbie's husband refers to Ernie affectionately as "the little punk." Ernie made the move to Florida with the family, and now he hangs out in the barn with all the other female cats. They all adore him now, and he knows it!

Some people have a conflict with their pets because they misunderstand an animal's motive. Psychic communication can help to alleviate these misunderstandings. Debbie gets many calls from frustrated people who complain that their cat is not affectionate: "She won't let me pick her up," or "He won't lie quietly on my lap." Believe it or not, one woman Debbie spoke with threatened to have her cat put to sleep if the cat didn't start showing her some affection, the way the other cats in the household did! (Yes, Debbie was horrified!)

Animals are individual beings, and like people, some are comfortable with giving and receiving affection, while others are not. A very shy person might feel completely overwhelmed by someone who constantly tries to hug and touch him. Talk about an invasion of personal space! Many animals also feel this way. It doesn't mean the animal will never change or get more comfortable, although some do remain more aloof or uninterested in physical affection throughout their lives. In some cases, patience and an effort to show understanding of who that animal is and what they are comfortable with gives the animal a space to begin breaking down the walls of protection.

> **Horse Sense** _____
>
> Remember to ask questions with an open heart rather than beginning by telling your animal what *not* to do. If your animal is practicing an undesirable behavior, first ask the animal why, before working out a solution. Then, give the animal something to do, rather than something *not* to do.

> **Cat's Meow** _____
>
> I feel invisible in a crowd. People look so big and they move by so closely. This is upsetting. I feel I need to be on guard, and I am worried they won't see me, and might step on me. I hug close to my people and bark when I get nervous.
>
> —Ralph, a Border Collie mix, when asked how he feels when he is in a crowd

Debbie often finds that when people tell their animals they understand that the animal is uncomfortable with being picked up or forced to sit on a lap, and agree to not do this until the animal is comfortable, amazing changes start to happen. The animal no longer feels threatened, and often eventually begins to seek out attention and affection!

Sometimes, we even have conflicts with wild animals, birds, even insects! Most homeowners know the feeling of seeing an ant … or a parade of ants … crawling across the kitchen cabinet or floor in the summer. Debbie had carpenter ants in her home, and these insects can cause a lot of damage to a house. Debbie didn't want to poison the insects, who were, after all, just doing what carpenter ants do. Poisoning any creature goes against everything Debbie believes. On the other hand, she didn't want to let them destroy her house, either.

Debbie frantically connected with the ants and explained to them the unfortunate outcome (a visit from the exterminator), should they decide to stay in her home. She asked them to leave and offered them many of the fallen trees outside her home for refuge.

After this connection, the ant population in Debbie's home dramatically decreased, but they were definitely not gone. When Debbie connected with them again to find out why some ants remained, they explained that the remaining ones were worker and warrior ants and that they had to do their job no matter what. They did not fear dying for their job.

Debbie continued to warn the ants when the exterminator was coming, to give them a fair chance to evacuate. Even though she still felt conflicted about using an exterminator, Debbie knew she had at least given the ants fair warning and that many of them had chosen to leave.

This kind of conflict, with wild animals, can also be turned to everyone's benefit. We can warn animals when they face danger. Debbie used to alert the deer that wandered onto her property as to when hunting season began. She then offered her property as a safe refuge.

> **Horse Sense**
>
> Whenever you see or sense an animal in danger, don't worry about going through the steps of connecting. Quickly shoot out a message of warning or preparation directed at the animal.

If Debbie sees a cat or dog dart out into the road while driving, she immediately connects with them telepathically to explain to them the dangers of the road, and to request that they avoid it for their own safety.

No matter what your conflict or the conflict within your unique family, telepathic communication will help everyone to see everyone else's point of view, making a resolution, and subsequently, all the family relationships, just a little bit stronger, more loving, and deeper.

The Least You Need to Know

- Although different species and different breeds share certain physical and behavioral characteristics, each animal is an individual with a unique spirit.

- Recognizing and exploring each animal's individual personality without prejudice will deepen your relationship with your animal and will help your efforts to communicate telepathically.

- Animals form relationships with humans, and also with other animals. Don't neglect to explore the way your animals feel about the other pets, and people, in the house.

- Telepathic communication can help to resolve conflicts between humans and animals as well as between animals.

Chapter 10

What's in a Name?

In This Chapter

- The significance of naming your pet
- The psychic face behind the name
- Asking your pet for input
- Exercises to help you find your pet's *real* name

What's in a name? More than you might suspect! Names label us, in ways that can shore us up or tear us down. Names make first impressions on others, and deeply influence, in many ways, how we see ourselves.

Humans have strong feelings about their own names, but sometimes name their animals without much thought. How would you like going through life with a name like Maniac, or Stupid, or Miss Prissy? Names can be insulting to the animal, or even become self-fulfilling prophecies. (How do you think *you* would act if everyone always called you Captain Trouble?)

We've met many animals with names that simply didn't seem to fit them. Some animals feel perfectly happy about their names, as long as their people speak them in a loving tone. Other animals have very definite ideas about their names, loving them or, in many cases, hating them! Some animals have strong ideas about what they would prefer to be called, or even what they consider to be their "real" name.

In this chapter, we'll look at the significance of your pet's name, and give you some tips for finding the right name for any future animals in your life.

A Rose by Any Other Name ...

How did you choose your animal's name? Some people keep the name a pet had from previous owners, or one that was given by a breeder or animal shelter worker. Some people have a name in mind before they ever meet the animal they eventually name. Some wait to meet the animal, and then give the name that seems appropriate.

When you know how to connect psychically to animals, you can even let them pick their own names! A friend of Debbie's bought a cute filly. She was trying to find the correct name for this filly, and asked Debbie to connect with her to see if she had an idea what she wanted to be named.

When Debbie connected with the young horse, she came through with a very strong personality, one of enthusiasm, great youthful energy, grace, and a charismatic presence. Debbie explained that her person wanted to give the opportunity to pick her own name.

At first, Debbie had trouble making out all the syllables because it was a name she had never heard before. Iza? Izza? Za ... Izador ... Izadora! Yes, that was the name. It felt just right.

The filly confirmed the name with enthusiasm and excitement. Izadora was exactly the name she wanted. Then she told Debbie that when she grew up, more than anything, she wanted to be a dancer. This excited her new owner because she had plans to teach this filly dressage, which is, in its highest form, a kind of dance between horse and rider.

Neither Debbie nor her friend had ever heard of the name Izadora before, but the friend agreed she would grant her filly's wish and give her that name. When Debbie and her friend went to the barn to see Izadora, they told the barn owner the name, and she laughed. "Well that makes sense," she said. "If she wants to be a dancer, she must know about Isadora Duncan!"

Debbie and her friend had never heard of Isadora Duncan, but later learned this extraordinary free-spirited woman, born in 1878 in San Francisco, founded modern dance as we know it today. Debbie couldn't help getting goose bumps at the realization

> **Cat's Meow**
>
> I have great coloring. I could be a circus pony, you know. I could be a singing circus pony.
>
> —Twinkle, a Shetland pony

that somehow, the little filly knew more than she did about human culture. Debbie and her friends expect some great performances out of that little filly!

A regular client of Debbie's named Sarah rescued a little kitten from a horrible dog fight, and the kitten, paralyzed from the middle of his back down, had an incredible attitude and a zest for life, despite his paralysis. Sarah wanted to give the little orange tabby the perfect name, the name he would choose for himself, so Debbie connected with this miraculous little guy and the kitten perked up immediately and told Debbie that his favorite name was Gulliver. From that day, Sarah has called him Gulliver the World Traveler.

Doggone! _____

Remember that many animals will live up to the qualities in the name you give them, so beware of naming your horse Bucky or Bullet if you want to be able to stay in the saddle! Steer clear of naming your dog The Terminator or Dumbo, or of bestowing on your cat names like Scratch or Tasmanian Devil.

Naming Your Pet

Consider the connotations behind any name you choose for your pet. Does the name really fit the animal's personality, as you know it? Does it "feel right"? Intuition can help guide you in choosing a name, but so can plain old common sense.

When Debbie adopted her two goats from the MSPCA, they came with names that just didn't seem to suit them. Debbie asked the two goats what they would like to be called. The big goat explained that because he was so intelligent, he wanted a simple human name, something that would reflect that he was smarter than the average goat. Debbie suggested "Sam," which he took to right away.

The smaller goat was a little bit shy. He asked, bashfully, to be called "The Kid." Debbie told him that sounded just wonderful. Now Sam and The Kid live happily with Debbie, and she can't help thinking the two names together sound like the perfect name for an old-fashioned Western movie!

Giving your animal a name that brings out his or her inner essence gives your pet a feeling of importance and respect. The animal will feel more connected to you if you grant a name that shows you understand who your animal is. Debbie remembers one consultation in which she asked a woman what her horse's barn name was, and she told Debbie the name was "Sir."

When Debbie called the horse's name in her head to get his attention, he came through with a bit of an attitude and told Debbie, with an air of disdain, that "Sir" was not his *entire* name, thank you very much, and he would appreciate the respect of being summoned by full name.

When Debbie told his person this, she laughed and said that his full name is Sirs Mirage! Debbie tried again, and got a much better response. Whenever Debbie communicates with Sirs Mirage, which she does periodically, she never forgets to use his full name!

You can choose a name with a positive and respectful connotation and still get a bad response from your animal. Some animals simply won't answer to some names, while other names seem to capture their attention immediately. Experiment with different names to see how your animal reacts. Even his or her body language can speak to you about which names your animal prefers.

Can't Find a Name? Just Ask!

If you have yet to name your animal, or can't seem to come up with the right name on your own, you can connect telepathically to find out what that animal would like to be called. You can also do this to find out how your animal feels about the name you have already given him or her, and you can ask if your animal has a preferable name, or an alteration or addition to the existing name.

Connect to your animal in the way we showed you in earlier chapters in this book. Relax and be open to whatever comes to you, and simply ask, "What is your name?" or "What do you think of your name?" or "What would you like to be named?"

You might not hear a name, per se, or it might take a while. Keep listening! You could get an image or some other sensory clue, a sound or a color or a moving picture. You might see the word spelled, or an image of some of the letters.

When Debbie asks an animal what he or she wants to be named, she doesn't necessarily get words. Often, the animal will try to get the meaning across with pictures or colors.

A woman named Joyce called Debbie about her new Rottweiler puppy. She wanted to find the perfect name, and when Debbie asked the puppy what name she would like, all she received was an unusual olive green color. The puppy was consequently named Olive.

Sometimes, people have their hearts set on a particular name. If this isn't the name your animal chooses, don't despair. Many times, animals will be content to live with your choice, or they might want to add a middle or last name. Debbie communicated with a horse named Travis, whose trainer wanted to know a good show name. Travis said he liked the name Travis, but wanted something in front of it, like "Tom." The horse is now called Tom Travis.

Another young thoroughbred filly Debbie spoke with sent Debbie the image of an unusual flower. Debbie wasn't sure what the flower was, so she did a little investigating on the Internet, and discovered it was a type of lily. The filly wanted to be called Lilly, and so she was.

A friend of Debbie's gave her a little, neglected cat she had rescued from a stable. The delicate little creature didn't have a name, and when Debbie asked the kitty what she wanted to be called, she sent Debbie a vivid scarlet color, then the image of a southern woman all dressed up.

"Scarlett," Debbie said.

The petite cat answered, "Yes, but don't forget the second part!"

"Of course … Ms. O'Hara!" Debbie smiled. "Scarlett O'Hara." And so the cat was named, and her name fits her to a T.

 Cat's Meow

Llamas hold the wisdom of the world. We will share it only with those who earn our respect and who give us respect. We have what others long for, but if they are true of heart, we will share it. Many miss out on our wisdom, and that's a shame, but not our problem. We are here for those who are ready to learn with open hearts and clear minds, without prejudice, preconceived notions, or bias.

—Cornelius the Llama, when asked what he liked about being a llama

Stories like this last one often fuel people's skepticism. A kitten knowing who Scarlett O'Hara is? Ridiculous! But wait. We are *not* suggesting that this little feline Scarlett O'Hara has watched *Gone With the Wind* and personally identified with Vivian Leigh's character. Of course not!

What happens when Debbie, or you, receive images like a scarlet color and a southern belle, is that your intuition is working with the energetic messages you receive to interpret them in a way you can understand. The energy works with your own personal frame of reference.

While we don't always understand why or even how an animal knows what he or she knows (we still feel amazement at that filly's knowledge of Isadora Duncan, but one can never know for sure all that an animal hears and perceives throughout its life), we can trust the communication process to work for us by staying open and letting the images in our own experience and knowledge work with the energetic messages as they come.

Sometimes animals will even give Debbie names from different cultures and different countries. This is still a mystery to Debbie. It might be a name they have carried with them through many past lives!

Doggone!

Debbie has spoken with animals that absolutely refused to listen to anything their human said to them *until* their names were changed to something more suitable. Some animals have negative associations to names given to them by people who mistreated them, or that they associate with an unpleasant time or situation, even from a past life! If your animal responds negatively to a name, it's best to find a better one.

The best way to let this process of naming happen without your interference is to pay attention to any images or syllables you get. You might suddenly see a picture of your Aunt Sue, but that doesn't mean your new dog knows Aunt Sue. Just as with Scarlet O'Hara, it means that your intuition is translating the images the animal is sending in a new frame of reference, one that you can best interpret correctly.

Psychic messages often come through in a manner personally pertinent to the receiver. It is all part of the process of spiritual energy speaking to spiritual energy, which uses the available images and sensory vocabulary of the receiver to best convey the true meaning of the message. In other words, your dog may want the name "Sue" and so your brain brings up the image of your aunt to help you find that name, that particular sound.

Cat's Meow

That's a silly dog trick. I give love by rubbing my head on you.

—Charles, a Newfoundland, when asked why he doesn't like to give kisses

Eve asked Debbie to ask Sally, Eve's dog, what she thought of *her* name, which came from the animal shelter where Eve adopted Sally. Sally didn't hesitate to say that, while she didn't exactly *mind* the name "Sally," she loved being called "beautiful," or "Bella." Surprised, Eve tried it out. "Bella?" Sally's ears perked right up, and she jumped on Eve's lap. She knew exactly who Eve was talking to! Eve doesn't know where Sally (um … Bella) came up with that name. Perhaps it was a name given to her by a past owner, or perhaps she simply liked it. Or maybe she lived in Italy in a past life! Eve may never know, but she still tells Sally she is beautiful, and calls her "Bella" once in awhile, just to make her happy. And, Eve's children call Sally "Bella" when they really want to get her attention. (Works every time.)

Name-Finding Exercises

To find a name, the *right* name, for your animal, sit quietly with your animal friend and a paper and pen. Make sure you both feel relaxed and comfortable. Connect with the animal, then ask your animal what name they would like to be called.

Pay attention to every perception, and write down everything that comes, so you don't forget. Even if the images aren't at first clear, write them down in the best way you can. You may get several names. Write them all down! If so, look at your list and ask your animal how he or she feels about each name. Let your animal send you a reaction to each name. One of the names will feel right to you. If it doesn't, keep listening for more names.

If you find that you still come up with nothing, another exercise is to find a baby name book, one of those with hundreds, even thousands, of names to choose from. Relax with your pet, and then slowly go through the book, saying different names to your pet and waiting for reactions, both physical and telepathic. It may take a while, but when you hit on the right name, you will feel a strong positive reaction from your pet. This means your pet likes that one!

Horse Sense

It's difficult to explain how it feels to know a name is the right one, but it is an intuitive process. The more you sharpen, refine, and develop your intuition, the more comfortable you will be about trusting your intuitive feelings about "rightness" and "wrongness." This valuable skill will help you in all aspects of your life.

You might find several names to which your pet responds positively. This might be a message from your animal that choosing the name should be a joint effort. Your animal will respond well to several names, then let you pick the one you want to use for your animal.

No matter what your animal's name, let your bond strengthen and grow through mutual respect and communication. What you call your animal is important, but even more important is how you talk to your animal, how you treat your animal, and how you love your animal. Let the name reflect the depth and unique character that is the animal you've come to know, and your animal will show you, in many ways, how much and how well that name fits.

The Least You Need to Know

◆ Names have an important impact on your pet. They can make an animal feel proud, ashamed, angry, insulted, or pleased, and they can also become a self-fulfilling prophecy if they suggest a certain behavior.

◆ Find a name that suits your pet by paying attention to your pet's individual personality and how he or she responds to different names.

◆ To find out what name your animal would like or prefer, connect telepathically with your animal, and ask.

◆ When listening telepathically for the right name, write down any impressions: names, letters, sounds, colors, and images. If more than one name comes, ask your animal how he or she feels about each suggested name.

Your Pet's Emotional Scars and Fears

In This Chapter

- ◆ Animals hurt, too
- ◆ Helping your pet through emotional issues
- ◆ Overcoming your animal's fears
- ◆ Discovering your adopted animal's past
- ◆ Using flower essences
- ◆ Homeopathic remedies to bring about healing

Once upon a time, not so very long ago, people didn't think animals had any feelings at all. Mainstream thought had decided that animals operated on instinct, didn't feel pain the way we do, and had no emotions. People who knew animals well have always known this isn't true, but society as a whole insisted that it was.

Today, however, mainstream thought has shifted. So many people include animals as part of their family and know animals so well that those who continue to believe animals have no emotions are in the minority. Just look into the loving eyes of your dog, the contemplative eyes of your cat, or the contented eyes of your horse, and you will know animals have more in common with us, emotionally, than used to be believed.

However, having an emotional life has a downside. Any emotional being can also become emotionally injured, by trauma, abuse, neglect, loss, and pain. Because our society doesn't value animals as much as it values people, many animals are cast aside and forced to experience conditions and treatment that would psychologically damage a human for good. Such treatment has the same effect on many animals, but others are able to pull out of their pain, suffering, grief, and fear to live happy lives again. A loving human family can be a big part of that healing.

Your Emotional Animal

Imagine you lost someone you loved as much as you loved life itself. Imagine someone beat you until you couldn't move, and left you to die. Imagine your family pushed you out of the car on a road trip and drove on without ever coming back for you.

And then, imagine that you finally found someone else to be your friend, but they became angry at you every time you acted fearful, or sad, or lost your temper because you were in pain.

When the people you love most can't understand why you have emotional pain, you will probably eventually learn that you can't trust anyone, or that you should shut down and never let anyone into your heart again. Or maybe in your eternal optimism, you will keep trying, again and again, to find someone you can trust, no matter how many times you get cast aside.

This is exactly what happens to animals who have suffered emotional pain. Each animal, like each person, reacts to emotional trauma in a different way, depending on their personalities. An animal's past is a blueprint of who they have become, but who they are in spirit influences the subtle shadings of that blueprint.

CAUTION **Doggone!** _____

Traumatic experiences can happen at any stage of an animal's life, but an animal's emotional life begins at birth. Just as humans are largely shaped by the physical contact, affection, and interaction they receive as infants, animals, too, learn much and are largely shaped by their earliest weeks, nursing, being cleaned by their mothers, and interacting with littermates. Early human contact also helps socialize young animals to humans, cementing the possibilities for future relationships.

Animals that are taken away from their mothers at too young of an age often suffer anxiety, strange habits (a cat suckling a blanket for comfort), or difficulty socializing with other animals. For example, many dog books advise never bringing home a puppy before the age of eight weeks, because those first weeks are so crucial to the puppy's development. For some animals, including some breeds of dogs, that period is ideally even longer.

Another common trauma stems from being attacked by another animal, and this kind of emotional damage plays out in many ways. Debbie has often seen dogs who were attacked by surprise and who consequently develop unpredictable personalities, randomly attacking other dogs. When Debbie asks them why they do this, inevitably they show her that they are so afraid of being unexpectedly attacked again that they are trying to ward off the possibility by attacking first. Other dogs only become withdrawn and frightened after an attack.

Dogs are not the only pets who respond to this kind of trauma. String Bean was a barn cat before Molly adopted her, and she had a really wired, destructive personality (the veterinary assistants would literally return with bandaged hands and arms after handling the cat). Molly and her family wondered what the reason was for String Bean's strange and "over the top" behavior. Molly decided to find out as much as she could about String Bean's early life, and she found out that String Bean's littermates were attacked by either a raccoon or a hawk and violently killed when String Bean was a very small kitten. Molly attributes String Bean's sometimes-violent reactions in her early life to witnessing this terrible sight. Molly and her family work to send healing messages of love and protection to String Bean, to let her know they are there for her and will do their best to safeguard String Bean from harm.

Losing home after home can have a more chronic, slow but insidious emotional effect on animals. Animals like to know their boundaries, they like to have a routine, and they like to feel secure (don't we all?). Animals with a history of being adopted then returned or abandoned are especially in need of reassurance that they at last have a permanent home.

Sometimes, a well-adjusted animal who loses the only family it has ever known can suddenly develop behavioral problems because of the loss. Even if the new home is a loving and supportive home, the animal misses its original people, and the simple upheaval of such a

Cat's Meow

Please tell them this is not a training issue. I can't do what they are asking. I am uncomfortable in my own body. The pains come and go, and sometimes, they are so severe, I explode, or just have to get out of it.

—Shadow, a registered Quarter Horse

change is enough to cause some animals great upset. Or the animal might fear that no home will ever be permanent again.

Cheyenne's Insecurity

Michelle adopted Cheyenne, a beautiful black Labrador Retriever, from a local animal shelter. Michelle called Debbie, concerned because Cheyenne seemed depressed. When Debbie connected with Cheyenne to find out if she was happy in her new home, Cheyenne perked up and told Debbie she had finally found a home with someone to love her as much as she loves them.

Yet Cheyenne still had a problem. Like some people who are afraid when something good happens because it surely means something bad is bound to happen to take it all away, Cheyenne was so happy that she feared she might accidentally do something wrong and be sent back to the animal shelter!

Debbie explained this to Michelle, and Michelle confirmed that Cheyenne had been placed in two previous homes, and had been returned to the shelter twice. Her perfectly legitimate fear was that this pattern would repeat itself again with Michelle.

Both Debbie and Michelle assured Cheyenne that she had a home with Michelle forever, and that she need not ever worry about being sent back to the shelter. They could work through any problems, and nothing she could do would result in a return to the shelter. She was Michelle's, no matter what. Now that Cheyenne has learned to trust that she has a permanent, loving home with Michelle, her depression has lifted and she has settled in to her new life, happy and content.

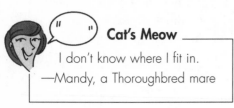

Cat's Meow

I don't know where I fit in.
—Mandy, a Thoroughbred mare

Blue Bell's Inferiority Complex

Blue Bell, a beautiful white cockatoo, lived with Martina, an experienced bird owner and rescuer. Martina called Debbie about the cockatoo, whom she had adopted six months earlier from a woman who could no longer care for the bird. Martina's concern was why Blue Bell kept ripping out all of her feathers. The problem started slowly but steadily increased, so Martina knew she had to do something about it.

When Debbie connected with Blue Bell, the cockatoo immediately poured her heart out to Debbie. She didn't feel pretty, and wanted to rip out all her ugly white feathers, in the hope that they would grow in green, like the other birds. Blue Bell told Debbie that the green birds were more special than she was. She was depressed and anxious that she was less important, and she thought that if only she could be a green bird, too …

Debbie asked Martina if she also had green birds in the house, and Martina confirmed that yes, she had two Amazon parrots that had been with her for eight years. She considered these two green birds her babies. Debbie explained to Martina that Blue Bell felt unimportant, unappreciated, and ugly. Martina and Debbie discussed ways of building up Blue Bell's self-esteem, so she could be proud of herself again.

Blue Bell had many feelings of inadequacy, not only because she had recently moved from the only home she knew, but also because in her previous home, she had been the only bird and the only focus of attention. In her new home, she was no longer the sole focus, and didn't understand how to handle such a change.

With a little patience and a whole lot of love, Martina was able to help Blue Bell feel important and pretty. Blue Bell no longer incessantly plucks out all her feathers, although she does occasionally revert to this behavior when she is upset about something. Overall, her confidence level has risen and she now understands that she, too, is a special part of Martina's family.

> **Horse Sense**
>
> Animals need the occasional ego boost, just as humans do. When you appreciate something about your animal, say so telepathically! Just make sure your affirmations are sincere, because if they aren't, your animal *will* be able to tell.

Communication for Emotional Health

Sometimes all an animal needs to hear is that you are in charge and will keep them safe and loved for the rest of their lives. How do you let your animals know they no longer have to worry or be afraid? By psychic communication, of course.

Frequent communication gives your animal a space to explore worries and fears, to explain undesirable behavior to you, and to tell you about what might have happened in the past. Just as with people, you may not get the whole story the first time. Give your animal time to talk about it and work through what has happened. Don't force the issue, but let the animal communicate to you when he or she is ready.

Through psychic communication, you can also offer your animal the crucial reassurance he or she needs to feel secure and safe again. Let your animal know, every day if necessary, that you are trustworthy, loving, and offer a safe, permanent home.

You can do other things to reassure an emotionally vulnerable animal. Animals, especially those who have suffered trauma, desperately crave boundaries, routines, and clear rules. They aren't sure what to do, they don't feel secure, they fear being abandoned again, and may develop severe anxiety, including separation anxiety from their people.

Clear rules and boundaries and a firm, consistent routine help these animals maintain a focus and feel secure and stable. Reinforce these rules, boundaries, and routines with psychic communication. Tell your animal, often if necessary, what they can expect from you. Warn them ahead of time when the routine will change, or from afar if the routine changes unexpectedly (such as if you will be late coming home from work). The more you communicate about what goes on in daily life, the more secure your animal will become.

Cat's Meow

I feel a bit chubby lately, and this bothers me.

—Frisker, a female Weimaraner

Emotional Rescue Routines

Although every animal can benefit from the following practices, implement these habits for your emotionally insecure animal, and watch your once-fearful friend slowly relax into happy security. (These routines could help *you* finally feel more secure and organized in your life as well … a happy bonus):

♦ Feed your animal at the same times every day.

♦ Go to bed at the same time every night, and get up at the same time every morning.

♦ Try to leave for work and come home from work (or, if you work at home, sit down to work and take breaks from work) at the same time every day.

Horse Sense

Whenever possible, talk to your animal and tell him or her what you are doing, or just chat about your day. Your animal understands more of what you say than you might think.

♦ Schedule a playtime and/or training time with your animal at the same time (or times) every day. Always end with a treat (food or a special toy).

♦ Give your animal an important job, whether that is to watch over the house, take care of another animal, sit next to you while you work, or work hard at learning training exercises. An animal with a job is an animal with a purpose.

The key to helping your animal move past fear, emotional blocks, and training barriers is to understand that blueprint that is the life and personality your animal now owns. But what if you don't know what happened to your animal in the past?

Finding out what happened in your animal's past can help you help your animal learn to feel safe. When your animal learns he or she has finally found someone to trust, life—and behavior—can turn completely around. But how do you find out about a trauma when it happened before you ever even met your animal?

Your Animal's Life, Before You

People often contact Debbie to find a way to fill in the missing pieces in their animal's past, especially when the animal has been adopted from an animal shelter and nobody knows anything about the animal's former life. Even if your animal seems happy and well-adjusted, you may be curious about where the animal came from and what happened in its life up to that time. Was your adopted shelter animal lost? Abandoned? Abused?

Debbie has heard many stories from animals about what happened to them before they found their current humans, and every story has, to some degree, enlightened the resident humans about why their animals do what they do, and how they can help them overcome emotional hurt from the past.

Horse Sense

Debbie never forces the issue of a past trauma. She lets animals tell her as much as they are willing and able to share. Some animals are eager and ready to talk about their past, and in doing so, they often experience a great release and the beginning of healing. Other animals aren't ready to share past trauma, refusing to go back to that place emotionally. These animals need support, love, and patience to release the problem in their own way and time.

Ralph's Anxiety

Becky had just adopted a wonderful mixed-breed dog named Ralph. Ralph was full of love, but Becky noticed that around men, Ralph became incredibly fearful. Becky lived alone, but often had male friends come over and Ralph would cower and sometimes even shake. Because Becky had adopted Ralph from a local shelter, she had no background information on him and she was anxious to know what had happened to this little dog to make him so frightened.

When Debbie first connected with Ralph, she told him how much his new person, Becky, loved him and that she thought he was a wonderful companion. This made Ralph feel great about his new home, and even about himself. Next, Debbie asked Ralph if he wanted to share anything about his past with her.

Ralph showed Debbie a picture of being in a home with a woman in her mid-30s. He loved this woman very much and she loved him. Then he showed Debbie a picture of a man, and a scene of the man yelling and hitting the woman. This frightened Ralph immensely. Debbie also got the feeling of knowing that alcohol was involved. She could feel Ralph's pain and fear, and his feeling of helplessness at not being able to do anything about his beloved human being hurt.

Debbie tried to comfort and reassure Ralph, and then asked Ralph if he wanted to tell her more. He did. Ralph conveyed his feelings to Debbie about how his fear grew so much that he became frightened at the very sight of the abusive man. Debbie asked Ralph how he escaped this situation and ended up at the shelter. Ralph told Debbie that one day, he simply left and didn't go back to that place. Debbie felt overwhelmed with sadness and admiration at Ralph's courage to finally leave his frightening and dangerous situation.

Cat's Meow

I don't know how to erase this pain, but I would gladly swap bodies if I could. I am not being bullheaded. I'm just fearful of what comes next.

—Sable, a Quarter Horse

When Debbie relayed Ralph's story to Becky, Becky was astounded and shuddered at the thought of her beloved animal going through such an experience. She continues to assure Ralph that no one will hurt him, *or her*, now that he is safe in his new home. "We are both safe here," she tells him often. Now that Becky knows from where Ralph's fears stem, she can take steps to help him overcome this fear by working with him to help him trust again.

In cases like Ralph's, Debbie always assures the animal that they are now in a loving, safe home and that it is okay to let those past memories go. Although releasing a painful memory can be difficult, with love and support and a safe, secure routine, many animals can successfully conquer their emotional traumas, finally healing and moving on to a new life. To help this process, sometimes, Debbie will recommend flower essences. (See later in this chapter for more on using flower essences and other natural remedies for emotional healing.)

Finnegan's Scare

Before Debbie bought her horse, Finnegan, he was in training to become a race-horse. He had trained at many of the tracks in Massachusetts and upstate New York. Although he had always been a very sensitive horse, he had an accident on the race-track that changed the way he looked at things from that day forward.

Finnegan had his exercise rider on his back and they were rounding the bend. A large white trash bag had blown onto the track and before the rider could steer clear of it, the wind blew it right at Finnegan. He attempted to dodge it, at which point the wind pushed it again and it got wrapped around his belly.

In their natural environment, horses are prey animals. Instinctually, the feeling of something wrapping itself around a horse's belly can be terrifying. Finnegan bucked and bucked to get the bag off of him, but instead, he unseated his rider. She was okay, but as she walked over to help him, he got scared again and double barrel kicked her in the chest. He was so frightened that his mind was no longer in control and his instincts were in overdrive, as if he was fighting for his life.

Since that day, Finnegan is terrified of anything that moves from the side while he is being ridden. Other horses might have been able to move past this without any lasting effects, but Finnegan chooses to hold his fears close to him, ever vigilant that he might again be caught off-guard.

Knowing about this incident has helped Debbie understand why Finnegan has so many fears. This knowledge has allowed Debbie to try different ways of desensitizing him. It has been a long road, but Debbie can finally say that Finnegan's tendency to spook has decreased dramatically since she first brought him home. When Finn nuzzles Debbie you can see the love and respect in this caring relationship. Every living being deserves and appreciates another's efforts to understand and support their deepest needs. We all need someone to believe in us—whether animal, human, or plant!

Debbie and Finnegan still have a long way to go. Overcoming fears takes time and patience for anyone, and it doesn't happen overnight. Sometimes, it can take years to get past an emotional trauma. Many animals who have been physically abused suffer long-term effects that might even manifest themselves as a mirroring of the aggressive behavior of which they were a victim. For animals (including humans), aggression can be an instinctual survival mechanism, whether it makes sense in the actual situation or not. Knowing your animal's past experience will help you to understand how to help them and what method of training will be most effective.

> **Cat's Meow**
>
> I scratch the furniture because when you don't respond to meowing, this always works to get some attention.
> —Meringo, a female orange tabby cat

Frisco's Fear

Mary called Debbie about her dog, Frisco, who barked constantly when she put him outside, even if for just half an hour. When Debbie connected with the beautiful, fawn-colored Boxer, she asked him why he chose to bark every time his person put him outside. He had a beautiful fenced-in yard, and every reason to relax and enjoy it.

Frisco told Debbie that in his former home, he was never let inside the house. He stayed outside, day and night, no matter how rainy, snowy, or cold. Frisco hated living outside. He only wanted to be with his people, but rarely was allowed to see them, except for when they ventured into the backyard.

Every time Mary let Frisco into the backyard, he was struck with the fear that she, also, would leave him out there and that he would never be allowed to come back inside. Debbie explained this to Mary, who had adopted Frisco from an animal shelter and knew nothing about his past. Debbie instructed Mary to explain to Frisco, each time she let him out, exactly how long he would be out there before Mary would bring him back in, and that he could always, always come back inside. Then Debbie got an idea. She suggested Mary get a doggie door so that Frisco could go in and out based on his own decisions.

> **Horse Sense** _____
>
> If you are considering adding another animal to your family, we hope you will consider visiting your local animal shelter. Many of the animals there have lost their homes through no fault of their own, and are well-behaved, loving pets who just want a forever-home.

Mary followed Debbie's advice. The doggy door empowered Frisco. Knowing he had the freedom to go in and out whenever he wanted, and that he would never be forced outside, helped Frisco to conquer the fear that haunted him from his past of neglect. Frisco now spends much of his days outside, happily watching over his beautiful yard, without any anxiety, fear, or unnecessary barking.

Sally's Story

Debbie and Eve are both big advocates of adopting animals from animal shelters. Although many of these animals have been neglected or abandoned and desperately want a secure, loving home, some were perfect family pets to other owners and were lost or displaced by mistake, or whose people had to give them up through no fault of the animal's.

These animals make excellent pets as well, and have often already mastered good manners and polite behavior. Eve's dog, Sally, is such an example, according to what she told Debbie.

Sally tells Debbie her past didn't involve any abuse. She lived happily with a gentle young man. One day, when they were on a long car trip, the car broke down in the middle of Iowa. Sally's person left the car to find help. He left a window cracked for Sally, and after waiting dutifully for a long time, Sally wiggled out and went to look for him.

> **Cat's Meow** _____
>
> I love my life!
> —Hank, a hound dog cross

Another young man found her wandering the highway, picked her up, kept her for a few days (she tells Eve she slept under his covers), and tried to find her owner, who was probably forced to continue his trip without her and was by this time far away. Because he lived in an apartment that didn't allow dogs, the new young man took the charming little terrier to the shelter, where Eve found her, staring intently at Eve as if to hypnotize her into an adoption. It didn't take much hypnotizing!

Eve hopes Sally's former human somehow knows Sally has a happy, loving home and a totally devoted human.

Uncovering Your Animal's Past

You can go to a professional animal communicator to help tell you the story of your animal's past. Or you can try it yourself. All you have to do is ask.

Set aside a quiet time to sit with your animal. Choose a time when you won't be rushed or distracted. Depending on your animal's past experience, the subject could be difficult, so it is important to focus fully on your animal, giving him or her your complete attention and open heart.

When you are both comfortable, begin the steps to prepare for a connection. Once you have connected, silently ask your animal if he or she would feel comfortable sharing with you something about the past.

Some animals prefer to wait until another time, some may not be ready, some will simply tell you "no," and others will flood you with information. Be patient, accept whatever you get, and acknowledge it back to the animal as you go. Instead of doubting any impressions that come through, keep your heart open and really be there to listen to your animal, and don't forget to write it all down after you are finished.

Horse Sense

When asking your animal about his or her past, you won't always get a lot of information. No matter what you get, be sure to thank your animal. Next time, your animal may be ready to tell you more.

Helping Your Animal Heal

Sometimes, letting your animal express and release a past hurt can be all it takes to heal, but sometimes, healing is more difficult. As with people, each animal has his or her own healing calendar. Some heal and move on more quickly than others, but that doesn't mean that you are helpless. By understanding an animal's past, we validate their experience, and that can help them to heal. But again, it may not happen quickly.

When you communicate with an animal about past trauma, abuse, or neglect, you need to acknowledge the pain as something real. If animals realize that another being actually understands their pain, they might feel a great relief. They might feel they don't have to expend huge amounts of energy constantly trying to show you they are afraid of something or fearful of reliving something, because now they see that you understand. This takes a huge burden off an already beleaguered animal.

You can also ask your animals what you can do to help them heal. Your animal might have a very specific suggestion or request that you wouldn't have considered. Don't overwhelm your animal. They might have no idea what you can do to help, and they might just need a little space for awhile. Give the animal what he or she tells you is needed, not what *you* think is needed.

Most importantly, don't put a time frame on healing. Allow it to happen at its own pace and don't get discouraged if it takes weeks, months, even years. Patience and understanding are the essential components to a nurturing relationship that gives the animal space and a safe place to heal.

Buddhist monk Thich Nhat Hanh writes in his book *Anger* that many people in difficult human relationships will give up too easily in their work to make the bond better, but at the same time will devote themselves to many years of effort to accomplish a goal such as getting an education or learning a new language. The monk quietly makes the suggestion that we might consider being equally devoted to the long haul of improving our loving bonds. Whether a human to human or animal to human relationship, we agree that the love and support we can give in a positive way toward healing a living being in pain or with whom we experience a difficult relationship is one of the best ways we can use our love and our time.

Horse Sense

As you and your animals work toward healing emotional pain, continue to interact with your animals in a gentle, loving way, seeing them for who they are, and trying to focus on their strengths, encouraging them to grow strong and build confidence. Help them find a purpose, so they feel necessary and focused. With love, patience, understanding, and acceptance, your animals can learn to love, trust, and even feel at peace again.

Healing with Flower Essences

Flower essences, or flower remedies, contain the energy essences of different flowers, distilled into an alcohol base (such as brandy). A few drops of the right remedy, mixed into water or food, balances or corrects emotions gone awry, for whatever reason.

People or animals can use flower essences (Bach flower essences is the most known brand), which are often recommended by a holistic health practitioner, but also available at most health food stores. They are completely nontoxic, can be mixed into cold or hot drinks or foods, have no side effects, don't interfere with conventional medicine, and anecdotal evidence suggests they really do work.

Many people use flower essences, especially a combination of different essences called Rescue Remedy, for anxiety, fear, and depression in their pets. Debbie often recommends flower essences to her clients. Flower essences can help an animal move through the healing process.

Flower essences work in conjunction with your, or an animal's, own body on the energetic and emotional levels. Debbie often gets an intuitive feeling about which essence will help each animal. With practice, a familiarity with the different flower essences, and an increasing trust in your own intuition, you can do the same.

> **Pet Speak**
>
> **Flower essences** are natural herbal remedies made from blooming flowers that are soaked or boiled in spring water then preserved in alcohol (often brandy). These essences are nontoxic and have no side effects, but the energy of the flowers remains in the remedy and helps to balance different aspects of the emotions.

Flower essences help the animal to heal on both an energetic and emotional level, but the effect is subtle. The one mistake people make in administering flower essences is not waiting long enough or giving the remedy often enough. Unlike drugs, flower essences don't have any negative side effects on the body. Some flower essences work immediately; others take effect slowly over time. In some cases, for multiple aspects of emotional healing, you can combine flower essences, but experts advise against combining more than six essences into one remedy. Too many combined seem to dilute the effect.

Bach flower essences are most effective when given a few times daily for a period of one week to a month, depending on the animal's needs. Putting drops of the essence in the animal's water is a great way to administer it because the animal can dose itself throughout the day. You may also want to include a water dish without the essence so your animal can choose which dish to drink from. If other animals in the home accidentally drink the water with the essence, no harm is done. If the animal's system doesn't need the remedy it does nothing. In this regard flower essences work very differently than homeopathy (which we'll discuss in the next section).

To give flower essences, put a few drops in your animal's water bowl, on a treat or sugar cube, or directly into the animal's mouth. For some animals, it will work to drop the essence on the paw for them to lick off. Some remedies are appropriate for rubbing on your animal's ears or around his or her nose. At this point, many animals will sigh—a sign the remedy is working.

Bach offers 38 flower essences, and studying these and their effects can be an interesting and fruitful project. For the purposes of this book, Debbie will advise you on some of the more common essences and their uses:

Bach flower essences:

◆ Rescue Remedy: This multi-purpose remedy works well before and after a stressful event, such as going to the vet, traveling, introducing a new animal, or immediately after any traumatic incident. Rescue Remedy is a combination of the following five flower essences, which can also be used individually for the purposes described. Rescue Remedy now comes in a spray bottle; you mist the air the animal is in, like the car if you are going on a long trip, or their carrier. Just inhaling the essence can be as effective as taking it orally. Avoid spraying into the eyes, however (yours *or* your animal's), due to the alcohol content.

◆ Star of Bethlehem, for trauma or shock.

◆ Clematis, for focus and consciousness.

◆ Impatiens, for nervousness, agitation, pain, stress, and (perhaps not surprisingly), impatience.

◆ Cherry Plum, to help an animal stabilize emotions, and for animals who are high strung, whose attention is hard to capture, and who can be destructive if their energy doesn't have a focus.

◆ Rock Rose, for terror or panic.

Other essences Debbie often recommends:

◆ Aspen, for animals who fear many things, spook or frighten easily, or feel compelled to be hyper-alert.

◆ Mimulus, for animals who have very specific fears, such as a fear of loud noises or small spaces.

◆ Vine, for the dominant animal or bully who pushes around the others.

◆ Beech, for picky animals or animals that don't tolerate new animals or people in their home, preferring their human to themselves only.

◆ Chestnut Bud, to help break bad habits and some obsessive behavior. This remedy also does well when combined with Cherry Plum and Rock Rose during training sessions.

♦ Crab Apple, a good remedy for cleansing the body of toxins and painful memories.

♦ Gorse, for depression, and a good grief remedy. For animals who appear to have given up or lost hope.

♦ Holly, a good remedy for jealous animals.

♦ Larch, to build confidence.

♦ Olive, for the animal that may be tired due to emotional or physical exhaustion, or after a long illness.

♦ Pine, a good remedy for grief, especially due to missing an animal or person. Also good for animals that cower or are very submissive, or try to hard to please at their own expense.

♦ Vervain, for animals with hyperactive energy that won't or can't relax.

♦ Walnut, to help animals feel safe and less vulnerable. Also a helpful remedy when moving to a new house or barn. This is also a good remedy to use with Rescue Remedy when moving or bringing a new animal home.

♦ Willow, for animals whose behavior may change when they are not getting enough attention. It's a good remedy for animals who feel a lot of resentment toward people or other animals.

Horse Sense

We highly recommend reading more about flower essences, and trying them on your animals … and yourself! You can buy flower essences at most local health food stores and some pet stores that cater to a holistic market. There is no risk of overdose when using flower essences. In the case of homeopathy or herbs, Debbie always advises a person to contact a holistic vet or homeopath; however, flower essences are incredibly safe. Unfortunately, most vets don't know much about them.

Let's look back at some of the stories in this chapter. Ralph, the dog who was afraid of men, could have benefited from Rescue Remedy, especially when moving into his new home. Mimulus could follow, to help address his specific fear of men.

Finnegan, Debbie's thoroughbred who had the traumatic accident on the track with the white plastic bag, is too late for Rescue Remedy, which is best used immediately after a traumatic incident. However, what Debbie can and does do is help him with his present fears, with aspen, mimulus, and larch: aspen for his general fears, mimulus for his specific fears (white bags), and larch to help build confidence.

Blue Bell, the cockatoo could benefit from Rescue Remedy to help her integrate into her new home, and whenever she becomes specifically upset about something. Larch would also help build her confidence.

These are only a few of the essences available. We mention them in this book because flower essences work on the energetic level, along a similar channel to psychic communication: spirit to spirit, energy essence to energy essence. Debbie has found flower essences to be a beautiful and effective adjunct to her practice.

Homeopathic Healing

Debbie also recommends *homeopathic remedies* for emotional and physical trauma. Debbie has seen homeopathy work wonders on animals when conventional medicine did not. Homeopathy does not mask symptoms. Rather, it addresses the cause of symptoms at its source, encouraging the body to balance and heal itself. It is important to use the right remedy and dosage for each animal and situation, which is why we recommend an experienced and reputable holistic veterinarian for the diagnoses of disease and the prescribing of homeopathic remedies.

In homeopathy, the reasoning is like cures like. Substances that can cause symptoms of illness in man or animal can also be used to trigger the body to heal itself when the condition shows similar symptoms. For instance, the homeopathic remedy Apis is made from the honey bee and is recommended for insect bites, hives, and irritated itchy skin. Humans and animals have the ability to heal themselves and homeopathy stimulates the body's ability to do this. Conventional medicine tends to focus on masking the symptoms of a problem or disease or to destroy the harmful agents or pathogens inherently present that create disease.

Homeopathy is based on the idea that the symptoms of a disease represent the body's own attempt at bringing sickness to the surface to try to heal itself. Homeopathic remedies work *with* the body, not *against* it. They are made from natural substances and diluted to minute amounts so the energy or essence of the substance is captured. The greater the dilution, the stronger the remedy! Homeopathic remedies are most often found in a small tablet form made from a sugar base. Some are also tinctures or

> **Pet Speak**
>
> **Homeopathic remedies** are made from various natural substances, which are then heavily diluted. These remedies are available from health food stores and holistic veterinarians without a prescription. A reputable holistic vet can help you use homeopathic remedies appropriately for your animal.

liquids, and others are in powder or cream form. Because of the extreme dilution of homeopathy it is relatively safe to use on animals, adults, and children. However, mastering the appropriate remedy and dosage in relation to the disease or symptoms at hand remains a challenge, and thus seeking the advice of a licensed veterinary homeopath is advised. Often the higher potencies of homeopathic remedies are not readily available in local health food stores and can only be obtained by a licensed homeopath.

Again, don't confuse flower essences with homeopathy. The flower essences we talked about earlier work in a different way than homeopathic remedies to heal the body. The Bach flower essences are made only from the essence of flowers. Homeopathy is made from various natural substances. Flower essences are liquid tinctures, while homeopathic remedies comes in several forms.

Horse Sense

A holistic, homeopathic veterinarian can prescribe the correct homeopathic remedy for your animal. Find a holistic veterinarian on the web at www.altvetmed.com, or ask around for recommendations.

You can, however, buy low-dosage homeopathic remedies in most health food stores. Debbie carries an emergency kit of homeopathic and flower essences that she often uses on every member of her family, whether two- or four-legged, before ever reaching for that bottle of "regular" medicine.

Always remember that when an animal suffers severe emotional symptoms, a physical problem could be at the root of the problem. Check with a vet to be sure you don't miss anything while at the same time addressing your animal's emotional needs. Keep talking. Keep communicating. Keep helping each other heal … because many an animal, in its own process of healing, has managed to heal his person at the same time.

The Least You Need to Know

- ◆ Animals have emotional lives and can experience emotional trauma just as people do.

- ◆ Psychic communication with your animal can help you to understand the reasons behind difficult behavior so that you and your animal can work on the problem together.

- ◆ Experiences your animal had before you adopted him or her can dramatically influence the animal's behavior and personality. Psychic communication can uncover this life before you and help solve problems.

- ◆ Flower essences and homeopathic remedies can help to heal animals emotionally as well as physically.

Want Happier Animals? Keep Your Pet Informed

In This Chapter

- ◆ Why you should tell all
- ◆ How to prepare pets for a trip or a move
- ◆ How to prepare pets for a trip to the vet, a performance, or other stressful situations
- ◆ Don't keep life changes a secret
- ◆ Intuitive methods for bringing new animals into the family

Animals pick up a lot from us, far beyond what we tell them. They can sense the energy and moods of all the sentient beings in the house, and when something happens or the routine changes, they can tell if you are upset about it, joyful about it, or just plain stressed out.

However, although they can tell when something is wrong or right or different, they don't understand the logistics, the details, or what will happen next—unless you tell them. All creatures, including humans, handle stress better when they are prepared for what's to come. The more you tell your animals, and the more you assume that they understand what you are telling them, the better they will adjust to changes in life and routine. Happy, calm animals help to reduce everyone's stress!

Tell It Like It Is

Sometimes, animals engage in behaviors we don't like simply due to misunderstandings that can easily be alleviated with some simple communication. Animals can feel insecure at a change of routine, a move, a change in the family, or the addition or loss of another animal in the house.

Ellen contacted Debbie, very excited about the addition of a new, splendid three-year-old cat that Ellen had adopted from the shelter. His name was Benjamin, but Ellen felt the name didn't suit him. She also was concerned about why Benjamin was spraying in the house.

Debbie connected with the new cat, and first asked him about his name. The cat confirmed that he didn't like the name Benjamin. Debbie felt the name "Santo" coming through, so she asked the cat if he liked that name, and he enthusiastically responded that yes, he was Santo.

Horse Sense

Before you move animals from one location to another, be sure each animal has an updated health record. Some states require this, just to enter the state, and all states require a rabies vaccination. Each animal should also have an identification tag with emergency contact information, just in case someone gets lost.

Next, Debbie asked why Santo felt the need to spray inside the house. Santo said that he could smell other cats in the home, and this made him nervous. He wanted to make sure his scent was there, too. Ellen confirmed that she had one cat, and another that had recently passed into spirit. Santo smelled the scents from two other cats. Debbie explained to Santo that he could only spray his scent outside, but could use his head and neck to rub his scent on things inside. Santo agreed, and told Debbie that he loved his new home and desperately wanted to do the right thing. Ellen began calling her cat Santo, and he responded immediately. He also stopped spraying inside the house, and has adjusted beautifully.

Debbie's Big Move

Because animals thrive on routine, moving to a new home or even a new barn on the same property can pose a real challenge. When Debbie had the daunting task of moving two horses, two goats, one dog, and three cats (two of which had been wild and never confined to a small area before) from Massachusetts to Florida, she knew she had a potentially volatile situation that would truly put her communication abilities to the test.

Debbie always advises people to tell animals, well in advance, about a move to a new home. In Debbie's case, several months before the move, she began to explain to all her animals about the exciting opportunity ahead of them. She acknowledged that they all loved their home, but that they were going to embark on a new adventure, moving to an even better home. She told her animals that she would keep them apprised of developments and let them know when moving day was coming.

As the move approached, Debbie continued to prepare her animals. Debbie's dog, Champ, hates riding in the car, so Debbie explained to him that, although they would have to drive for almost three days, they would stop often so he could get out, run around, stretch his legs, and have a bathroom break.

Debbie knew her cats would enjoy the move even less than Champ. They would have to stay in their cat carriers in the car. Debbie explained this to the cats, but also assured them that they would be let out, one at a time, for a stretch, and that everyone would get to come out and look around and have some free time in the hotels each night.

> **Doggone!**
>
> Animals may be reluctant to eat or drink while traveling, which can result in many different problems. Bring along some favorite treats to encourage them to eat. A can of chicken broth can help rehydrate an animal and is gentle and palatable. Also bring bottled tap water, because a sudden change in water supply can upset an animal's stomach and make him reluctant to drink.

Debbie also explained to Champ and the cats all about hotels, and that they would actually sleep in places the animals had never been before, but it would only be for two nights. She told them that they would be in a different place, so that it was very important to stay back from the door whenever it opened, and not try to run out, because they might not be able to find their way back.

Weeks before the move, Debbie brought the cat carriers into the living room so the cats could get used to them. She put food and catnip in the carriers so the cats would explore them, inside and out, and associate them with a pleasant experience.

A week before the move, Debbie had the horses and goats professionally shipped, so they arrived in Florida first. Debbie arranged for the woman who owned the house they had just bought to take care of them for that week. Her husband was also there to ensure the horses and goats arrived in good shape and were comforted by a familiar face. She also communicated to them what the trip would be like and stressed the importance that they drink water whenever they were offered it during the long haul to Florida.

It was a three-day trailer trip for the horses and goats as well, with an overnight stop, and very stressful, but they arrived in good condition. Horses, especially, can get very sick if they don't drink enough when being shipped long distances, so Debbie continued to emphasize to them the importance of drinking whenever possible, whether they were thirsty or not. Finnegan hates trailers, but he marched dutifully right on.

When moving day arrived, Debbie used a bottle of Rescue Remedy (the flower essence combination we told you about in the last chapter) to spray in the car, the cat cages, and on the animals and herself. She also brought the bottle along, to use in the hotel room, to help everyone stay calm and relaxed. They loaded up the clan, and off they went! The move went better than Debbie could have imagined.

Your Moving Day

On the day of a big move, your animals will sense the excitement, the stress, and the change in the air and in you. They will also see the movers, the boxes, and the suitcases, and that alone is enough to make anybody nervous! Animals who already know what is coming will be better prepared than animals with no preparation, but even so, everyone in the house is bound to be at least a little nervous, wound-up, or uneasy.

Be aware of your animals on this important day. Make sure they are secure in a safe area so they can't accidentally get out. With all the loading, an animal could easily slip out the front door, and a nervous, frightened animal can be hard to find and to communicate with. Explain to your animals the importance of staying in the house on this day, and keep reassuring them that, even though there may be a lot of chaos in the house, it will soon be over and you will be on your way.

To help ease your animals' anxiety and keep them safe, you should secure them in a room that the movers will not be entering and post a sign on the door to alert movers not to open the door. When Debbie was packing the car for the move she kept each cat securely locked in their cat carriers so that they were extra secure should someone accidentally open the door to the room they were in. Extra precautions should be taken to make sure your animals are secured, because many animals are known to "take off" on moving day. If you don't have a secure place to keep your animals while the movers are working, consider bringing them to a friend's house or to a kennel for safe keeping until the movers have finished.

Also, acknowledge your animal's fears and even grief about leaving an old home and setting out to a new home. You will miss your old house, your neighborhood, and your friends; and your animal might also feel the loss and sadness at leaving one environment behind, not to mention the fear that often accompanies any new foray out into the unknown. Keep in touch throughout the day, no matter how busy you get, so your animal knows that you are in charge and you will make sure everything is okay.

> **CAUTION**
>
> **Doggone!**
>
> In the car, be sure to secure your animal in a pet seat-belt, carrier, or crate large enough for the animal to stand up, turn around, and lie down in. This keeps the animal safe in case of sudden stops or an accident, and can also keep you safe and free to drive undistracted by a pacing or worried animal.

Packing a special overnight bag just for your animals can also help ease the stress of being on the road. Whenever traveling with your animal, whether to a new home or just on vacation, certain essential supplies can mean the difference between an uneventful trip and a stressful catastrophe. Be sure to pack the following things when on the road with your pet:

- Your animal's regular food
- Can opener and a plastic fork, if feeding canned food
- Bottled water
- Nonbreakable bowls for food and water
- Health records, including vaccination records
- Rabies and other vaccination certificates
- Collar and leash
- Baggies and paper towels, to clean up waste at rest stops
- A spray bottle of Rescue Remedy or other calming flower essence
- Your pet's regular medications, including heartworm, parasite control, any prescriptions, and carsickness remedy (ask your vet what to use if your animal gets carsick)

◆ A favorite toy or other object with a familiar smell, such as one of your unwashed T-shirts

When traveling with your pet, arrange ahead of time for pet-friendly hotels along the way, and tell them exactly what animals you are bringing and how they will be secured. Some hotels charge a pet fee, others don't, but always observe etiquette by keeping your animals safe and secure, not leaving them alone in the room unless necessary, and always cleaning up after your animal.

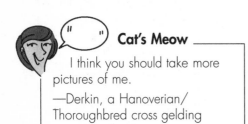

Cat's Meow

I think you should take more pictures of me.

—Derkin, a Hanoverian/ Thoroughbred cross gelding

Also, try to get a room that opens into a hallway instead of a parking lot. A frightened escapee will be easier to find inside than outside. Also check that doors and windows are closed. A frightened animal can claw or push through a screen.

During the drive and the transitions in and out of hotels, keep explaining to your animal exactly what is going on, and the importance of staying with you because you will keep everyone safe.

Brand New Home-Sweet-Home

Before you arrive at your final destination, help your animals get familiar with the new house by sending them mental pictures of the house, inside and out (assuming you've seen it yourself), and by talking to them about what the new house will be like, where they will sleep and eat, and how their routines will still be the same, and which other familiar animals and people will be there.

For some easily stressed animals, once in the new home, introduce them to just one or two rooms at a time, such as the room where they will sleep or eat (this works well for cats), so they can establish their own comfort zone and not be overwhelmed by the whole house at once. Walk your dogs around the whole house and yard on a leash, letting them take their time and smell all the new smells. Explain to your animals that it is time to cut their ties to the old house and begin to put down roots here in the new house. Cats sometimes take longer to adjust to a new home than dogs. Just give them time, and keep explaining the new rules and routines for the new home.

If your cats urinate or spray in the new house, explain to them that although the new smells might be foreign, one rule of the new house is that they must still use their litter box and that they can put their own smell on things in the new house by rubbing them with their head and neck. Cats have scent glands in their faces and necks that transfer their scent through rubbing, so they will often accept this suggestion as an alternative to spraying.

Explain to dogs the rules of the home as well, and the importance of listening to you at all times. Dogs get very excited in new environments and might wander away and get lost if you don't pay attention.

Keep outdoor cats indoors for at least two weeks, so they have time to feel safe and secure and get used to the new home before getting acquainted with the new outdoor surroundings. Give everyone time, be patient, keep a consistent schedule, and most importantly, keep communicating, visualizing positive behavior, exuding calm feelings, and expressing your happiness at the new location. If your animals feel secure in the notion that you have everything under control and are happy with the new house, they will feel better able to adjust in their own way to the new environment.

Before letting your animals outside on your new property, inspect all fencing and surrounding areas for dangers. If you allow your cats to roam, check for possible dangers and warn your cats to avoid these areas.

When Debbie moved to Florida, into a rural area on a large property where her animals were able to explore, she had a host of new things to warn her animals about. Debbie told her animals to watch out for water, especially moving water (Florida has a huge alligator population), to ignore the frogs (some frogs can be poisonous, even deadly, to dogs if eaten), that all animals must come in when it is dark, and that black lizards can also be toxic when eaten. Explain any cautions and dangers to your animals to help keep everyone safe, especially for those animals who aren't confined to a fenced-in area (generally, confining animals within a secure fence or indoors is the safest option, although your animals may not like it!).

Because all of the cats Debbie has now were once wild, they insist on being able to roam outdoors. They love to be outside, and Debbie respects this wish. However, she would not advise letting your cats outside at all if you lived on a busy street! The dogs, when let outside, stay on the property as well, but Debbie also has fencing along the perimeter.

Cat's Meow

I am on board with the move. I would like to set the ground rules right up front with the new people, though. They need to respect my space, especially my stall, and always ask permission to do things. This will make everyone's life easier. Also, they should say my name before they do anything with me, like, "Hi, Cookie, here is your grain. Hi, Cookie, I am going to turn you out now." That's the way it should be done!
—Cookie, a small Welsh pony

Easing Into a New Life

Sometimes, animals take longer to fully adjust to a new home than you might think. Communicating with the animal about what he or she is holding on to from the previous environment can go a long way toward helping the animal resolve old feelings and let go of the past.

A woman named Lynne called Debbie about her cat, Tusk. He was a dynamic orange tabby with double paws and a macho attitude. She adored Tusk, but a few times a week, he would wander a few blocks away to hang out at the house they used to live in. This worried Lynne because Tusk had to cross a few streets to get there and she was concerned with his safety.

Debbie connected with Tusk to find out why he was still visiting his old house, long after they had moved to a new house. He showed Debbie that he liked to hang out by the big tree there. Lynne confirmed that the old house had a big oak tree in the yard. When Debbie asked Tusk why he was so attached to that particular tree, he said, "I don't want to miss her should she return, because she doesn't know where we moved."

Debbie relayed this message to Lynne, who said that just before the move, Tusk's sister, Tabitha, had died and that Tusk missed her very much. She was buried under the big oak tree. Debbie explained to Tusk that Tabitha had gone over to spirit and that she could find them, in this form, wherever they were. He didn't need to go back to the old house to see if she was waiting. Tusk expressed great relief to Debbie to finally understand what had happened. Since their conversation, Tusk hasn't once wandered back to the old house, and spends much more time inside with Lynne, entertaining her with his antics.

> **Cat's Meow**
>
> It's unstable here. Shifty. Lots of things contradict reality. I don't see this as my forever home.
> —Charlie, a Holsteiner chestnut gelding

Vacation Preparation

We already talked about how to handle going away on vacation in Chapter 8, but as a reminder, when you go on vacation, whether or not you take your pet, you can waylay much anxiety and worry by telling your pet everything about what will happen ahead of time: where you are going, who will watch them or where they will stay when you are gone, or where you will go and how long you will be there if you are taking your animal along. Also remember to check with your animals telepathically, sending them messages of "hello" and images of where you are (those "mental postcards"), to help them feel more connected to you and to keep them from missing you and worrying about you.

Give your animal a job to do while you are gone, such as watching over the house, resting, or keeping the other animals calm. Picture in your head what will happen the day you return: all your animals being so excited to see you, relaxing, and spending some quality time with them. Send your animals this image, which can remain with them should they begin to doubt that you will come back.

By preparing your animals for these sudden changes in routine, they will trust you more and know what is going on, instead of feeling deceived and abandoned.

Preparing Your Animal for Stressful Situations

Life isn't always easy. Sometimes, stressful events necessarily arise, whether pleasant or unpleasant. Even fun events can be stressful. Preparing your pet for stressful situations, such as a trip to the vet or a competitive performance in a show, can help your animal to handle the stress more effectively.

When you've got a vet visit ahead, picture for your animal what will be involved: getting into the cat carrier, putting on the leash, having a relaxing ride in the car. Then, picture as much as you can of what procedures are going to take place, and always send them pictures of coming home afterwards and getting a big treat and lots of love and attention.

Fully preparing your animal for something unpleasant, such as a visit to the vet, won't necessarily mean that your animal will willingly jump in the car, suddenly eager to go get those vaccinations. What it will do is keep them informed about what will happen and why, so they don't feel frightened about the unknown. Remember, communication builds trust.

When preparing for a performance, such as a dog show or horse show, it's important to explain to your animal the entire process, even if he or she has performed before. Tell your animal how long the trip will be to the show grounds and what to expect when you get there. Visualize with your animals the routine: parking the trailer, unloading horses or dogs and/or equipment, walking them around to see the area, having a meal or a treat, the necessary grooming, warm-ups, and so on.

You might explain to your animal that the first class is at 10 A.M., and that this will be a

Horse Sense _____

During and after a performance event, be sure to acknowledge that your animal has done well, even if you don't do as well as you would have liked. Show grounds are hectic, scary places with lots of distractions, so give credit where credit is due! This will only help to build your relationship and improve future performances.

dressage test, a jump course, an obedience trial, or an agility course. Mentally go through the whole test, course, or routine in your head with your animal. Try to picture the maneuvers the way you would imagine them being executed. Positive visualization goes a long way when at a show or performance. Push all negative thoughts and doubts and fears aside and let the positive, confident, fun thoughts surface and take precedence. Try not to get too serious, and try to stay calm. Remember that animals feel what we feel and sense our fears, which can serve to compound theirs.

Rescue Remedy (one of the combination flower essences we mentioned in Chapter 11) for you and your animal might be a good beginning to a day of performance! Debbie is always a nervous wreck at horse shows, but she tries to visualize the perfect day: she and her horse Finnegan feeling calm and serene, jumping a clear course. She always pictures her horse jumping everything, even if he feels unsure. She pictures him sailing over each jump with confidence, to help build his confidence. Then, she pictures rewarding him, all the people admiring how handsome he is, going home to his stall and getting a special dinner, and being able to tell all his friends how well he did.

When Life Changes

Every life has landmarks: a new job, a new house, a new car; a marriage, a new baby, a new pet; a divorce, separation, loss, death. No matter what changes in your family and in your life, whether gradually or suddenly, letting your pet know everything you know will show that you respect and honor his or her intelligence and emotional life. The more your animal knows about major life changes to come, whether you perceive them as negative or positive, the more he or she can move through these transitions smoothly, even helping you to transition with greater ease and clarity.

Bundle of Joy

When you realize you are expecting a new baby, you know your life will change drastically, but the lives of the animals in your family will also change. Explain to your animals the exciting news, and let them know that you might be a bit preoccupied during this time, but that they still have important jobs in your life and that it doesn't mean that you love them any less. Let them feel your excitement and anticipation, and let them share in it, too, so that they feel the new family member will be an important and positive part of their lives.

During pregnancy and just after childbirth, make a commitment to set aside quiet time with just you and your animals, to enjoy each other. This is a relaxing way to unwind after a long day, and it can help you and your animals to touch base and stay connected. Explain to dogs and cats that the house will take on some new smells with the arrival of a new baby, and that they will also hear different noises that shouldn't alarm them. Help them to define their new roles in the family, as protector, helper, and emotional supporter. Explain to them the proper behavior with a baby. If you can, expose your animals the sounds of a new baby by bringing home a tape of a crying child, so they get used to that unique sound.

When you are in the hospital, if possible, have someone bring home clothes or blankets from the newborn for the animals to smell, so they can get used to and accept the scent before they ever meet the new baby. Send your animals mental pictures of the baby, and explain exactly when you will be bringing the baby home.

> **Cat's Meow**
>
> We could both be the babies! I think this sounds like a fun project.
>
> —Casey, a female Shih Tzu, when asked what she would think of a new baby in the house

When you do bring home the new baby, introduce the animals to the new tiny human by being loving, supportive, gentle, and affirming to your animals as they meet the new one, and helping them to keep themselves under control. Also be prepared for the stress and fatigue you will feel in the early weeks with a newborn. You may feel so overwhelmed that you don't always deal with your animals the way you would at other times.

If your animals get too excited around the new baby, or even jealous, you may get frustrated with their behavior, and even yell or get angry with them. You may forget to pay attention to them at all! However, if you and your animals are both prepared for this stressful but joyful time, everyone will be calmer and prepared for this life change.

Marriage and Divorce

Marriage and divorce can both play with the emotions of your animals. But, like any other life change, proper communication can go a long way toward alleviating fears your animal might have that he or she will be left out of your new relationship or will be abandoned when a family seems to disintegrate.

> **Doggone!**
>
> Animals, like children, will feel much better if they understand that a divorce is not their fault, or that a new man in Mom's life or woman in Dad's life will not replace them in their human's affection. Tell them!

Debbie gets many calls from clients facing an impending divorce, trying to find out who their animal wants to reside with or how they feel about shared custody. This is always a hard decision for everyone involved, but as long as there is plenty of love to go around on both sides, it doesn't have to be as painful as you may think.

Debbie knows a lot of dogs who are happy spending time with both people after a divorce, and others, of course, who prefer one over the other as a caretaker if they must make that decision. Sandra called Debbie, concerned about which dogs wanted to stay with her and which dogs wanted to remain with her husband after the divorce. Sandra was moving to another house with a large yard, and David was, for the time being, remaining at the house they shared.

> **Cat's Meow**
>
> I love protecting my house and family, but it's not the same. It's quieter. I miss my friends, but I don't want to leave Daddy alone. I need to watch over him. He works late and is tired. I am concerned for him. He is depressed and distant, and he isn't eating well. It's my job to watch over him.
>
> —Rose, a Great Dane

Sandra had four dogs, three of which wanted to stay with her. The last dog, Brisko, a Boxer mix, wanted to stay with Dad. He said that someone had to look after Dad during this time, and although he would miss his siblings, he chose to watch over him. Sandra was surprised but also relieved, as David was having a difficult time adjusting to the divorce, and really did need some loving support from Brisko.

Choosing an Animal to Join Your Family

If you would like to bring another animal into your family, the first thing to do, to help make such an addition be a positive experience for everyone, is to tune in to the animals already in your home to see if they are open to the addition of another animal. (See Chapter 13.)

Also, be clear and honest with yourself about what you are looking for in an animal companion. And, check with the new animal, too, communicating telepathically to see if you feel a connection, and if your home and family and situation seem like what the new animal is also looking for.

When Debbie was looking for a horse to add to her family, she knew the kind of personality she wanted in a horse. She was looking for a horse that was easygoing and that would be safe for her husband or for kids to ride. He needed to be okay with not being ridden every day, and be a friend to Debbie's other horse, Finnegan, who can be difficult, gets nervous and spooky, and gets very attached to other horses. Finnegan needs to be ridden often and is the "king" of the barn, and the new horse would need to respect this role and position, not be dominant and disrupt the hierarchy in the barn.

Debbie set her intention toward finding the right horse for her home. She was scanning some Internet ads for horses one day, and one ad caught her eye. The ad didn't say much, but she had a feeling she should e-mail the woman who had placed the ad, to get a picture of the horse so that she could connect with him to find out what he wanted in a home and if his personality would fit into what she was looking for.

The horse in question was a Spotted Walking horse (Debbie had never even heard of the breed before)—not exactly what she was looking for, but Debbie couldn't ignore her feeling that she should find out more. When Debbie connected with him, his personality said it all. He was gentle and sweet, and admitted that he could be easily frightened by things, but that he would listen to his person when scared. He said he didn't like ring work but liked an occasional trail ride and that he was happy just being with other horses, and that he didn't need to be the boss or be ridden every day.

> **Horse Sense**
>
> Debbie often gets calls from people to connect with a new horse prior to purchase, to see if the horse has the personality and body to hold up to what the person has planned for the horse. Some people want a show horse that will take them to the top, and it takes a certain personality to be able to do this without falling apart.

Debbie explained her situation to see if he would be interested, and he was willing to check it out. She arranged a trip to go meet him, and sure enough, she fell in love. Sunset Stroller, a.k.a. Sonny, has been a wonderful addition to Debbie's home and family. He was everything he said he was, and more.

Sometimes the animals in your home will tell you exactly what type of animal they want you to get. Deidre and Mike called Debbie to find out if their cat Tazz wanted another cat in the home. They feared that Tazz was lonely after the loss of his long-time companion, Sweetie. When Debbie connected with Tazz, he liked the idea of having another cat in the home to keep him company while his people were gone during the day.

When Debbie asked him if he had any specific requests, he said, "I would like the cat to not be a kitten. Kittens are too much work, but I also don't want the cat to be too old so that all they do is sleep. I would like a black and white cat much like me, but make sure he knows I am the boss. Also I would like a male. Females can be too complicated and I want someone I can lounge around with." Deidre and Mike started their search for the perfect cat for Tazz, and we are happy to report that Deidre, Mike, Tazz, and Manie are all doing fine, and engage in plenty of lounging.

Eve wondered if Sally might like another dog to play with, and Sally immediately told Debbie that she thought it was a wonderful idea, since Eve's two young boys sometimes overwhelmed her. Sally thought that a new dog might distract the boys, and that they could pour all their attention onto the new dog, so that Sally could have more time alone with Eve.

Eve found a little terrier mix puppy for the boys, and although they do spend quite a bit of time petting, playing with, and carrying little Jack around the house and yard, and although Sally does have more alone time with Eve, Sally has found herself quite surprised at how much fun *she* could have with a new puppy! They go everywhere together and sit in the sun out on the lawn, shoulder to shoulder, sniffing the breeze and keeping an eye on the perimeter for neighbors to greet, other dogs to bark at, and rabbits to chase. Sometimes they squabble, as siblings will, but the household is certainly livelier!

Even though animals don't always know how things will turn out or what they will and won't like, when considering a prospective new animal to join your home, you can learn a lot by connecting with the new animal and asking some questions:

◆ What is your personality like?

◆ What do you like to do?

◆ How do you get along with other animals in your species, and other animals in general?

◆ What do you think of children?

◆ Is there anything that makes you nervous or frightens you?

◆ What are your goals in life?

◆ What things do you want in a home or barn?

◆ What do you like and dislike?

◆ How does your body feel?

◆ Do you have any injuries or pains that come and go?

◆ How do you feel about showing/performance?

◆ Would you like to tell me anything about your past?

◆ How did you end up at the shelter, and how long have you been here?

Sometimes, despite all logic, you might find yourself inexplicably drawn toward a particular animal. Even if you can't explain why, you might find your heartstrings are crying out that "this is the one!" Pay attention to this feeling, while also paying attention to your own limitations in space, time, and energy. Often times, these intuitive leanings result in the most meaningful partnerships between humans and animals. Animal communication is all about learning to trust your instinct, so if your instinct tells you that an animal belongs with you, pay attention!

The Least You Need to Know

- The more you explain to animals about life changes, the better they will weather those changes and the more they will trust you.

- Communicating ahead of time about moving, vacations, vet visits, or performance events can ease your animal's anxiety and help him or her prepare mentally for what's ahead.

- When your life changes in a major way, such as with the addition of a new baby or pet, or because of a marriage or divorce, share everything with your animal so that the transition is easier for everyone.

- When considering bringing a new animal into the family, ask your animals what they think about it first, and ask the new animal if he or she would like to join your family.

Part 4

Welcome to Your Pet's World: The Animals Speak

This part of the book gives you a peek into the minds and hearts of pets all over the world. Debbie reveals what cats, dogs, horses, and birds complain about most, what they would like us to know, and how much love and sometimes exasperation they feel for us. We'll also talk about how to dissolve common communication blocks between humans and animals, and how telepathic communication with your pet can help reveal the cause of, and often the solution for, the most common behavior problems. Finally, we'll show you exactly what to do when your animal gets lost, and how to increase your chances of a happy reunion.

Common Complaints from the Animals

In This Chapter

- Animals have their gripes, too
- Common complaints from cats, dogs, horses, and birds
- The upset of having other animals come and go
- Using telepathic communication to discover and address common complaints

Even animals have their gripes. Don't think they don't notice that cheaper food or that so-called deodorized cat litter. So you believe your parrot likes all those dangly chew toys or your horse just *loves* that new trainer? Think again!

Domesticated animals in particular, living as they do in such close quarters with humans, frequently complain about many of the same types of things. In this chapter, Debbie will tell you about some of the more common complaints she gets from cats, dogs, horses, and birds, and how you can best address them.

Complaining Cats

Cats live with us, but sometimes they seem like they don't care much for human company. Or they become suddenly starved for our affection. Humans might think that cats mostly complain about getting too much affection, or not enough, but cats have plenty of more specific complaints than that!

The complaints Debbie most often hears from cats who live with humans fall into a few specific categories: those related to the litter box, food and water, and of course, foolish human behavior. Some cats can border on intellectual snobbery, but then, so can some humans, so who are we to talk?

Here's what Debbie often hears from cats.

Litter Box Complaints

Cats spend a lot of time in the litter box. (Just think how much time you spend in the bathroom.) Of course they don't like a dirty one, who would? Here are some common litter box complaints:

> **Doggone!**
>
> Remember that cats are fastidious. They like a clean box, and they want their own individual box (or no more than two cats to a box, if the box is big and cleaned at least once or twice a day). How would you like it if you couldn't flush the toilet yourself and someone else only flushed it for you once every couple of days? Yuck.

- You aren't keeping my litter box clean enough.
- You have too many cats for one litter box. We each need our own!
- I hate the perfume-y smell of this cat litter.
- I hate how the cat litter clumps to my paws!
- The sides of the litter box are too high. It's hard to get in and out.
- The box is upstairs, or downstairs, or otherwise too difficult to get to.
- The litter box is in a vulnerable spot and it makes me uncomfortable.

Litter boxes should be easy to enter, and you should avoid litter filled with perfumes that can irritate cats' sensitive olfactory systems. It's better to get a litter that absorbs odor rather than masks it, and clean the box frequently. Keep the litter box well away from food bowls, preferably in different rooms. Also, because cats are naturally vulnerable when using the litter box, they get nervous if they feel too exposed. Many cats like covered litter boxes, which feel safe and secure. However, don't forget to clean them! If a covered litter box means you won't see the litter and will forget about it, then get another kind of box. The smell can really build up in there!

Feline Food-Related Complaints

Those cat food commercials about finicky cats don't come out of nowhere. Cats can be very finicky, and they like food that is high in quality and delicious in taste. (Then again, who doesn't?) Here's what they say:

- This is an inferior food. I need something that is higher quality.

- You don't give me enough variety in my diet. I'm bored with it.

- My water isn't clean enough.

- I prefer running water.

Cats can be prone to allergies and urinary tract infections when they regularly consume inferior foods. Many of the foods found in supermarkets are made with fillers and additives that complicate the animal's sensitive system. Always use a premium cat food, made with ingredients approved for human consumption, to avoid these health problems in the first place. Some brands we recommend for sensitive cats: Wellness, Innova, Felidae, Evolve, and Noah's Kingdom, to name just a few. If you aren't sure, read the label. Cats are carnivorous and real meat should top the list, not meat by-products. As for dry food versus canned food, as long as the food is high in quality, it doesn't really matter. Choose a complete, balanced, premium food that your cat enjoys.

> **Cat's Meow**
>
> Please ask my person to give me my own water bowl. Buster likes to stick his paws in the water and gets it all dirty, and I refuse to drink it!

What Cats Think About You

Cats do love us, even when they don't act like it. However, they also have a few criticisms about the way we do things. Here's what Debbie's feline clients frequently tell her about their people:

- I don't like it when you move me out of my spot!

- You don't nap enough.

- You sleep too long and waste the morning. The best hunting is at the crack of dawn!

♦ I don't like it when you let people stay in our house.

♦ I don't approve of moving out of our home!

♦ Why are people always trying to pick me up? I don't enjoy it.

♦ You walk too hard on the floor. It makes me very nervous.

♦ Can you fix this wobbly scratching post? It's not satisfying when it moves around like that.

♦ This scratching post isn't high enough to get a really good stretch. I need to be able to get a really good stretch.

♦ Our veterinarian isn't very smart.

Cat's Meow

I am a wise guy, the pleasure is *all* mine!! I am a one-of-a-kind cat and basically do as I please. They love my attitude and coloring. They think that I am very special.

—J.D., a gray Manx cat

Cats don't care for change, whether that means being moved from a sunny spot on the couch or being moved into a new house. Some of them can have a bit of a superiority complex, too! Explaining to your cats well ahead of time when change of any kind is imminent will help them to deal with that change better.

They will also appreciate it if you stick to a routine and try not to clomp around so much. If you walk a little more like a cat, your cats will be pleased. They will also appreciate it if you get out of bed at the same time every morning. The regularity of a consistent schedule makes cats feel secure.

Dissed by the Dog

Cats aren't the only ones with complaints about being four-legged creatures in a two-legged household. Dogs have plenty to complain about, and sometimes they give Debbie a real earful! Dogs want to be with you, they want to be appreciated, they want to feel secure, and they love to play, have fun, hang out with friends, and eat really good food. In other words, dogs aren't all that different from people!

Here are some of the most common complaints from our canine friends.

Living to Eat?

Sure, dogs love their dinners. Some are pickier than others, but many of them have something to say:

- Could I please have some hamburger/steak/bacon instead of this dried crunchy stuff?

- This new food tastes too healthy.

- I just know my buddy is getting better food in his bowl than I'm getting in mine.

- Cat food tastes *way* better than dog food.

- People food is way better than dog or cat food. I think I should be able to eat more of it.

Despite what your dog may tell you, stick to a high-quality, premium diet for good health, one that lists real meat at the top of the ingredient list.

Horse Sense

Some dogs do very well on a homemade diet of simple, healthy people food, such as boiled chicken and rice with ground-up vegetables. However, because dogs have specific nutritional requirements, don't just give them any old food. Research how to prepare a homemade diet that will keep your dog healthy and free of nutritional deficiencies. Many good books show you how to do this. See Appendix B for a list.

Dogs Just Wanna Have Fun

Dogs have a beautiful, playful sense of fun and they want us to join in their light approach to life. They also love nothing more than to be with their people. Here's what they tell Debbie about their approach to life and the way their people sometimes don't share it:

- I would really like to be able to go outside more and socialize. I like to socialize!

- You are working too much. Can't you take more breaks to play?

- I really need more playtime in my life.

- I love getting all muddy and wet. Why do you get so worked up about it?

- I wish the whole family was together more often. I love that.

- I wish we could go on special outings more often, like picnics or trips to the park.

◆ You are way too serious during training/dog shows! Lighten up, will ya?

◆ I like to run off and smell things whenever I want. I don't like to have it planned first. Can't I just act on the spur of the moment? Do I have to wear that leash?

◆ When we walk with the leash, you walk too slowly. I wish we could pick up the pace.

◆ I want to greet you at the door when you come home *first*. I wish those other dogs/cats would get out of my way.

◆ I hate it when you leave. Can't you just stay here all the time, or always take me with you?

◆ I did such a good job today, and you didn't even seem to notice!

Cat's Meow

I love playing, and then coming back and having all my toys around me. I like lazy days, too. I can be a couch potato. I love T.V.

—Hansen, a Rottweiler

Discomfort Zone

Although dogs aren't as obsessed with their physical complaints as horses (as you'll see in a moment), they do have their share of gripes about their environment and the way it makes them feel. Dogs like to feel safe and in control, and when they don't, they'll tell you about it:

◆ I hate to get my feet wet and when it's raining, I'm just not going to go out there. (This complaint is especially common in small dogs.)

◆ The floors are too slippery! I'm afraid of slipping when I walk on them.

◆ That medicine really stinks.

◆ My legs are achy and weak; the stairs are hard for me.

◆ I do not like other dogs to come too close to me, it makes me feel vulnerable and oftentimes I will get defensive and on guard.

Remember that your dog wants nothing more than to be with you, loves a steady and regular routine, wants to feel secure, and simply adores having a really good time. If you need to change something, or everyone needs to get serious for awhile, psychic communication lets you explain this to your dog, who may not necessarily like it or agree to your conditions, but at least everyone will know what's what.

Haranguing Horses

The sociable horse has many complaints about life with humans and with other horses in that social network that is the barn. Horses tend also to have more physical complaints, overall, than dogs and cats. Some are fairly temperamental, as animals go. Here are some of the most common complaints Debbie hears from horses.

Let's Get Physical

Horses are very body-aware. They notice how things feel more acutely than some other animals, and they will tell you all about it. They also have sensitive taste buds. For instance:

- My saddle doesn't fit right. It's too tight and it hurts.

- I really dislike this blanket. It doesn't fit right. It doesn't feel good.

- Let me tell you about my aches and pains … (horses go into lots of detail about this!)

- I hate all these bugs! They're driving me crazy.

- I hate that bug spray! It burns my skin and my eyes.

- The supplements you put in my food make it taste funny.

- I have a sophisticated palate and this hay is not high enough quality for me.

- I really would like to be able to eat more grass.

- More treats, darn it!

- I prefer the other bit, it has a better flavor of metal and does not pinch my mouth like this one does.

- Be careful taking my blanket off, sometimes it zaps me. (Static electricity!)

> **Cat's Meow**
>
> Life is extraordinary. Life is precious. Live each day. Take nothing for granted.
>
> —Preppy, a horse fighting a terminal illness

The more you tune in to your horse to determine his or her physical level of comfort, the more you can make things feel better. Psychic communication can provide you with the opportunity to explain to your horse that some discomforts are just part of life and will soon pass, while others are definitely important and need to be addressed, and that you will do so immediately.

Irritating People, Irritating Horses

Horses get easily annoyed with us and with their fellow horses, too. Here's what they say:

◆ I don't enjoy having to sit on the cross ties while you stand there and chit-chat with people.

◆ I hate being fed late! Can't you bring me my food at the same time every day? Is that so hard?

◆ My stablemate really annoys me.

◆ That horse over there won't settle down in his stall. It's irritating.

◆ I would really prefer to be outside more.

◆ I really don't like waiting and waiting to do something I know we're going to do. Can't we get on with it?

◆ The blacksmith doesn't realize that I need more chances to put my leg down to rest.

◆ My trainer isn't very nice.

◆ My trainer is way too inflexible. He/she needs to see the big picture and adjust to methods to fit my personality.

◆ Now that I'm retired, I feel like I don't have a job anymore. I don't feel like I'm worth anything anymore.

> **Cat's Meow**
>
> I don't need a stronger bit, just a different saddle. It pinches my achy areas and I have stiffness in my back. I hollow it, which makes it hard for me to round. When my back is stiff, I compensate by hollowing and raising my head. This relieves the tension in my back muscles.
>
> —Hank, a gray Arabian horse, when asked why he was running through the bit

Sure, sometimes horses do have to wait or deal with less than perfect people (don't we all?). However, talking with your horse can sometimes uncover problems you hadn't realized existed, such as with trainers or blacksmiths. It can also make you more aware when a horse is truly bothered by the behavior of a stablemate.

When Birds Berate Us

Birds have some of the complaints you might expect would come from someone living in a cage, but one Debbie doesn't often hear is the desire to *not* live in a cage.

Birds like to have their environment just so, and (like most of us), they would like a little more attention, thank you very much:

♦ I don't see you enough!

♦ You have too much stuff hanging inside my cage. I don't have room to move around.

♦ I can't see outside from where you have my cage.

♦ I get really bored during the day when nobody is around.

♦ I wish I was in a place where I could get more sunlight.

♦ I wish people weren't always putting their hands in my cage and invading my space.

♦ Why do you tell me to be quiet? I'm just sharing my voice with you.

When Other Animals Come and Go

Finally, one of the things that most upsets animals is when the animal friends they make leave them. Animals form strong attachments with each other, and they can become very upset when they lose their animal friends. Pet psychic communication is an effective way to prepare an animal for the sometimes-inevitable loss of another animal friend, or, when this isn't possible, to explain afterward exactly what happened.

Debbie's horse, Finnegan, gets very attached to other horses. So much so, that he will become frantic and hysterical if Debbie takes another horse out of his sight. When Debbie communicated with him to find out why, he showed her that at a young age, his best friend, another bay horse, was taken out of his paddock and he never saw him again. His friend was sold, and Finnegan never even had the chance to say good-bye.

Debbie's heart went out to her horse, who is very sensitive and a real worrier. Just like some humans, some animals bond particularly strongly to their friends and feel their losses with particular intensity. Because of this experience, Finnegan is reluctant to trust that when a horse is taken out of his sight, he will ever see that horse again.

> **CAUTION**
>
> **Doggone!**
>
> Because horses are so emotionally and physically sensitive, it is important to be emotionally open, nonjudgmental, and sensitive but truthful when communicating with them. If horses sense you aren't sympathetic or think you are lying, some might close themselves off to communication with you. Others might get angry with you.

Finnegan's new best buddy was an Appaloosa mare named Peggy. They spent their days grazing together. He would run the fence, calling to her in a frantic manner if she was even taken in the barn to be groomed, let alone taken out for a ride. But Peggy's owner was in the process of relocating to Maryland, and Peggy was also going to be moved. As soon as Debbie found out this information, she told Finnegan. She told him every day that Peggy would soon be leaving. She told him how many days until she would be moved and gave him plenty of time to say good-bye.

Debbie made every effort to prepare her sensitive horse for his friend's departure. On the day Peggy was to leave, the barn was so silent, you could have heard a pin drop.

Horse Sense

When considering bringing a new animal into the home, be sure you recognize your limitations and expectations. For instance, if you live in a tiny apartment and don't have much or any yard, it would be unfair to bring a large, active dog into your home, unless you know you can provide the animal with plenty of attention, interaction, and vigorous exercise.

Peggy was taken out to the trailer, loaded up, and off they went. Finnegan never once whinnied or moved from his stall. He was silent and still as he watched her drive away. Debbie couldn't believe the silence, and she mourned for Finnegan, knowing that he might never see his friend again, and that he was losing yet another. However, she feels Finnegan handled the loss with much less trauma than if he hadn't been prepared for it.

Finnegan continues to get attached to other horses, and Debbie always tries to do her best to let him know the status of each resident. If a horse is going to leave, Debbie will try to give Finnegan as much notice as she can, so that he has a chance to say good-bye.

Some animals will also complain about the addition of a new animal to the family, becoming resentful and distant if you go against their wishes. Imagine being a young child and having your parents quite suddenly telling you that they were bringing home a new brother or sister, and that you would have to share your food and your room with them.

Some children would be excited, but others would be angry and hurt. Again, be sure to prepare your animals with lots of conversation about what will happen, what is expected of them, and what their special and very important jobs will be when the new animal joins your family.

The Least You Need to Know

- Animals have complaints about their lives, just like people.

- Cats tend to complain about the condition of their litter boxes, the quality of their food, and the enigmatic nature of human behavior (and we thought *they* were the mysterious ones!).

- Dogs tend to complain about not getting enough time with their people or enough chances to have fun and play with their people.

- Horses are fastidious about their schedules, their stablemates, and their bodies. They tend to go into great detail about their physical complaints.

- Birds complain about invasion of their cage space by hands and too many toys, as well as boredom and not getting to be with—and share their lovely voices with—their people enough.

Chapter 14

Going to the Source: Behavioral Problems

In This Chapter

- ◆ Behavioral problems always have a cause
- ◆ Using pet psychic communication to address separation anxiety, housebreaking issues, and aggression
- ◆ What to do when your animal's behavior suddenly changes for no apparent reasons
- ◆ Addressing wandering and destructive behavior

This book is filled with stories about behavioral issues and how telepathic communication has discovered the cause and resolved the problem. In this chapter, we'll pinpoint some of the specific behavioral problems domesticated animals tend to have, and how you can best address them by going right to the source: the animal.

Just like humans, animals don't always understand why they do the things they do or have the feelings they feel, but together, you and your animal can work to solve problems, create solutions, and design compromises that improve family harmony.

Separation Anxiety

Bryan called Debbie about his dog Harley, a friendly Lab/Shepherd cross. Harley had recently begun to exhibit some destructive behavior in the house while Bryan was at work. When Debbie connected with Harley to find out why, Harley said that Bryan had other interests and was gone too long. When Debbie relayed this information to Bryan, he mentioned to her that instead of coming home right after work, he was going out with his girlfriend. He said that he had the neighbor come by to let Harley out, but obviously that was no replacement in Harley's eyes to actually seeing his person. Bryan made some changes in his schedule and he and Harley are a happy pair again.

Although not all vets recognize separation anxiety as a valid medical condition, many people experience this problem with their animals: when they leave, the animal becomes inconsolable, wracked with fear, anxiety, chronic barking, agitation, and sometimes extremely destructive behavior. Children sometimes have this problem, too, and in human circles, it's considered a treatable psychological condition.

The problem is common in dogs, especially those that have been abandoned to shelters or rescue groups. Although most domesticated animals love to spend time with their people, some dogs tend to form extremely intense emotional connections to people, and they fear that when their beloved people leave, they will leave forever. You can hardly blame those dogs who have experienced this very scenario before: People left them without warning, or left them in a strange place and never came back.

Separation anxiety isn't just your dog not liking to be left out in the yard alone or whining for a few minutes at the door when you leave or when you put him in his doggy den or crate. It isn't a bored dog barking or chewing up the sofa cushions when you leave him alone in the house, and it isn't even a dog yelping and barking because you've changed the routine and suddenly started leaving at a different time than usual. These are all natural behaviors that are easily resolved.

> **Doggone!**
>
> Sometimes, what looks like separation anxiety is actually a medical problem, so have your veterinarian check out your dog to make sure he is healthy, even if you are pretty sure the problem is separation anxiety.

Separation anxiety is more serious than that. It is a problem in which your dog loses control and becomes seriously fraught with anxiety.

Traditionally, people were often at a loss about what to do when their pets experienced separation anxiety. Some stay crated for their own and the furniture's protection, but spend the day full of fear and anxiety. Some dogs won't stop barking, and some have even been known to chew their way right out of a plastic crate in their desperation. At a loss regarding what else to do, vets sometimes prescribe serious drugs to treat the symptoms of separation anxiety, when the answer is usually fairly simple.

When addressing separation anxiety with your dog, it is very important to acknowledge him or her and ask for cooperation in solving the problem. Let your dog share her fears with you. Does she fear abandonment? Talk often about the problem. Sometimes, just being able to tell you, through telepathic communication, why they are reacting the way they do will help animals begin to resolve separation anxiety on their own. You can help in other ways, too:

♦ Every time you leave, tell your animal where you are going, why you are going, and how long it will be until you return. Picture yourself coming home and greeting your dog in a calm, happy way. Send your animal that picture.

♦ Give your dog a purpose or job to do while you are gone. Explain the job in detail, and emphasize how important it is to you that the dog do that job well. Some examples might be to watch over house, take a rest, work on healing, watch over other animals in the house, or keep the house in order.

♦ Never use "don't" in your visualizations or instructions about jobs or about your absence. Your words and images should be positive. Show what you would like your animal to do, *not* what you hope he *won't* do. If you visualize the anxious behavior, your dog will become more anxious, not less. Visualize the healthy behavior.

♦ Have Rescue Remedy on hand, the flower essence that helps to calm animals and people emotionally. (See Chapter 11 for more on flower essences.)

♦ In some cases, dogs can be desensitized to your necessary absences. Begin by leaving for very short periods of time, even just a few minutes. Come back. Greet your dog calmly and happily. A few hours later, leave again for a few minutes, then come back. Extend the time you leave each day by a little bit.

♦ Always act calm and pleasant when you return, not fraught with emotion yourself. If you act overly emotional about leaving and returning, your dog will pick up on those intense emotions, and such behavior on your part can even cause or worsen separation anxiety. Some trainers suggest completely ignoring your dog for 10 minutes before leaving and when returning, casually saying hello after you've put down your things and can turn your attention calmly to your dog; or you might casually say good-bye, then putter around a bit to find keys, purses, etc., before you leave. Leave without ceremony. Arrive without ceremony. This sends your dog the additional message that your coming and going is no cause for alarm of any kind. Don't sneak out; simply act calm so that your animal doesn't pick up on your emotion over the situation. Remember to tell your animals where you are going and when you are coming back.

♦ When you are away, send your dog occasional messages of reassurance and updates on when you will be back. Keep your messages calm and pleasant. Thank your dog for watching over the house while you are gone, or for doing her or his job in your absence and then tell your pet when you will return.

♦ If, after all these measures, your dog still experiences severe separation anxiety, consider contacting an experienced and reputable animal behaviorist who can give you additional ideas about alleviating the problem.

Bathroom Issues

You go to the bathroom indoors. Your dog might think, why shouldn't he? Why does your cat stop using her litter box? Why does your puppy look you straight in the eye while urinating on your bed pillow?

Puppies and kittens need "potty training" just like human children, but when an adult animal suddenly has a lapse in training or a puppy can't seem to learn after a few months, the first thing to do is rule out health issues.

Missy, a white Persian cat, had recently started going to the bathroom outside of her box. She was usually a fastidious kitty, and her owner always kept the box impeccably clean. When Debbie connected to Missy to find out why she had suddenly stopped using her box, Missy showed Debbie that she had to urinate often, but that when she did, only a little came out. Then she told Debbie that she experienced a burning feeling while urinating. Debbie instructed Missy's owner to take her to the vet to have a urine test done, and that she suspected Missy might be suffering from a urinary tract infection. Missy's person, Karen, took the advice Debbie had gleaned from the information Missy had sent her, and sure enough, the vet found that Missy had a mild urinary tract infection that was treatable with antibiotics.

Doggone!

Debbie estimates that 80 percent of the cats and 50 percent of the dogs she has communicated with about bathroom issues have health issues, so have your vet give your animal a clean bill of health first. With the remaining animals, Debbie has found that emotional issues stemming from past or present problems lay at the bottom (so to speak) of undesirable bathroom behavior.

Common health issues that can cause animals to lapse in their bathroom training include the following:

- Urinary tract infections

- Urinary stones

- Disorders of the kidney, including infection, stones, even renal failure

- Diabetes (usually but not always accompanied by noticeably excessive thirst)

- Intestinal parasites like giardia, a protozoan that can cause uncontrollable diarrhea

- Mobility problems such as bad hips or spinal disk ruptures that make getting to the right bathroom spot difficult or painful

- The animal has a general feeling of sickness

- A new medication that is causing incontinence

A vet can discover and address each of these issues, so again, don't wait to schedule a checkup, and mention the bathroom issues to your vet.

Some of the emotional reasons Debbie has discovered from animals about why they won't use a litter box or go outside to eliminate include the following:

- The litter box is too dirty for a fastidious cat.

- Too many cats to one litter box.

- Cats say the litter hurts their feet or burns their eyes.

- Many cats who have been declawed have intense sensitivity in their paws and often find using a litter box excruciatingly painful. Declawing your cat should be avoided at all costs.

- Cats associate the litter with a feeling of painful urination or constipation, either from a past or present illness.

- The animal feels fearful or angry about something and responds in this way.

- The animal has a lack of boundaries or doesn't understand the rules.

- The animal is trying to get your attention, and negative attention is better than no attention.

- Another animal in the house is doing it.

- It is wet or cold outside and the animal doesn't like the discomfort of going out into those conditions.

♦ Sometimes, animals think you really don't mind very much if they go in the wrong place because you may overlook it once, and therefore, they feel it is okay. Debbie finds that people who don't set clear boundaries and overlook dogs, especially, going to the bathroom inside, or make excuses for them (not health related), allow holes in their boundaries. Thus, the problem of the animal going to the bathroom inside begins to escalate.

> **Cat's Meow**
>
> I respect cats. I learned the hard way. I know my boundaries.
>
> —Gypsy, a female mixed-breed dog

After you have identified the root cause of bathroom misbehavior, you can take steps to resolve the problem. Talk openly and honestly with your animal. If the problem is medical, explain this, and explain that you aren't angry because you know your animal is ill and you are doing your best to help. If the problem is emotional or a basic misunderstanding, address the problem and explain how important it is to you that your animal go in the proper spot, whether litter box or yard.

These other good ideas ensure good bathroom habits:

♦ Set clear boundaries and establish firm rules. Explain them to your pet and send telepathic reminders, often if necessary, until your animal understands and accepts the rule.

♦ Visualize the acceptable behavior and send the picture to your animal. Keep the images positive. For example, don't send a picture of a housetraining accident and your angry face. Instead, send a picture of your animal doing what you want her to do, with lots of positive energy.

♦ Change your own behavior! For example, if your cat isn't using the litter box because it is too dirty, come to a compromise. Promise to clean the box more often or get a separate box for each cat, if they promise to use the box.

♦ Explain to the animal why this behavior is unacceptable and what the options are.

♦ For animals who have simply developed a bad habit of eliminating indoors (not due to a health problem), Debbie has found that the flower essence combination that works well is cherry plum and chestnut bud.

Aggression and Physical Resistance

Sometimes, animals behave aggressively for an obvious reason: They are being attacked, threatened, cornered, challenged, or abused. However, when animals behave aggressively or physically resist something they usually accept, Debbie has found that most of the time, the behavior stems from both physical and emotional pain.

Many people call Debbie when a horse starts bucking, rearing, kicking, pinning ears back, or otherwise acting aggressive and/or resistant. Debbie usually finds that the horse is in physical pain, and once the pain is removed, the behavior resolves. Pet psychic communication can help you to pinpoint the source of pain, which can help the veterinarian or veterinary chiropractor discover and address the physical problem.

> **Cat's Meow**
>
> They have no respect for my space, I constantly have to warn them not to come closer.
>
> —Fabio, a male Doberman

Sometimes, aggression stems from emotional abuse. Animals experiencing aggression due to severe emotional trauma require a lot of patience and understanding in order to release the experience and begin to trust again.

When animals aren't aggressive toward humans but do display serious aggression toward other animals, the causes can be many: jealousy, dominance, insecurity, delusions of grandeur, an adolescent phase, a power struggle, etc. Finding out the root cause and explaining the reality of the situation to your animal can help everyone work toward harmony. For instance, you can work to show one of your cats that he needn't be jealous of another cat because he is equally valuable in the household. (Back up this talk with action, which speaks, as we all know, louder than words—even telepathic words!)

Or you can explain to your dog that she needn't worry about the other dogs walking by on the other side of the fence because they are no threat to her property or people, they are just walking by, and aggression isn't necessary.

Again, Debbie has also found that giving each animal in the house or barn a very specific and important job can help to alleviate aggression by giving each animal an individual purpose on which to focus.

Flower essences can also help alter aggressive or resistant behavior, once you get to the root of the problem and identify the appropriate essence.

Because of the nature of our current society, aggression is extremely dangerous. You could get sued, and your animal could be taken away and even killed by court order.

You must address aggression and not take it lightly. Call in the experts. Working with a professional animal communicator, a vet, and an animal behaviorist specializing in aggression, you will be much more likely to resolve the problem and head off disaster. Don't make the problem worse by allowing your own emotions to get out of control. Remain calm and take the necessary steps to address this issue.

Part of your job can be to explain to the animal what acceptable behavior is, and then visualizing it. Many times, Debbie has been faced with the daunting task of outlining for the animal an ultimatum: If they continued to attack people, they will end up being euthanized. They must change this behavior immediately. In these situations, Debbie visualizes how she expects the animal to behave around people, and that if they feel the urge or need to attack, they need to retreat or go to their person's side for support.

Dogs with a lot of aggression usually have a warped view of what their space is. A healthy view of space is about two feet around the animal's body. A dog with an unhealthy view of space will think his space is the whole room or street. As a result, if another dog or person enters what he perceives to be his space, he feels the need to protect that space. Often times, by explaining what a healthy view of space is, and readjusting it for these animals, the behavior can be modified.

Animals with a very small view of space, one that literally hugs their body, are usually very insecure and nervous. They may bite out of fear because they constantly feel vulnerable. Again, by helping them understand where their space is and how they can protect it without violence, these dogs can feel confident enough to self-modify their behavior.

Carla contacted Debbie about her dog Rasta, a Rhodesian Ridgeback. When Carla and Rasta would go walking, Rasta often tried to lunge at other dogs, even if they were on the other side of the road. Rasta is a very large dog, and Carla constantly feared that one day, he would break free from her grip and attack someone's dog.

When Debbie connected with Rasta, he explained to her that his job was to protect his person, and that he didn't even want other dogs looking in their direction. He felt that if he made a big enough scene, everyone would know that he was serious. Rasta had one of those personalities you might have met in humans: larger than life and a bit pushy at times. Rasta showed Debbie that he felt "his space" encompassed any area he was in. He said that any animal within sight was justifiably in his space and he wanted to set them straight.

Debbie chatted with Rasta for awhile to explain to him what his actual "space" really was. She also explained to him that his job was to walk proudly next to Carla when they went on their walks, and to ignore other dogs unless they came within a foot of his "actual" space, at which time he could warn them verbally, i.e. with a growl, but could not exhibit any physical aggression (like lunging).

Debbie explained to Rasta that if he didn't change his behavior, he could no longer go on walks with his person and would be forced to stay home. Rasta loved his walks, so this ultimatum made him stop and think. Carla's job was to reinforce the revised "job description" that Debbie discussed with Rasta, and to verbally remind him of it prior to each walk, stating the ultimatum as well.

Carla noticed a big change in Rasta after that. She watched him try very hard to ignore other dogs, and Carla always acknowledged this with positive reinforcement. There are still occasions when Rasta feels threatened and tenses up to react, but Carla picks up on this, too, and helps to calm Rasta down so that he can focus again on his job. Both Carla and Rasta are better in tune with each other, now that each knows what the other one is thinking during the walks. Rasta has progressively gotten better, but it certainly is a team effort!

> **Doggone!**
>
> Because aggression can put other people at risk, take extra precautions with an animal working through aggression issues. Be aware of the laws in your area, but most importantly, if your dog is working through aggression and you don't feel able to control him or her in public, keep the dog away from other people or dogs until the problem is resolved.

Uncharacteristic Behavior

Sometimes, life seems to be going along nicely. Then, suddenly, an animal might begin to act different than usual. A usually tractable horse might start biting, kicking, bucking, bolting, or refusing jumps. A gentle dog might begin snapping at people or biting himself for no apparent reason. A seemingly well-adjusted cat might begin hiding, crying out more, or constantly demanding food. A bird might begin plucking out feathers. These are just a few examples of sudden behavior changes in pets.

Betsey ran a riding program for children and contacted Debbie about one of her school horses, Bronson. Bronson was a favorite among the kids, tall and black with a white blaze everyone loved to pat. Lately, though, Bronson acted differently. He was reluctant to work and when he did, he became uncooperative and cranky. Betsey was concerned that Bronson wanted to retire and was unhappy in his job.

When Debbie connected with Bronson to find out how he was doing, Bronson confided that he was having terrible headaches and that his body ached all over. He said he was cranky lately but still loved the children. Betsey and Debbie discussed the many areas of pain that Bronson highlighted. Debbie suggested Betsey contact a chiropractor for Bronson, but something also told her to advise Betsey to have him tested for *Lyme disease*. Betsey agreed to both. The chiropractor found that Bronson's body was indeed very sore, and worked in many of the areas that Bronson mentioned.

A month later, Bronson's Lyme test came back confirming that he did indeed have Lyme disease, which was making him feel even more sore than usual. The Lyme disease also explained Bronson's uncharacteristic lethargy. Bronson was treated for the Lyme disease and has resumed his job as a school horse, but is now working a much reduced schedule.

Pet Speak _____

Lyme disease is the most common tick-borne illness in the United States. Both animals and people can be infected. Most common in wooded areas of the northeast, upper Midwest, northern California, and the Pacific Northwest, Lyme disease in pets often causes sudden lameness, swollen joints, and sometimes, fever, weakness, lethargy, weight loss, and loss of appetite. Ticks must be attached for 5 to 20 hours before they can transmit Lyme disease, so prompt tick removal can prevent the disease. Veterinarians prescribe antibiotics to treat Lyme disease. In susceptible areas, pets can receive Lyme disease vaccinations.

When an animal experiences behavioral changes, the first thing to do is to use your telepathic skills to find out what is going on. Often, when we are worried about a behavior change in our animals, our minds begin to fabricate all kinds of reasons for what could be wrong. It is important, to get a clear telepathic response from your animal, that you still your mind as best you can and stay open to whatever comes. If you still feel unclear, find a quiet area, sit outside perhaps, and focus on relaxing and quieting your mind.

Ask your animal if you can imagine that you are in his or her body, to help you find out what is wrong. Take a minute to visualize going into the animal's body. Relax and feel what it is like to be your animal. Then, imagine yourself doing the strange behavior, and take a minute to try to understand why "you" are doing this.

It could be that your horse is biting because he has a bad headache and feels awful, or that your horse is bucking because the saddle is pinching him, or bolting because he has back spasms, or refusing jumps because his hocks are sore and he is just plain tired of showing.

Your dog might be growling because his stomach aches from ulcers, or biting at himself because his joints are achy or his skin itches. Your cat might be crying out more because she is trying to let you know she is constipated or demanding more food because she has a thyroid imbalance that is driving her to eat.

The causes of behavioral changes can be as vast as there are animals, but tuning in to find out why your animal has altered his behavior is your privilege. If you suspect that your animal is ill, please seek the counsel of a qualified vet, but also, take that minute to tune in to your animals so that you can help to direct your vet's attention to something he or she might otherwise miss. Remember, you know your animals better than anyone else, so go with your gut instinct, and give your animals a chance to tell you what is wrong.

The Wanderer

Wandering, or roaming, is an important issue for animals because of the many dangers they face when heading out alone beyond the boundaries of their homes. Animals wander for different reasons: some for adventure, some to follow a scent or chase something, some to find a mate, others to socialize, but it is important that you do what is necessary to ensure your animals are safe and secure, especially while you are not home. We don't recommend tying your dog to a pole or a tree, especially unsupervised. We do recommend proper dog fencing so that your dog has the freedom of exploring the yard, without the fear of getting loose or lost.

Cats can be more challenging, but many people make the decision to keep their cats indoors, only taking them out on a leash. We recently saw a cat stroller covered with a netted tent for walking your cat in the fresh air, and an elaborate, netted system of walkways and climbing towers to set up in your backyard for cats to use in their explorations without getting away. Depending on where you live, you may decide to let your cat roam, but talk about the dangers and the rules involved with this kind of freedom. Try to enlist your cat's cooperation so that he will abide by your request.

When talking to a wanderer, Debbie often explains, in vivid detail, the many dangers the animal faces and the trouble the animal could encounter when he wanders, to help him understand how important it is to stop this behavior, and why his people feel so strongly about him staying close to home.

Sure, sometimes the animal tells Debbie that he or she is careful and not to worry. Nevertheless, animals often don't understand the dangers of the modern world. When an animal wanders away, many things could happen, such as ...

- Being hit by a car

- Getting attacked by another animal

- Getting lost

- Being picked up by the dog officer and going to the animal shelter

- Being picked up or stolen by another person and not being allowed to get home again

After Debbie explains these dangers to wandering animals, she then asks them to stay within the boundaries of their home, and gives them a job that relates to this, such as watching over the yard which, obviously, they can't do properly if they wander away.

Further, Debbie visualizes the boundaries of the yard for the animal and shows that they need to stay within this perimeter. This can help the animal better understand exactly what "wandering" means.

Eve has always been concerned about the way Sally leaps over her chain-link fence as if it wasn't even there (springy little Rat Terrier!) to wander around the cul-de-sac and visit the neighbors. Eve lives next to a bus line and she feared Sally would try to cross the street and get hit, particularly if she eyed a rabbit. Debbie explained to Sally how important it was that she watch the yard and stay in the yard. Sally told Debbie that she didn't go very far, but Debbie insisted that she stay in the yard nevertheless, so she could do her job of guarding the yard.

Sally's behavior improved somewhat, but it wasn't until the puppy, Jack, came into the family that she stopped leaving the yard altogether. She later told Debbie that her job was both to patrol the perimeter, and to keep an eye on Jack. The little Pomeranian mix can only aspire to leaping over the great heights of that fence, so Sally stays put to keep an eye on him.

Appetite for Destruction

When your animal engages in destructive behavior, it benefits no one. Destructive behavior can be anything from your dog tearing up the house while you are gone to a horse constantly kicking the stall, a bird plucking out his feathers to a cat clawing your couch.

Destructive behavior can stem from a number of reasons, and that is why communication is so important in finding the root cause. Maybe your dog is destructive due to separation anxiety, or plain old boredom.

If your animal is bored during the day, give him a job and lots of things to do: interactive toys with treats he has to work to release, ribbed rubber toys smeared with peanut butter, and chew toys that take a lot of work to finish. Also consider coming home for a lunch or hiring a dog walker or pet sitter to pay your bored animal a visit if you are gone all day.

A horse kicking his stall while inside could be doing this out of boredom, out of pain, or out of dislike for the horse stabled next to her. Again, you probably won't have much luck just asking the animal to stop without finding out the reason for the destructive behavior. Once the reason is uncovered and addressed, you can talk about solutions.

Your bird might be plucking his feathers due to anxiety, because of a health problem such as itchiness, or just to get attention. Find out why so you know what to do about the problem, and be sure to tell your bird how beautiful and healthy he looks when he keeps his feathers. If your bird isn't getting enough attention, well, that's something *you* need to address in your own schedule!

You might feel completely frustrated by your cat's destructive scratching on your furniture, but such behavior is completely normal for a cat. Cats need to sharpen their claws, and couches, chairs, or other pieces of furniture you think of as "yours" often offer the perfect size for a good stretch and the perfect scratching surface. Provide your cat with a sturdy, tall scratching post and send her visual images of her using the scratching post. Reward her when she uses it.

One of the best ways to address destruction, just as with many other behavioral problems, is to give your animal a purpose. Remember, once again, to keep it positive. You don't say, "Your job is *not* to chew the rug!" Instead, phrase it more along the lines of: "You have an important job in the house and that is to keep things in order and protect the house. If you feel the need to chew on something because you are anxious, please use your rubber toy." Or, "If you feel the need to scratch, remember your lovely scratching post!" And of course, don't forget to say thank you!

> **Cat's Meow**
>
> My scratching post is too wobbly and small. The rug gives me a good stretch and the proper resistance. It's perfect!
> —Princess, a calico kitten

Whenever you give your animal a specific job, make sure it is one he or she can actually achieve. For instance, don't tell your little toy poodle, who is only comfortable with you and who is terrified of people he doesn't know, to be the greeter of the home. A more realistic job would be to give and receive love, or to help you relax, or to bring joy into the home.

Always acknowledge when your animal did a good job when you return home. This reinforces the good behavior. You can remind your animal of his job as often as you feel it is needed.

It is important to make animals aware of the fact that they are responsible for their actions. Give them a choice. If you have an outdoor cat, for example, you might explain (as Debbie did to her cat) that the cat can go outside, but will have to come in before dark or lose outside privileges.

Go on to explain to them why you need them to do this, so they understand the reason behind the rule. Like children, animals want to be told everything. "Why?" is a big question for them. Be true with your word, because your animals know when you are bluffing and will call your bluff every time!

Finally, the message we most want you to come away with from this chapter is that behavioral problems always have a cause. Whether physical or emotional, your pet can often tell you exactly what's wrong. Sometimes the best solution will involve a behavioral change on *your* part, but being open to compromise and a discussion about the problem will improve, rather than erode, your loving relationship with your animal.

The Least You Need to Know

♦ When animals have behavior problems, frank and nonjudgmental communication can help you determine the root of the problem.

♦ Common behavioral problems in animals that pet psychic communication can help to address include (but are not limited to) separation anxiety, housebreaking issues, aggression, wandering, and destructive behavior.

♦ When your animal's behavior suddenly changes, rule out a medical problem, then work with your animal to determine the reason and the possible solutions.

♦ Sometimes you have to compromise to find a solution to behavioral problems, but the more you communicate with your animal, the more your relationship will grow.

Chapter **15**

Overcoming Communication Blocks

In This Chapter

- When the behavioral problem is *yours*
- Self-care for better psychic communication
- Overcoming communication blocks
- Enlisting power animals and spirit guides to help you

Animal communication is a constant process of learning and growing. You don't get it all exactly right the first time—or every time—no matter how experienced you are (although you *will* get better at it!).

As you practice and learn, you will be challenged to face things that might hurt, emotionally and spiritually: things that come from your animal, but also, things that come out of yourself. The key is to acknowledge what comes so you can grow and learn.

What's Holding You Back?

Certain things can limit your ability to communicate with animals. To really become proficient and comfortable with animal communication, it is important to address your own fears and issues, especially if you feel they are directly getting in your way.

Jettison Your Baggage

Anyone who has lived for more than a few years has some emotional baggage. That's all part of life and what makes us who we are. But, as anyone who has slogged through the airport with too many suitcases can attest, too much baggage can wear you down fast and slow down your progress.

If your baggage keeps you from trusting, opening your heart, or believing in things without scientific proof, then these things can stand in your way. Personal work to release this baggage and free up your heart for the future can help you to move past these issues

Fear of Pain

Many people fear using an animal communicator or learning the process themselves because they fear what their animals might tell them about themselves, or fear the pain of hearing about an animal's abusive past. If you are afraid of hearing or feeling these things, then you will inhibit the communication process and can inhibit your own as well as your animal's healing process.

Cat's Meow

When the heart is raw, it will be heard. Fine-tune this strength. Pain helps us to grow.

—Kayla, a tortoiseshell calico cat, in spirit after her passing

By understanding that healing takes place on all levels for everyone involved when you open yourself up to whatever your animal wants to tell you, you can all move into a better place and a more trusting relationship. Dealing honestly with communication that will be painful for you to hear or experience, even empathetically, can open you up to an entire realm of knowledge you might never have experienced.

Debbie's Life Lesson

Animals have a unique gift of teaching us both amazing and, at the same time, difficult lessons in life. When Debbie first started communicating with animals, she had to contend with a deep-seated fear of the pain of a dying animal. She had lost so many animals in her life already, she just didn't think she could face the situation again, especially not with the full ability to listen to the dying animal's feelings and pain. How could she ever bear it?

Debbie has learned that we draw the things we fear nearer to us. So, of course, many of her initial cases were people struggling with the euthanasia decision, calling to see if their animals were ready to pass over or wanted to keep fighting for life. Debbie doesn't believe in coincidences, and thinks that everything happens in our lives for a reason. And so, she soon had to deal with the loss of an animal on a deeply personal level. It was a life lesson sent to her, and so she will share it with you.

Jimmy James was Debbie's beloved cat (we've mentioned him occasionally throughout this book) whom Debbie rescued after he was trampled by an aggressive pony at a stable where she worked many years ago. Debbie rushed the injured cat to the hospital, his little body limp in her hands, and they took him right away. They told her that his brain was swollen and that he might never recover fully. Yet in just a few short days, he seemed to be doing better and Debbie took him home to live with her. Since that first meeting, Debbie and Jimmy James became soul partners.

Debbie loves Jimmy James with all her heart, and he managed to steal the hearts of all who met him. Their relationship continued to grow, and with the development of Debbie's animal communication skills, it really flourished! Jimmy James sat with Debbie through her many consultations, adding his two cents and advice where he felt it was needed. He especially liked to meow very loudly and bite Debbie's feet when he thought she was taking too long.

One day, a dear friend of Debbie's lost her cat. Debbie tried to help her friend through the grief, but kept thinking to herself that she would never be able to handle the loss of her Jimmy. Her fear of something happening to him consumed her, and she worried about him daily. She came home every night and hugged Jimmy tightly, telling him how much she loved him and how much she wanted and needed him to stay safe.

Debbie and Jimmy James had their daily routine: Jimmy woke Debbie at 5:30 with his gentle nuzzling, and they would go outside together. He explored the yard while Debbie fed the horses and goats, and he'd wait for Debbie's cue: "Time for breakfast!" These words sent him running back to meet Debbie at the door, so they could go inside for breakfast. Then, Jimmy James would venture off to his favorite spot in the sun for a nap until Debbie returned in the evening.

Cat's Meow

I will always be your baby. I will return to you the same way.

—Jimmy James, in spirit

The morning started like any other morning, except this morning, Debbie's life changed forever when she called out those familiar words: "Time for breakfast." Jimmy James ran a few strides toward her, then suddenly shot like a rocket, dragging his hind legs behind him. Debbie caught up to him and saw the terror in his eyes. He seemed paralyzed from the middle of his back down. She saw it happen: one instant he was fine, and the next he wasn't.

Debbie took Jimmy James from hospital to hospital and the diagnosis got worse and worse. Jimmy James was diagnosed with a blood clot in his spinal cord, causing him paralysis from the middle of his spine back. An emotional wreck, Debbie cried at night, asking God to help her through this horrible ordeal: *Please let Jimmy James pass on if it's his time, or please help him to be cured. Please, please don't make me have to decide,* she pleaded.

Because she was so close to the situation, Debbie decided to consult with a friend who was also an animal communicator, to make sure she really understood what she thought Jimmy James was telling her. She knew he wanted desperately to get out of the hospital and come home, and this is just what he told Debbie's friend. Jimmy said he had a lot to tell Debbie, but that it was between the two of them, so she needed to get him out of the hospital and take him home immediately.

Debbie honored this request and took him home with her. She set up a little bed for him by the sliding glass door where he loved to lie in the sun, and she stayed with him on the floor throughout the night. The two of them talked, and Jimmy James told Debbie that they had been together many times before and that they would eventually be together again. But right now, he was so happy to be home.

CAUTION

Doggone! _____

Making the decision to put an animal to sleep is never easy, and in this age of veterinary medicine, many more options exist to help animals out of illness and injury. Vets are much less willing than they once were to end an animal's life when that animal can be saved, but when the animal is beyond the realm of modern medicine, animal communication can help because you can ask the animal's wishes. This can alleviate much of the guesswork and consequential guilt.

The next day, Jimmy James seemed uncomfortable, and Debbie felt greatly conflicted about what to do. Jimmy told her that they both knew he was not going to be in this body for much longer, but that he needed her to relax and go about her day as usual. Debbie relaxed a bit and decided it would indeed be best to stick to her normal routine. This seemed to relax Jimmy James, also. When the cat's medication wore off, he seemed even more peaceful. Debbie gave him some homeopathic remedies to help him feel more comfortable, which seemed to help as well.

During this time together, Debbie came to terms with the situation. She had feared the death of Jimmy so much, but the experience transformed her fear into love. Suddenly things started to make sense to her. She realized there is so much more to this world than she can ever comprehend. During the entire ordeal with Jimmy, Debbie's husband Scott had been away on business in London, but called nightly to check in on Jimmy and Debbie. Debbie still believes this also happened for a reason, because the process was one for she and Jimmy to share alone.

The evening Debbie's husband returned, he greeted Jimmy with a big kiss. Jimmy was happy to see him, and Debbie felt relieved that Scott was able to see Jimmy again before he passed over. The next day, Jimmy seemed to sleep more, and the day after that he became increasingly uncomfortable. On December 6, Scott and Debbie stroked Jimmy as he peacefully passed over with the help of a sensitive vet. Debbie knew that he had a lot of work to do on the other side. Scott cried as he and Debbie left the office with Jimmy's body, but Debbie smiled tearfully at the sky, knowing that the connection between them remained deeper than ever. She acknowledged that she would miss Jimmy James's physical presence terribly, but she also knew that if she let herself get stuck in this grief, she would hinder his progress in coming back again.

Debbie smiles every time she thinks of Jimmy James. She smiles a lot lately, and knows that she will find him again. His passing continues to yield lessons to Debbie. In the circle of life, there are so many daily miracles, and Debbie chose to see and embrace this one. Without seeing, feeling, and hearing the pain of her beloved friend, she would never have gone through the dark valley of fear and loss to emerge wiser, happier, and closer to the universal spirit of all life. Debbie knows that all of us are students in this life, and she has decided that she will let animals teach her their wisdom so she can use that wisdom to help others. Debbie and Scott eagerly await the return of Jimmy's spirit into their lives. They believe they will recognize him when they meet him again.

Protecting Yourself

Some people fear that opening up their psychic doors will lead to a whole host of other problems: spiritual vulnerability, over-sensitivity, too much feeling. But opening yourself psychically isn't like

> **Horse Sense**
>
> If you feel lightheaded after a telepathic connection, it is important to ground yourself by placing both feet on the floor, imagining roots growing out of your feet into the earth. Go for a walk outside, touch the earth, eat something, or do some stretching exercises. All these things will keep you grounded.

opening Pandora's box. You can take steps to protect yourself while still learning and hearing your animal's pain.

If you feel that becoming psychic makes you vulnerable or too open to feel things, try this simple exercise Debbie teaches her students to do after each telepathic exchange or conversation, if they feel the energy of the animal is lingering on afterward: Simply picture yourself in a cocoon of white light. Let it swirl around you from head to toe. The white light offers a form of energetic protection to your personal energy field, pushing out any negative or lingering energies that are not yours to keep.

The Guilt Complex

Some people harbor deep-seated guilt and fear when it comes to their animal, when they feel that they have done, or might have done, something wrong. Maybe they feel they didn't do enough to save an animal that passed over into spirit. Maybe they feel guilt for relinquishing an animal or losing an animal. Or maybe they feel they made a mistake in training, lost their temper, or misunderstood the needs of their animals.

To truly connect effectively with your animal, you must forgive yourself. By letting go of the guilt and accepting that even though you might have made a mistake (like we all do), you can learn something from it, you will open yourself up to better, truer communication. Animals are great teachers and healers, and they will challenge us to be the best we can on all levels, physical, emotional, and spiritual. They are also usually quite willing to forgive us. If you admit and acknowledge the mistakes you have made along the way, and learn from them, you are honoring the animal involved in this situation in another way. The true crime is never learning from your mistakes. If you find a problem or behavior keeps following you around, take a hard look at yourself to see what lessons you may not be learning.

Moving On, Feeling Better

If you feel that you have a lot of baggage or fear or guilt inhibiting your ability to hear your animals, try writing down exactly what you are feeling, clarifying exactly what is blocking you. Then, picture what you would have done differently in the situation that bothers you. Forgive yourself out loud: "I forgive myself for _____." Then, thank your animal for helping you to learn this lesson. Do this for each animal you feel that you need to release any pain, fear, or guilt with.

Another important way to move on from your own emotional baggage and negative feelings is to take care of yourself. If you don't take care of yourself, you will not be able to give your animal the best care possible.

When life gets too crazy, set aside 20 minutes to take a walk, sit outside and listen to the sounds of the world around you, absorb the energy of the sun, or bask in the light of the moon. If you think you don't have time, we challenge you to find the time. Can you skip a half-hour of veg-out television time tonight? Go to bed just a little earlier? Leave the laundry, just for tonight? Or take a relaxation break instead of a lunch break?

By taking this time to just sit and relax, you will regenerate your soul. Only then can that little voice inside you, the one so often out-shouted by your worries and the stress of life, have the space to speak to you again. Take time out to let your soul sing, you will not regret the changes in your life.

> **Cat's Meow**
>
> My dad doesn't like being alone, so sometimes I have to keep him company. I don't mind this and he appreciates it. I'm his girl.
>
> —Gypsy, a mixed-breed dog

Are You Just Too Logical?

Can you be too analytical, too practical, too *logical* for pet psychic communication? Some people feel that they are too "left brained" to be able to successfully receive psychic messages. The left hemisphere of your brain governs analytical thought, language, and objectivity, whereas intuition and nonverbal, spatial awareness emerge from the right hemisphere.

If you are left-brain dominant (many people are), that doesn't mean you can't develop your intuition. Your brain still has a right side, you just need to learn to tap deeper into its resources.

Here is a simple exercise to get both sides of your brain working together, whenever you are feeling too left-brained to access your intuitive side: Draw an eternity figure on a piece of paper (a figure-eight tipped on its side). It may not be as easy as it sounds because this figure requires right-brain concentration to draw. Whenever you feel that you are in too much of a left-brain mode of thought, pull out a pen and start drawing your figure eights; it will help you get both sides of your brain in sync.

Chakra Awareness for Inner Balance

Another great way to get your body more receptive if you feel you are blocked is to learn about and become aware of your *chakras*, those energy centers along the center of your body that govern your energies, passions, instincts, and spirit. When your chakras get out of balance, your life will also lose balance and your ability to communicate with your animals could suffer.

The body has many energy centers or chakras, but seven primary ones along the center of the body from the base of the spine to the crown of the head. Each chakra has its own vibrating energy and color. When a chakra gets blocked, it can slow down and fade from lack of spiritual energy, while a too-open chakra can flood with too much energy.

Balancing and opening your chakras frees spiritual energy that can help you connect psychically with other living beings—both animal and human.

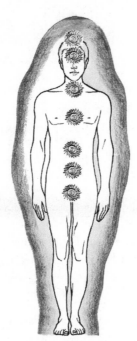

Pet Speak

Chakras are spinning energy centers in the body that correspond to certain biological and emotional processes. Energy runs between the chakras in meridians. Acupuncturists use the chakra/meridian energy system to determine which points to stimulate in order to release energy blockages.

Using various meditations, stones that match the chakra colors, and visualizations, you can check in with your chakras to see how they look and which areas needs attention. Some holistic healers can also do this for you if you are interested and the subject is new to you.

Each chakra represents certain basic aspects of our physical, emotional, and spiritual lives. Each chakra tends to cause certain states when it is too open or too closed, as well as an ideal balanced state. To help you understand where your chakras are and what they do, here is a quick rundown:

Chakra	Location	Color	Governs:	When Too Open:	When Too Closed:	When Balanced:
First	Base of spine	Red	Primal energy, instinct	Aggression	Fear	Deep inner contentment
Second	Behind the navel	Orange	Creativity, inner fire, what you consume	Over-intensity, burn-out	Inability to let go, compulsion to hang on to things	Healthy digestion and ability to process problems then move on
Third	Solar plexus	Yellow	Gut feelings, interaction with life	Becoming too vulnerable	Becoming inaccessible	Balanced interaction with the world
Fourth	Heart	Green	Emotions	Over-emotional	Coldness, inability to love	Healthy immune system, comfortable giving and receiving love
Fifth	Throat	Blue	Communication	Talking too much, not listening	Inability to express yourself verbally	Free-flowing, balanced communication
Sixth	Forehead/third eye	Deep blue/indigo	Intuition, imagination, psychic ability	Mistaking imagination for reality	Inability to access intuition	Deep inner connection to self and to the spirits of others, including animals
Seventh	Crown of the head	Violet	Enlightenment, understanding	Loss of awareness of physical world as part of your current existence	Isolation, believing life has no meaning	Ability to recognize your connection with all of life, perception of universal unity

Each of these chakras is always moving, spinning, and changing. Sometimes in the course of a few minutes, a chakra can swell and shrink, spin faster and slower. The color can grow dull and then brighten: that swell of conversation that flowed out of you, a wave in your fifth chakra; that sudden feeling of pulling away from someone, a "low tide" in your fourth chakra. These things happen to us all the time. We just don't usually think about the chakra connection to everything we do and feel.

When we get a blockage or an excess in a chakra that becomes chronic, however, our lives can begin to change in negative ways. For example, a blockage in the sixth "intuition" chakra, due to any number of reasons, can hinder your ability to communicate psychically with your animals. Rather than feeling like victims of circumstance or of our own wayward minds, however, we can instead take control of our chakras and help them to regain balance.

One of the best, and easiest, ways to help rebalance your chakras is through meditation. If you feel you have a blockage in a chakra, or can trace a particular negative feeling or behavior in your life to the chakra with which it is associated, spend some time each day meditating quietly on that chakra and imagining its color brightening, its energy spinning, and the channel widening to open the blockage, or falling back into line, to contain an overflow.

 **Horse Sense** _____

You can also balance your chakras by placing stones or crystals matching the color of the chakra over the part of your body where the chakra lies. For example, if you feel your heart is blocked, wear a necklace with a green stone long enough to hang over your heart. If you feel your intuition is blocked, relax for a few minutes while holding a deep blue or indigo stone on your forehead.

Chakra Meditation for Inner Balance

Sometimes Debbie leads her classes through the following chakra meditation, to help clarify and free their energy and open their hearts before attempting pet psychic communication, or to help them remove blockages when communication suddenly seems difficult. Read this out loud on a tape, or have a friend read it to you while you sit comfortably or lie down on your back, relax, listen, and focus on doing what the words say.

1. Take a deep breath in through your nose, slowly filling up your belly and chest. Exhale deeply through your mouth.

2. Inhale again to the count of three and exhale slowly through your mouth.

3. Inhale deeply again through your nose to the count of three and exhale slowly through your mouth, exhaling all the tension and worries you have built up inside your body. Exhale them away.

4. Inhale again, imagining a crisp cleansing white light entering your body. Exhale out any remaining negative energy you are harboring.

5. Let this light expand inside you. Imagine the white light circling your body.

6. Now focus on this white light. Imagine it beaming down on you from above, a beam of light flowing over and into the crown of your head, connecting you with positive energy and love from the universe.

7. Imagine the white light rinsing over you, clearing you of problems, imbalances, and blockages. As the light flows into your seventh chakra, imagine the light slowly turning into a vibrant violet color, energizing and balancing your sense of spiritual awareness and connection with all of life.

8. Now, imagine the white light gently moving down into your forehead, or third eye chakra, and swirling softly. Feel it circle your forehead and see it turning a beautiful indigo color as it clears, energizes, and balances your sixth chakra, allowing your intuition to ring clear and true.

9. Next, the white light moves down into your throat, circling your throat and energizing your fifth chakra. Imagine the light turning a beautiful sky blue, spinning in your throat, clearing any blocks. Let the light purge you of communication blocks, balancing your ability to relate to and communicate with the other sentient beings around you.

10. Now, the white light pours down into your heart, filling your heart with light as it turns the color of a forest. As the green light flows into your fourth chakra, let it penetrate and heal your heart. Feel your heart shifting into balance, beautiful and full of love.

11. The white light continues, moving downward into your solar plexus like a waterfall from your heart. As it hits this center, it turns the golden color of the sun and beams into your third chakra, filling you with a calm, balanced sense of self and a clear vision of your place in the world.

12. Next, the white light flows into your pelvis area, and as the light begins to glow the color of fire, setting your second chakra alight, you feel your energy rising and your inner fire glowing with warmth, affection, and creativity.

13. Finally, the powerful white light moves all the way down into your first chakra and as it does, it begins to glow red, aligning and balancing your instincts and

your most primal sense of being. You feel deeply balanced, aware, and in tune with your physical, emotional, and spiritual self.

14. Now the white light fills with all the colors of all the chakras, becoming an intense rainbow of color and energy that makes you your unique self and the entire universe of which you are an essential part. This colored light flows down your legs and into the earth below, anchoring you to earth as it continues to beam into you from above. The light flows in a continuous river of white to violet, blue to green, yellow to orange, red to full-spectrum white. You are here, and real, and essential.

15. Now, take a moment to relax and feel how balanced and at peace you are right now. Let your mind take you wherever it wishes to go, or let it simply stay here in the river of light. Stay here for as long as you like, and when you are ready, slowly begin to wiggle your feet and hands. Feel yourself anchored to earth, connected to heaven. Slowly open your eyes.

> **Cat's Meow**
>
> I would like you to use your hand to press into and massage my poll area. The rest of my body gets too sensitive, but this area needs it.
>
> —Mandy, a thoroughbred mare

Fear of Failure

What if you fear you just can't do it? What if you and your animal will never communicate well, psychically or otherwise?

If your relationship together seems to have hit a wall, it might be wise to step back from the situation and see it through your animal's eyes. It's easy to get so caught up in our own perspectives that we forget any others exist.

Rather than trying to talk to your animal through psychic communication, simply relax, breathe, and ask permission from your animal to see things from the animal's perspective. Keep breathing and imagine your spirit moving inside your animal and looking through those eyes you know so well from the outside. What does the world look like from here? Look at yourself from your animal's perspective. What is he thinking about you? What does she feel is the communication problem?

Also remember that animals tend to act as mirrors for us, reflecting back our own fears. This is one way they help us, and also, a way they suffer for us because they are so sensitive and so deeply bonded to us. A behavior you find irritating could actually be linked to your own behavior, and until you change, your animal will not, or cannot, change either.

Debbie got a call from a woman named Miranda about her dog, Bandit. Bandit loved doing agility competition, and was very good at it. Lately, however, Miranda noticed that Bandit's attitude had changed and he was not as confident or happy performing as he once was. Miranda called Debbie to see if she could find out the reason for Bandit's shift in attitude and performance.

When Debbie connected with Bandit and posed the question, he simply stated, "First her attitude changed. She is not sure about our talent anymore. She's concerned about what everyone thinks. It used to be fun and lighthearted, but not anymore."

Debbie relayed this message to Miranda. Miranda thought for a second, then confessed that they had advanced to another level of competition. As a result, she enlisted the help of a new trainer who was very demanding and intense. Miranda felt insecure around this trainer and wanted to impress her, but was worried that she would do something wrong. Bandit picked up on these worries and this pressure, and what had once been fun, lively competition became a stressful situation. Until Miranda changed her own confidence level and perception of the situation, Bandit himself would not be able to change. He was so closely connected to her that he mirrored back what she felt.

> **Horse Sense** _____
>
> Animal sports are meant to be fun. If the competition gets too intense and neither you nor your animal are enjoying it anymore, it might be worth reassessing whether you really want to continue the activity. Maybe something less competitive would be good. For some animals, however, the more competition, the better! It all depends on your own and your animal's individual personalities.

Help From Above

Another way to handle communication blocks is to ask for help from your spirit guides, angels, power animals, or whatever sources you rely on for spiritual guidance. Debbie taps these powers when she has a difficult consultation, including them in her stated intention and asking for their guidance and assistance. When you have a difficult situation with your own animals and you need clarity, ask your power animal, your spirit guide, and/or your angels for help.

We introduced you to totems and power animals in Chapter 2, but we would like to talk a little more about these and other spirit guides now. In Debbie's classes, she helps her students enlist the help of their power animals specifically for animal communication support through a brief relaxation meditation, and the following exercise, using a deck of animal cards (see Appendix B for some suggestions).

Tapping Your Power Animal for Better Communication

Try this exercise for extra help in reaching and effectively communicating with an animal when communication seems especially difficult. You can do this exercise alone, or with other interested friends. With a group, each person in turn draws a card then returns it.

Place your deck of animal cards face down in front of you, get comfortable, and relax:

1. Relax and breathe deeply.

2. State your intention out loud: "My intention is to meet my power animal for help with animal communication." Continue to breathe deeply while stating your intention.

3. Fan the deck out and find a card that you feel drawn to while repeating your intention silently to yourself.

4. Pick up the card that draws you and look at it. Notice if it is right side up or upside down, then put it back, face down, on the deck.

5. Take a few moments to contemplate the animal card you drew. What does this animal want you to know? How can the qualities of that animal aid your communication? Consult Appendix A for help, or simply use your intuition to think about the animal you drew.

6. If the animal appeared upside down, the qualities of that animal might be the ones that are hindering your communication. How can you use this information to help you remove your blocks?

Horse Sense

Pay attention whenever an animal crosses your path. If you see the same animal several times—deer at the edges of the road, rabbits leaping across lawns, cardinals—you might be recognizing one of your power animals, or an animal that holds a message for you.

Many of us have a few power animals that assist us with different areas of our lives. You can discover your band of helpers through this exercise, or by going on a meditation journey. This is a meditation in which you visualize traveling deep into the earth and meeting the power animal that appears to you. You can do this many times in different stages of your life to collect your group of spiritual helpers.

You can further honor your power animal and keep it in your mind and heart by putting images of that animal around your home. You might collect statues of that animal, hang pictures, even donate money to an organization that supports or protects that animal.

Meeting Your Spirit Guides and Angels

Not everyone believes in spirit guides and angels, but many of us feel that we know they are among us. Debbie has always known she had a spirit guide, but she didn't necessarily have a feeling of who it was. Then, she did a meditation to meet her spirit guide and learned that she had an amazing Native American warrior with her, whose gentle eyes assist her with her communications, guiding her along the way.

Even then, Debbie wasn't entirely sure of her vision until she visited a psychic named Laurie for a reading. The first thing Laurie said to Debbie was, "Did you know you have an Indian around you? He is very muscular and a warrior type. He shows me that he helps you with the animals." Debbie's jaw dropped. The psychic, who had no idea that Debbie was even an animal communicator, had confirmed her meditation vision.

We all have spirit guides helping us with various aspects of our lives. Rita Berkowitz, author of *The Complete Idiot's Guide to Communicating with Spirits*, has the gift of being able to draw your spirit guide intuitively, as well as the spirits of loved ones who have passed over, and a consultation with her is truly a remarkable experience. Debbie had another psychic friend tell her that she saw one of Debbie's spirit guides with her: an older Asian woman who was an herbalist. Debbie took this with a grain of salt until she met with Rita Berkowitz. She asked Rita to do a drawing of her spirit guides, and Rita drew for Debbie an aging Asian woman. Rita told Debbie that she saw her preparing herbal remedies. Well ... Debbie couldn't argue with that!

Spirit Guide Meditation

Perhaps you are curious to know what spirit guides surround and assist you in your life. To help you see and meet them, try this spirit guide meditation:

1. Find a comfortable place where you can relax and be completely quiet. Try to relax completely, allowing your thoughts to come and go as they please but without letting them engage you. Just notice them.

2. Take a deep breath in and hold it. Pause for the count of two.

3. Breathe deeply again and as you do, gather up the tension in your body and release it with your exhaled breath.

4. Take another deep breath, and as you exhale, let go of anybody else's energy or thoughts you might be carrying with you. Breathe in new energy ... breathe in new possibilities ... and allow your body to fill with lightness.

5. Feel your body becoming lighter and lighter as you relax more and more. Relax deeply, going deeper, feeling lighter. You're feeling very light now, so light you could almost float away.

6. Imagine you are walking down a wooded path. Notice the plant life on either side of you and the wildlife that might cross your path. Notice everything around you.

7. As you walk down this winding path, smell the fragrant flowers that bloom on either side of you and the smell of the crisp air, the leaves, and the sun on the branches.

8. You come to an opening at the end of the path and you notice it is a circular clearing. In the middle of the clearing is a beautiful, sturdy, inviting bench. Beside the bench is a small water fountain trickling pure, clear water.

9. You approach the fountain and let the cool water splash over your hands and onto your face. You feel utterly refreshed.

10. You walk over to the bench and sit down. You close your eyes and as you relax, you ask a question of the universe: "Today, may I meet my spirit guide (or angel, power animal—whomever you desire to meet)?"

11. Repeat the question in your head a few times. In the distance, you hear someone approaching, coming closer.

12. In this place you slowly open your eyes to see who it is. Take a moment to focus on the picture of what you see before you.

13. You introduce yourself to this being standing before you. Perhaps you will ask for a name, or guidance. Take some time to explore, peacefully and gently, this new level of your relationship with your spirit guide. Ask what you feel you need to know. Take your time.

14. Now, it is time to bid farewell to your spirit guide and this magical realm. You thank your spirit guide for coming to you in this way, and say good-bye.

15. You walk back down the winding, wooded path and as you do, you feel yourself coming back into your body, feeling more centered and grounded in the physical world again.

16. Wiggle your toes and fingers, feet and hands. When you feel ready, open your eyes.

After you have pictures in your mind of your spirit guides and power animals, you can speak to them in much the same way you communicate with animals. When you need guidance, just ask, then wait, with listening ears and an open heart, for the wisdom they have for you.

The Least You Need to Know

♦ Emotional baggage, fear of pain and vulnerability, and guilt can all hinder animal communication.

♦ Working out your emotional issues will help you to communicate with your animal more easily.

♦ Take care of yourself on all levels, from giving yourself enough rest and eating well to keeping your chakras balanced. A healthy, balanced body will be more in tune to natural intuition.

♦ Your power animals and spirit guides can help you with your animal communication. Find them through exercises with animal cards and the spirit guide meditation in this chapter.

Chapter 16

Connecting with a Lost Pet

In This Chapter

- ◆ What to do when your animal is lost
- ◆ Barriers to communication with a lost animal
- ◆ Intuitive methods for helping your animal get home again
- ◆ Building, strengthening, and accessing the energy cord of love between you and your pet

Sometimes, despite our best efforts—even if we keep our cats safely indoors, our dogs securely fenced and inside when we are away, our birds' wings clipped, and everybody i.d.-tagged and microchipped—our animal friends lose their way. Whether a wandering cat, a dog who digs out or jumps over a fence or scoots out of an open front door, a bird that flies out a window, or a hamster that manages to wiggle out of his cage, animals don't always stay exactly where we put them. They are living creatures, and sometimes they wander, explore, chase things, or just run for the pure joy of it and find themselves suddenly in an unfamiliar place.

In some cases, animals get stolen, lost on a trip, or otherwise taken far away. We don't always know what happened to them, and sometimes we may never find out, but pet psychic communication can make finding a lost animal, or at least finding out what happened, a lot easier.

However, communicating with a lost animal has its challenges, too. A lost animal can be frightened or panicked. A lost animal can misunderstand what happened and be angry at you, thinking you abandoned him or her. A lost animal might even have passed into spirit and not be aware of it, making locating the animal particularly challenging. In this chapter, we'll help you to stay calm and deal with the loss of your animal friend in the most effective way possible.

Practical Strategies for Finding Lost Animals

Most of us who live with animals know that sinking feeling of realization that your animal is no longer in the house, yard, or enclosure. Although it's easy to panic or become paralyzed by worry in such a situation, following some initial steps, even before you attempt to communicate telepathically with your animal, can give you the best chance to find your animal again:

◆ Stay calm. Take a deep breath. Think exactly when and where you last saw your animal. Has it been a few minutes? A few hours? This information could be helpful later.

◆ Talk to neighbors to see if anyone saw anything—your dog jumping the fence or running down the sidewalk, someone looking into your backyard, your cat wandering somewhere outside the yard. Figure out when your animal was last seen.

◆ Call the animal shelter, or visit, every day. Busy shelters don't have time to call you back if an animal arrives that resembles your description. If you keep checking, your animal might turn up there eventually.

Horse Sense _____

Websites such as www. petrecovery.com, www. petfinder.com, and www.sherlockbones.com can be of great help when trying to locate a lost pet. Many cities and states have regional online pet-finding websites and systems, too, and most are free. Hiring a pet detective costs money, but is well worth the cost if the person you hire finds your pet.

◆ Check the newspaper daily. Many people who find lost pets post a free "found pet" ad. If your area has more than one paper, check them all.

◆ Post flyers in the surrounding area and key traffic points outside your area. Dogs can travel far, so don't rule out areas that seem out of reach. Try to put a picture of your animal on the flyer, with your contact info, and when and where the animal was last seen. Many pets have been recovered due to flyers.

◆ Throughout the search process, try to connect telepathically with your animal. When you are upset and your animal is possibly scared and lost, this can be a challenge, so read on for some hints and tips to make connection with a lost animal easier and more effective.

The Challenges of Communicating with Lost Pets

When you realize your animal is lost, you can try to communicate right away, or you can take some concrete steps first, but attempting to communicate with your pet as soon as possible can help you to take action when you don't have anything else to do but look and wait.

Debbie got a call from Beverly, who was in a panic that her cat, Precious (a white Persian), who always comes right back inside, did not come home that evening. Beverly was beside herself, fearing the worst. When Debbie connected with Precious, Precious revealed that she was very upset. The house was too noisy and that she was hiding out until things got back to normal.

When Debbie told Beverly what Precious had confided, Debbie confirmed that she had guests over the night before for a dinner party. Precious did not take kindly to such an invasion of her personal space! When Debbie connected back to Precious to explain to her that Beverly was truly sorry for the commotion last night and that she was worried about her and needed her to come home quickly before it got dark and dangerous, Precious accepted the apology and marched right up the back steps while Debbie was still on the phone with Beverly! Beverly was, of course, delighted, and Precious was happy to be back home, safe and sound.

Because people often feel incredibly stressed when their animals are lost, the quiet relaxation necessary for effective communication can be difficult to achieve. Remember that your animal might be just fine and it won't help anything to get distressed and upset. If you want to reach your animal, you need to relax. Here are some strategies to help:

> **Cat's Meow**
>
> I am now a bit farther from home than I was. I have tried to make my way back, but there is a yellow cat that has become territorial in my yard. I don't know what to do.
>
> —Samson, a missing gray tabby cat

- Take a hot bath or shower, and try to connect when you start to relax in the warm water.

- Meditate for 10 minutes in a quiet room, focusing on your breathing, before trying to connect.

♦ Visualize your fear and worry being surrounded by a bubble, then push it to the side. These emotions interfere with communication and contribute to your animal's anxiety if he or she detects them in your communication.

When you feel ready to connect to your pet, attempt to do so. Remember that your animal may be frightened as well as disoriented, tired, or injured. They may also be angry or upset, which could be the source of why they left. Or perhaps they are feeling just fine and simply decided to have a little adventure. Keep all these possibilities in mind as you attempt to connect, allowing your mind to stay open and keeping your anxiety out of the way.

> **Horse Sense**
>
> When Debbie connects with a lost animal, she usually asks to look through their eyes, going psychically into the animal's body and looking out. This can help you to determine your animal's condition, and it can also help you to look around to see where your animal might be.

Debbie once asked a lost cat named Ginger if she could go into her body to see where she was. The cat agreed and when Debbie did so, she saw a dark room around her and smelled gasoline. She felt dirt under her feet and could hear people talking and dogs barking in the distance.

The woman who had lost her cat went to the neighbor's house to investigate, where she knew there was an old barn that housed a few antique vehicles. Ginger cat was hiding under one of the floor boards in the old barn, afraid to come out because the neighbor's dogs had chased her in there.

When you connect with your animal and go inside to see how your animal feels, notice how you feel. Do you feel tired? Nervous? Does anything hurt? These feelings can help you to determine your animal's physical and emotional state.

Also, in your mind's eye, look around you. What do you see? Are you in a dark area, under something, locked inside somewhere? Are you in the woods, in a cage, in someone else's house?

Focus on what you hear, what you feel, and what you smell. Unusual odors can help pinpoint a pet's location.

> **Cat's Meow**
>
> I am fascinated by people. They are so silly and so colorful. They make such strange sounds.
> —Chester, a black seal

You might just get a quick flash of a picture that might be a hint as to where your animal is. When Debbie's cat, Scarlett, was missing, Debbie was worried because they had just gotten a few feet of snow and normally the cat would come right home in inclement weather. This time, Debbie feared she might be stuck somewhere.

Debbie felt intuitively that Scarlett was physically fine. Then, suddenly Debbie got a quick flash of the two-story barn next door. She and her husband walked over and went into the barn. They began calling for Scarlett. Debbie could hear her crying, and then she jumped down a hole from the second story loft and all was well.

What to Ask

When connecting with a lost animal, you will accomplish more if you ask very specific questions. Here are some suggestions:

- **Can you hear anything?** Sounds your animal hears could give you a clue to where a lost animal is.

- **What does the ground feel like under your feet?** A dirt floor, a carpet, grass, concrete—these can all provide clues for locating your animal.

- **Is it dark? Can you see any light?** The lighting conditions can also be informative. Darkness in the middle of the day could mean your animal is stuck inside something: in a barn, under a porch, or in a basement.

- **Can I look through your eyes?** Can you look around for me? This can help you to get those flashes and images. If you see what your animal sees, you might be able to determine where your animal is.

- **How did you get here? Can you show me how?** A very frightened animal might not know or remember or understand what happened or how he got where he is. However, in some cases, animals know exactly where they are and exactly how they got there, and that can help you to find them and bring them home.

- **How does your body feel?** This question can help you to determine if your animal is injured or not. Remember to pay attention to any sudden feelings of pain or discomfort in your own body when you ask this question, because your animal might send you those feelings.

- **Did you leave for a reason?** Just like Precious, some animals leave on purpose because they are angry about something, or feel excluded, or got scared, or simply wanted to explore the neighborhood.

> **CAUTION**
>
> **Doggone!**
>
> If your animal is lost, don't assume, while trying to communicate, that your animal wants to come back. If your animal left for what she perceives is a good reason, she may not want to come home again. You can find this out, and find out why. This can also help you with resolving the conflict so your animal will want to return.

Communicating with your animal about the issue can help resolve it so your animal feels willing and able to come back home.

- **Do you have a message for me?** Sometimes you might have trouble determining more concrete details about where your animal is, but you might receive a specific message, something your animal makes sure you want to know. This can also be important if your animal has passed on and needs to tell you he is okay or what happened, or if he wants to say good-bye.

- **How can I find you?** Your animal might not know where she is, but she might be able to tell you how to get to where she is, depending on what she remembers and how calm she is. If you ask this question, you might suddenly know exactly where to go.

> **Cat's Meow** _____
>
> I don't like being told what to do, and I let them know in a dramatic fashion.
> —Lady, a half-Arab mare

As you continue to look, continue to talk. Stay in touch with your animal and keep asking questions. Also, remember to keep your own feelings in check and to offer reassuring, comforting words to your animal if you sense fear and anxiety. You really can help to calm your animal through psychic communication.

Connecting the Energy Cord of Love

When people call Debbie about a lost animal, she will always advise them to take the steps we've mentioned (posting flyers, contacting shelters, talking to neighbors, etc.). She also asks that they do something very specific in addition to these actions: She asks that they connect their animal to themselves with an energy cord of love.

> **Horse Sense** _____
>
> Whenever you think of your animal, visualize an energy cord of love between you. If you frequently visualize this energetic connection, even when your animal is with you, it will become a habit and a connection your animal will understand and draw strength from in difficult situations, whether they are lost or simply away from you for awhile, such as at the vet or while you are away from home.

To do this, relax, breathe deeply, then picture a braided cord of light going from your heart to your animal's heart. Visualize the cord and this energetic attachment between your animal and you. Then, as if the cord was a telephone line, simply send love through the cord, from human heart to animal heart, and ask the animal to use this energy to help him find his way home.

This exercise is simple but powerful. It can actually help a lost animal to find his way home, and it can also give a sick, frightened, or tired animal enough energy to stay safe until you can find him.

Find Them in Your Dreams

When your animal is lost, you won't feel much like sleeping, but before you go to bed at night, ask for information about your animal or the animal's location to come to you in a dream. Sometimes, we have noticed details or clues that we don't consciously recognize as relevant. If we set our intention to discover these while dreaming, they often rise to the surface.

Also ask to remember your dreams well. Once, when Debbie's cat Scarlett was missing yet *again*, she came to Debbie in a dream and showed her that he was just fine. She came back two days later unharmed, after what was certainly an interesting but apparently safe adventure. When Debbie first inherited Scarlett she was used to being a barn cat in her former home and coming and going as she pleased. Debbie found it difficult to convince this strong-minded feline that coming inside every night is essential to being a part of Debbie's family. Scarlett did, however, tame her wild ways, and Debbie is happy to say that although Scarlett loves being outside, she also comes in every evening now. No more missing-in-action episodes, thank goodness!

Debbie got a call from Theresa about a horse named Comanche she feared had been stolen. Theresa had allowed a couple to take the horse on a trial basis, but when she went to the house to collect the money, the horse and people were gone. She contacted Debbie to find out if she could help track down Comanche.

When Debbie connected with the horse, Comanche told Debbie that she was physically fine. Debbie asked Comanche to look around to show her what the surroundings looked like, so that Debbie could get a better idea of where the horse was. Comanche proved to be quite helpful in this effort, showing Debbie very specific details: a chain link fence, some old farm machinery scattered about the yard, a small shed with a ramp, and a small ranch home at the front of the property. Across the street, she showed Debbie miles of cornfields.

Debbie described this to Theresa, who said that was an exact description of the house where she had just been, the house she thought was abandoned, and that Comanche had not been there. Debbie connected with Comanche again and she continued to show her the same pictures. Theresa decided to pay one more visit to the house, just in case. Sure enough, when she arrived, she found Comanche alone on the property, and promptly brought her home.

When Your Animal Isn't Okay

Lost animal cases unfortunately do not always have happy endings. Sometimes an animal dies suddenly, and even they don't know that they have passed over, which makes communication confusing. The animal can be frightened and wanting to come home, yet won't understand where he is.

Karen called Debbie about her cat, Fluffy, a Maine Coon cat that had been missing for three days. When Debbie connected with Fluffy, he kept telling Debbie that it "happened so fast." Finally, he showed Debbie his body lying limp at the side of the road.

Debbie could hardly believe what she was seeing, and of course didn't want to believe it! But then, Fluffy sent Debbie the taste of blood in her mouth, and Debbie realized that Fluffy must have been hit by a car and was communicating to her in spirit.

> **Cat's Meow**
>
> The end is another beginning waiting to unfold. It holds in its awakening old loves, new friends, and bold adventures.
>
> —Leo, an orange tabby cat, regarding death

Once Debbie realized this, she continued to talk with Fluffy, who assured her that he was okay, but that he hated to give up such a good-looking body. Debbie conveyed this information to Karen, who had felt in her heart that something bad had happened to Fluffy. Karen was relieved to know that he didn't suffer and that he was okay on the other side.

Connecting with a lost animal can be challenging at best. Because both sides of such a communication can be in a state of extreme emotion, fear, and panic, the connection can be hard to receive. Information may not necessarily come in chronological order but in bits and pieces, and the animal may not know whether he is still alive or has passed over into spirit.

Despite these bumps, Debbie has been a part of some success stories of telepathic communication, bringing lost pets and their humans back together. By learning how to connect yourself to a lost animal, you might not only be able to locate your own lost animals, but might even be able to help friends and neighbors, in the event that their animals get lost.

The Least You Need to Know

♦ When your animal gets lost, combine pet psychic communication with vigorous efforts to find your animal, including asking neighbors, posting flyers, contacting shelters, checking the newspaper, and looking at "lost and found pets" websites.

♦ Psychic communication can also help to give you clues about where your animal is. Ask your animal specific questions, such as what the animal sees, hears, and smells. Ask what the ground under the animal's feet feels like, and whether the animal remembers how he got to where he is.

♦ Ask if the animal was upset about something, left on purpose, or wants to come home. Sometimes you can resolve a conflict psychically, and your animal will then decide to come home on her own.

♦ Other intuitive methods for finding a lost pet include asking to go into your animal to look through his eyes, visualizing a cord of love connecting your heart to your animal's heart to give your animal strength and an understanding of the way home, and setting your intention before sleep so that your dreams might reveal clues to where your animal is.

♦ If your animal isn't coming back because she has passed over, you may still be able to communicate with your animal in spirit. However, some animals, especially those that passed over quickly and unexpectedly, might be unaware that they have passed over, so such communication can be challenging.

Part **5**

The Sacred Bond Between Animals and Humans

This part explores the many ways animals heal humans, from dolphin therapy for children to dog therapy for nursing home residents to horse therapy for people with disabilities. We'll also explore the ways we can help to heal our animals holistically, how to decide if your animal is ready to pass on, how to manage your own grief and the grief of the other animals in your family when an animal passes on, even how to keep on talking with an animal who has passed into spirit. Finally, we'll celebrate the sacred bond between humans and animals with ideas for how to be an advocate for animals in whatever way works for you and your life. You can live in peace and harmony with the animals in your life and with the natural world as a whole, preserving, honoring, and rejoicing in it. It all begins with an open heart and a simple willingness to reach out and communicate.

Chapter 17

Out of Love Come Miracles: What Our Pets Teach Us

In This Chapter

◆ How animals heal us

◆ Stories of dolphins, horses, and dogs that heal and help

◆ Your own animal is ready to heal you, too

◆ Let your animal show you your own soul

Humans and animals have come together in an understanding for a reason. We help each other and form relationships that are valuable to everyone. Animals help us understand our interconnectedness with the life cycle, and they show us how much they are like us, even as they show us how unique each of us can be.

Although we often think about keeping our own pets healthy with regular trips to the veterinarian, healthy food, and lots of love, we might not always realize the healing power, teaching power, and helping power animals have for us. Animals live with us, stay with us, love us for a reason. They help us and teach us because they can, and if we let them, we can experience profound healing, wisdom, and even spiritual growth through our relationships with them.

Animals Who Heal

Everyone knows it feels good to stroke a cat, cuddle a puppy, or gaze meditatively at a tank full of fish, but today we also know that interactions with animals actually can have a profound effect on human health. Studies have demonstrated that people with pets have lower blood pressure and lower levels of stress hormones.

People who have pets heal faster after illness or surgery, and several national organizations exist solely for the purpose of training animals to work in a therapy setting. Dogs visit nursing home residents and hospital patients. Cats curl up on the laps of patients in psychiatry offices. Dolphins help to increase speech and motor skills in children and adults diagnosed with developmental, physical, and/or emotional disabilities, such as mental retardation, Down syndrome, and autism.

Animals work in schools with children who have disabilities. Some work as full-time assistance dogs for people with impaired sight, hearing, or mobility. Some dogs have been trained to detect oncoming seizures, heart attacks, even cancer cells, alerting humans to impending trouble. Horses trained in hippotherapy—the practice of using horses for therapy on humans—help people with various physical, psychological, and behavioral problems through horseback riding, the horse empowering the patient.

Sometimes, animals who have suffered abandonment and abuse find a new life helping humans with disabilities, and these animals seem to have an uncanny sense of suffering and a sensitivity and empathy with humans who need their help. One such rescue, rehabilitation, and education organization is called StillPointe, a llama sanctuary in Carlsborg, Washington.

> **Cat's Meow**
>
> If we could actually see each other's souls, there would be no hate.
>
> —Demetrius, a llama

Even in your own home, your animals can help you to feel calmer, more loving, and less stressed, and they can even help you heal more quickly. The power of animals to heal is proven as well as miraculous.

Debbie had the opportunity to meet a group of therapy dolphins in Key Largo, Florida, and found them nothing short of amazing. Their capacity to love, heal, and accept have had a miraculous effect on the people who visited.

If you have ever been in the presence of a dolphin, you already know the pure joy they can impart. Debbie finds the feeling indescribable. Dolphins also do remarkable work through such programs as the Child Empowerment Program at the Human Dolphin Institute in Florida. The parents of many of the children in this program remark at the difference they see in their children after each session with the dolphins. The goal of this program is to empower the children by enhancing their intellectual, emotional, and physical well-being. Scientists have found that when dolphins interact with humans, the humans experience a greater harmony between the left and right sides of the brain, and this can help children improve their ability to learn, their interest in learning, and their communication skills.

We believe the more that humans positively interact with other forms of life on our planet, the healthier, more balanced, and more spiritually evolved we become. The proven healing power of animals, even when we are merely in their presence, is the perfect demonstration of this belief. The more we know and love and spend time with animals, the more we understand the unity of all life.

Horse Sense

For more information on dolphin-assisted therapy, please see the following websites:

- ◆ AquaThought Foundation: www.aquathought.com/index.html
- ◆ The Human Dolphin Institute: www.whaleguide.com/directory/humandolphin.htm
- ◆ Cetacean Society International: http://csiwhalesalive.org
- ◆ Island Dolphin Care: www.islanddolphincare.org

Horses Who Heal

Debbie has also witnessed the effect horses can have on abused or abandoned children. Children often feel an immediate bond with horses, who can teach them respect, friendship, trust, and love—all things they may never have received from the people who have come in and out of their troubled lives. The guardians of these children often report that the children, who once wouldn't look anyone in the eye, are able to make eye contact after therapy with the horses. Children who refused to talk become excited and talkative with the horses, telling them about their day. They are better able to interact, with other children and with adults, with confidence and respect.

Horses also work wonders with handicapped children, helping them to bond with another being. The children see progress in each class, in their ability to handle such a large animal with control and ease. Some children have smiled for the first time in their lives while on a horse during this kind of therapy,

Horse Sense

Anyone who has ever had a bond with a horse knows that they heal and teach us on very deep levels.

and horses, too, seem to enjoy this important job. Therapy horses have told Debbie that they take pride in and feel rewarded by the need and love they feel from the children they help. It takes a special kind of horse to do this kind of work, and these unique animals have an abundance of patience and love.

Horses heal people in ways other than through structured therapy programs. Jane had gone through a rough divorce. She had stayed in her marriage much too long, trying to make something work that she finally realized would never work. She felt defeated, and she blamed herself for her failed marriage. And then, Jane met Maxx.

Maxx was a 17-hand Hanoverian Thoroughbred cross with big, soulful eyes. Jane and Maxx had a unique bond. Maxx was not an easy horse to ride and Jane was a beginner, but she was determined to ride him. As their bond grew, so did Jane's pride and confidence in herself. She went from living her life for someone else with no direction and no fulfillment, to living her life with pride and direction, with confidence and a sense of self. Jane's soul came to life again because she was doing something she deeply desired to do, something that challenged her and touched her heart and soul. This made her happy.

Jane received everything that she gave to the relationship with Maxx back from him, in a truly mutual partnership. This was something her marriage had lacked. Maxx adored her and she adored him. He was the stability and love she needed during a difficult time, and this relationship helped Jane heal. Maxx was a great teacher in her life, and went on to be a great teacher and soul mate to another woman after his job with Jane was completed.

Horse Sense

Miniature horses have been trained to help blind people in their daily lives, much as an assistance dog would do.

Jane still thinks of Maxx often and thanks him for helping her to see who she really was. Maxx taught her to have the courage to move forward in life and to meet each challenge and bump in the road with determination and courage.

Dogs to the Rescue

Dogs can do therapy work, too, and many dogs are formally trained in therapy work. These therapy dogs must pass certain tests to be certified as therapy dogs, showing they have the right temperament and are trained to behave in a hospital or nursing home setting.

Many of these dogs, from large to small, smooth to fluffy, regularly visit children's hospitals and nursing homes with their people. Some dogs light up the room when they enter, then patiently make their way around to see each person. Many lonely elderly people look forward to their weekly meetings with their furry friends. The therapy dogs make them smile, bring back memories, and help them feel loved. These visits give people something to look forward to, especially when they don't often get any visitors.

Debbie had the opportunity to speak with a wonderful yellow Lab named Sadie. Sadie would go to the hospital with her person once a week to visit the patients there, many of whom were terminally ill. Sadie's person, George, became concerned because he noticed Sadie becoming depressed on the way home from the hospital. Sadie's down mood would continue for a few days after the visits. George wanted to make sure Sadie still wanted to do therapy work, so he called Debbie.

When Debbie connected with Sadie, Sadie told her that although she loved her job, she felt helpless. She knew the people she visited were in pain and that some of them were dying, and she wished desperately that she could help them more than just providing a soft coat to pat. She would dwell on the experience for days afterwards, she explained.

Debbie explained to Sadie that her job was not to cure these people, but simply to show them love and friendship, and that this was exactly what they needed from her. Now, after each visit, George tells Sadie she did a wonderful job, and that now she is off-duty until next time. This reminder after each visit keeps Sadie enjoying her job without bringing home the stress she often felt. She understands now that her job is to be herself and to love the people she visits for who they are.

Cat's Meow

I dance for you in a tango with the wind, round and round.
—A dragonfly

For more information about therapy dogs, or for instructions on how to train and certify your own gentle canine friend for therapy work, contact the Delta Society about their Pet Partners Program. Find them online at www.deltasociety.org/dsa000.htm, or write or e-mail them at 289 Perimeter Road East, Renton, WA 98055; e-mail: info@deltasociety.org.

For a list of additional regional and national therapy organizations, visit the Dog-Play website (www.dog-play.com), which lists many different activities to do with your dog and organizations involved in each activity.

Some dogs have even more specialized training than therapy dogs. These assistance dogs help people with sight, hearing, or mobility impairments do the everyday tasks that can be a challenge for them. These dogs must pass rigorous training, and many who enter training programs don't finish, but those who do have great intelligence, dedication, patience, and a desire to help the people who need them.

Some dogs have also been trained to detect a stroke, heart attack, or seizure before it happens. Others can even smell cancer cells.

Of course, you probably know the dog's sense of smell is far more developed than the human's. Dogs use their sense of smell, as well as their intuition, to follow scents for miles; to detect illegal contraband, weapons, or even land mines; and to find people who have been buried under snow or rubble. After the terrorist attacks on the World Trade Center in New York City on September 11, 2001, many search and rescue dogs endured burning smoke and huge piles of rubble to search for survivors. Thousands of dogs work side-by-side with humans every day to help us, save us, and heal us.

Your Very Own Animals

Even if they haven't undergone a single minute of specialized training, our own animals have the ability to heal us, too. Animals open our hearts and teach us how to love unconditionally, just by their example. Animals teach us joy, how to play, and how to live in the moment. They teach us respect, humility, patience, and above all else, love. When we work to help heal an abused or hurt animal, we can also experience healing on many levels.

One of Debbie's dearest friends, Rose, once told her the story of how her horse, Mountain, set her on the right path for her life. Mountain was a thoroughbred off the racetrack that had many bad memories and flashbacks from that difficult time in his life. He was a hard horse to train and even harder to ride. Nevertheless, Rose only had eyes for him, and the bond was instantaneous. They were meant to be a team.

Rose's biggest challenge was keeping Mountain comfortable due to the injuries he sustained having been on the racetrack. Rose's mission was to find a way to help her horse. Unfortunately, traditional veterinary medicine could do nothing for Mountain's pain. The only thing that seemed to help him were chiropractic treatments, but Rose and Mountain lived in an area with no local horse chiropractors, and Rose was forced to trailer Mountain three hours each way for an appointment.

Finally, Rose decided that she would make her commitment to helping Mountain wholeheartedly. She went to chiropractic school herself to learn the appropriate techniques, and has now become one of the most widely sought-after chiropractors in the Northeast. Rose took what she learned and successfully treated her horse to the point where he was pain free. Mountain is still Rose's most valued teacher and friend.

Mountain was a healer in more ways than through his bond with Rose. When Debbie first brought home her horse, Finnegan, and moved him into his new boarding barn, the other horses picked on him incessantly. Finnegan was already insecure, and the most dominant horse in the barn seemed to have a score to settle with the new horse. That's when Mountain stepped in and protected Finnegan. That first day when the dominant horse named Nick ran Finnegan out of the herd, Mountain went to Finnegan's side and protected him from Nick for each day thereafter. Their bond was special. Of course, Nick was just asserting his own strong personality! He was the alpha horse of the herd and wanted to make sure Finnegan came nowhere near his mare friends. Even horses feel the need to stick up for their shy, sensitive friends.

Mountain and Finnegan soon became best friends. Mountain helped Finnegan grow up in many ways, and as a result of their friendship, Debbie met and developed a strong friendship with Rose. Sometimes animals enrich our lives in ways that even they didn't intend!

> **Cat's Meow**
>
> My purpose in life is to help people fall in love again with the spirit of the horse.
> —Silver Dollar, an Arabian gelding

Reflecting the Inner You

Because they are so intuitive, so bonded to us, and so sensitive, animals mirror us in many ways. Sometimes they reflect back to us the very behavior we need to change or address in our lives. We might think the animal has a behavior problem, when in reality, we are the ones with the problem and they are just trying to show it to us.

Sometimes animals will mirror a health issue that we have, even one we don't yet know exists. Some animals have even developed the same illnesses as their people, out of an extreme psychic empathy and in the hope that by taking on the disease, they can take it away from their person.

> **CAUTION**
>
> **Doggone!**
>
> Before you decide that your animal has a behavior problem, stop for a moment and make sure the animal isn't just mirroring your own fears, problems, inadequacies, or insecurities. Work on these issues in yourself, and they might quickly resolve in your animal.

Our animals heal us and teach us in many ways, and the best way to fully bond with and be healed by your own animals is to keep an open mind, an open heart, and a listening ear. Communicate frequently, spend lots of time together, and just be in each other's presence. You and your animal can heal and teach each other, and that will make your relationship even more special than it already is.

The Least You Need to Know

♦ Animals heal people by forming relationship with them as pets and by communicating their intuitive knowledge about us. Their greatest gift is their unconditional love. Love in its purest form is a great source of healing.

♦ Animals also help and heal people in more structured ways: by working as therapy animals with people in need; by working as service animals to help people with sight, hearing, and mobility impairments; and by being trained to detect seizures, heart attacks, stroke, or cancer.

♦ Animals also work in search and rescue and other scent-related detection jobs.

♦ Your own animal can heal you by mirroring your own emotional and even physical conditions.

Chapter 18

Helping Animals Heal: Scanning for Pain

In This Chapter

- ◆ How you can help heal your animals
- ◆ Body scanning techniques and visualization
- ◆ Stories of healing the mind-body-spirit
- ◆ How you can support your animal's healing efforts
- ◆ Alternative veterinary care

Just as our animals can heal us, we can heal them. When our animals have been injured, become sick, or when we rescue them from abuse or neglect, healing them can also help to heal us, and the mutual healing process is a miraculous yet common effect when humans and animals come together in a relationship.

You can use telepathic communication as part of the process when working with your animal toward healing. In conjunction with other natural techniques and practices, you might find yourself working wonderful changes in your animal as well as in your relationship to each other. This chapter will help guide you.

The Body Scan

A body scan is a technique you can use during telepathic communication with your animal that will help you uncover areas of pain or dysfunction in your animal's body.

Body scans are an active part of each consultation Debbie does, and they can be extremely effective in helping your animal communicate to you what areas need attention.

With practice, you can do body scans on your own animals, as well as on yourself and your family members, to check on how they are feeling on a regular basis. Debbie does body scans a few different ways, and you can, too. You can ask the animal to send you a picture of his body or how he moves his body, to demonstrate a problem. Or you can ask the animal to allow you to go inside the animal's body, to determine for yourself what hurts or feels wrong.

> **Cat's Meow**
>
> I am afraid I won't meet your expectations. I feel bad for setting you back this year because I didn't show a lot. You are very serious and focused and I feel like I sidetracked you. I am very afraid you don't have faith in my recovery.
>
> —Kat, a Warmblood mare

Journey Within

To do the body scan in which you go inside an animal's body, you can use the same basic technique Debbie uses. Here's how it works:

1. Breathe deeply. Focus on your body, paying attention to what your body feels like, and whether you have any noticeable aches and pains. If you recognize what physical sensations are unique to you before connecting, you won't mistakenly attribute these to your animal.

2. Open your heart. Be ready to feel and accept anything at all.

3. State your intention. Verbalize in your mind exactly what you want to accomplish.

4. Call out the animal's name in your mind.

5. Ask for permission to do a body scan on your animal.

6. When you feel you have your animal's permission, ask if she can send to you any pain she feels in her body or to tell you where she hurts.

7. When you go inside the body, simply imagine that you are the animal, seeing through the animal's eyes, feeling what she feels.

8. When you're inside, visualize making your way through the body, starting at the tip of the tail or the crown of the head, whichever you prefer. Gradually work through the body, focusing on one part at a time and paying attention to subtle signals in your own body, such as a quick ache in your knee, an itch in your shoulder blade, a sudden awareness of your stomach.

9. Don't discount anything! Stay open.

10. Write down all the sensations you feel and all the things you feel draw your attention. Write as you go, so you don't forget anything. This is not the time to analyze your intuition. Just trust it, and write it down.

11. When you are done, imagine yourself coming out of the animal's body and back into your own body. Surround yourself with white light.

12. Don't forget to thank your animal for communicating with you in this way.

Horse Sense

During the body scan, if you feel a sensation in your right hand, that corresponds to your animal's right front paw. If you get an ache in your left knee, that corresponds to your animal's left hind leg, hock (knee), and so on.

As you do the body scan, you can use this worksheet as a template to keep track of each part of the animal, as you focus on it.

The more experience you get doing body scans, the more you will start to recognize feelings that come up again and again, representing similar problems in different animals and people. You might also learn to recognize certain recurring symbols. These feelings and symbols, unique to you, will become part of your own intuitive vocabulary, just as Debbie and other animal communicators have learned to recognize certain symbols, feelings, and patterns in their own body scan readings, unique to them.

Remember that your own consciousness "translates" these spirit-to-spirit messages in ways you can best understand, so you will discover that certain patterns emerge. Practice is important to becoming efficient at doing body scans. The more you practice, the easier it will become.

Animal Body Scan Worksheet

Record what you feel while performing the animal body scan in the spaces below, or adapt this information to a format that works better for you. Remember to notice any feelings, sensations, words, images, colors, symbols, or anything else that emerges when you go into each body part. Trust that you are making an intuitive connection with your animal; consider all that comes up and document it faithfully—even if it doesn't seem to "fit." Each detail may prove valuable as you work to understand and heal the circumstances surrounding your animal's health.

Body senses and structure/mobility (joints, muscles, tendons, and ligaments)

Head:_____

    Eyes: _____

    Ears: _____

    Nose: _____

    Mouth: _____

    Teeth: _____

Neck: _____

Shoulders: _____

Front legs: _____

    Knee: _____

    Ankle: _____

    Paw/foot/hoof: _____

Back: _____

Belly: _____

Hips: _____

Rump: _____

Tail: _____

Hind legs: _____

    Stifle: _____

    Knee/hock: _____

    Ankle: _____

    Paw/Foot/Hoof: _____

Misc.:_____

Body functions/organs

Throat: _____

Esophagus: _____

Lungs: _____

Heart: _____

Blood: _____

Stomach: _____

Intestines: _____

Liver: _____

Spleen: _____

Kidneys: _____

Bladder: _____

    More thoughts, impressions, sensations:

_____

_____

_____

Watch and Learn

Sometimes, you may feel you didn't get enough information from the body scan technique in which you try to go inside the animal. Another technique Debbie frequently uses to find out where an animal hurts, especially if she feels she isn't getting much information from the body scan, is to ask the animal to show you an active picture of himself moving, like a mental video.

Often, an animal will be very dramatic in showing you where he or she hurts. For instance, when Debbie communicates with horses, she asks them to show her how they look walking, trotting, and cantering for her. They proceed to show Debbie which leg is stiff or which side is more difficult to bend. They might also send a picture that zooms in on a particular body part, to let Debbie know that this is the source of pain. It is like a movie playing in Debbie's head, and she is simply observing the film. The animal is the director and the star, and Debbie just takes notes. To do this, just connect with your animal and ask for this information.

Horse Sense

Sometimes, all you need to do is ask your animals how they are feeling. Some questions to ask:

◆ How long have you felt this way?

◆ When did it start?

◆ Why did this happen?

◆ What helps it and what aggravates it?

◆ What can we do to make it better?

Many times when Debbie first connects with an animal, the animal will go on to tell her that the person called Debbie because he or she was worried about the animal's health. The animal will then go on to explain why. Animals are very perceptive about what we are trying to do for them!

The best method for you might be different than the best method for someone else, so just see what works best for you, and then customize it to work for you and your animal.

Animal communicators cannot diagnose illness, and are ethically bound not to pretend they can. What they can do, however, is tell you where the animal hurts or what particular complaints the animal is making. Your vet or chiropractor can then use this information to help treat the animal.

Solving Medical Mysteries

Debbie was called to connect with a 2-year-old Appaloosa filly named Matoose. Her person was worried because her legs were swollen like balloons, and the vets could not find anything wrong with her.

When Debbie connected with Matoose, she showed Debbie that she did not have an accident or fall, but that her legs were experiencing an allergic reaction. When Debbie asked her what she thought this could be from, she began to show Debbie something being added to her grain. It was a dark green color.

When Debbie asked Matoose's person, Tina, if she had recently started her on a new supplement, she said that she just put her on a daily wormer four days ago. Tina had said that she mentioned this to the vet originally, but that the vet did not think this was the cause because she had never seen a horse have an allergic reaction to it before.

Debbie explained to Tina that Matoose's system felt weak to her. Her liver seemed to be working too hard. Tina said that Matoose had been on steroids a week prior. Tina agreed to take Matoose off the daily wormer to see if her condition improved. Within one day of stopping this medication, Matoose's legs started to return to normal.

When an animal's liver is working hard, as in Matoose's case, it might be due to the amount of steroids/medication the animal had been given. Matoose's little body had a hard time handling it. Her liver was so overworked that it couldn't adequately process the addition of a daily wormer to the load. If her liver had been functioning properly, she might have been able to handle the daily wormer, but in this case, her body reacted adversely.

Because Matoose was able to communicate an image of exactly what was causing her problem, Tina was able to cure Matoose. You might be able to uncover a similar medical mystery through animal communication.

CAUTION

Doggone!

Some people are more sensitive to feeling sensations in their bodies sent from an animal, and might have a harder time feeling "back to normal" after a body-scan communication. When Debbie first started communicating with the animals professionally, headaches she would sense from animals would linger with her long after the communication. Clear your energy field by visualizing a surrounding white light, and by shaking your hands and feet.

The Mind-Body-Spirit Link

Animals, like people, become ill on different levels, and heal on different levels, too. Sometimes a physical problem is caused by an emotional upset. Unprocessed emotions can become buried and manifest as physical symptoms, even years later. Unless the animal heals the emotional aspect of the illness, the physical manifestation of it may not respond well to treatment. Also, many times a serious emotional upset can weaken a system enough for a physical condition to surface.

Animals also heal on a spiritual or soul level. This might take many lifetimes to achieve, but each lesson and challenge they face in this life becomes imprinted on their soul or karma, to be faced, or built upon, later.

Sasha's Mind-Body

Debbie communicated with a wonderful Arabian horse named Sasha who was particularly in tune with his body. Sasha gave Debbie a detailed run-down of his physical condition, so she could communicate Sasha's situation to his person Fran. Here's what Sasha shared during his body scan from Debbie:

- He experienced a past stifle injury.

- He has a colon problem.

- He had an injury both emotional and physical from an old trailering accident.

- He has occasional difficulty breathing.

- He experiences allergies and respiratory problems around mold and pine at certain times of the year.

- He experiences some puffiness in the right hind fetlock area.

- He feels weak and stiff on the right side of his body and also on his lower right front leg. He showed that he needed supportive boots and that concussion to this area could be damaging.

- He experiences achiness in right front knee toward the outside.

- He paddles a bit when trotting in front.

- He has a hard time digesting sugars and alfalfa.

- He has other digestive problems. Coarser hay is better, he says. Alfalfa is hard on his system.

- Gently tugging on his tail helps his back.

- He said his person had been wondering about his shoes, and he wanted her to know that the soles of his hooves are thin. This bothers him.

- He has a really sore spot on his back, at the base of the withers, off to the left.

- Again, his right front leg is stiff and feels achy like arthritis.

- He is sensitive behind his right front elbow and in his rib area.

- His left hind is stiff in the stifle area and along the muscles at the point of his rump.

- He has a sore spot above his left hind hock, on the inside of his leg.

- He has a twist in his step when his left hind leaves the ground.

- Check the left hind hoof, he seems to be bearing more pressure on the inside wall here.

- He says there is a saddle pad his person uses that he does not like as much as the others. He prefers the thinner pad. He also says his person sits heavier to the right side and sometimes the saddle twists that way.

- He says he stumbles a lot and it would help if his person didn't shift her weight as much.

- He feels a sensitivity in his stomach on the left side in the lower abdomen.

- He is a bit gassy.

- He also has problems with other foods like oats and sweet feed. Pellets are easier.

- He says he enjoys camping and wants to do more.

- He says he used to be afraid of the dark, but not anymore. Now he has to be the brave one. (He lives with a horse who is blind in one eye.)

> **Cat's Meow**
>
> She does so much for others all the time. I worry about her. We heal each other; this is part of our love.
>
> —Sasha, about his person, Fran

Fran also asked Debbie to ask Sasha why he dislikes the trailer, and Sasha explained that he had a trailering accident in the past—not in the trailer he has now, but in an older trailer. Fran also wanted to know what happened to his legs because he has scars on both. When Debbie asked Sasha about the scars, he showed her a picture of getting caught on a fence. He said he was calm when it happened, but as he tried to get free, it tore the skin deeper. Another horse had been involved and he was upset with the other horse.

Sasha is an amazing horse and the love he and Fran share is beyond words. Fran shared with Debbie after the session was done that Sasha had surgery to remove a large enterolith (tumor/stone) from his colon. The enterolith was as hard as a bowling ball and the size of a grapefruit. After Fran did extensive research to find out what some of the causes to this are, she realized that it is a calcium phosphorus build-up, and the stone had a high alfalfa content! No wonder Sasha kept mentioning that alfalfa, she thought.

Fran immediately pulled Sasha off alfalfa hay and is now very careful about his diet. Fran also does a lot of endurance riding with Sasha and they both enjoy camping together. Sasha is getting older, and Fran does whatever she can to relieve his aches and pains. The love and friendship they both share is truly wonderful. Both Fran and Sasha have gone through their share of personal challenges, but together they help each other to be strong. They really do help each other heal.

Here is the letter Debbie received from Fran after the consultation was completed:

Dear Debbie:

The afternoon of August 7, 2003, changed my whole outlook of the animal world. You opened that door for me. I've heard other animal communicators speak to groups and demonstrate their beliefs, but I was never convinced that these people truly had the ability to go beyond a physical appearance of what the animal was saying.

Debbie, you are a sweet, sincere, and gifted person. I felt like I was in shock after you told me things that were absolutely, astonishingly accurate about my horse. As you know, Sasha had been behaving strangely and so, when I came across your website, I was curious.

I was apprehensive about our session, but I became intrigued when I asked you why Sasha was so afraid of trailers and you told me about the accident from his past. The real turning point, however, was when I asked you about the scars on Sasha's back legs. I knew how they got there, but you didn't. I fully expected you to say they were caused by the trailer accident, but instead, you fell silent, then with surprise in your voice, said, "A fence!" When you described the wounds in exact detail, a chill came over me, my jaw dropped, tears formed in my eyes. I knew right then that you could actually see and hear what Sasha was telling me! It was exactly that! Eight years ago, Sasha struck out with his hind legs at another horse across a wood fence and got hung up on the top rung for quite some time before someone from the training facility came to his aid.

I would recommend you to anyone who ever wanted to know more about their pets. You are the one. Thank you so much.

Sincerely,
Fran
Palm Beach Gardens, Florida

Fering's Transformation

Sheryl contacted Debbie about her horse, Fering. Both Sheryl and Fering live in France (remember, telepathy can transcend any distance, even the barrier of languages, because it is a spirit-to-spirit communication). Fering was Sheryl's blind horse who was becoming more and more aggressive toward Sheryl. It was becoming impossible to give Fering the medicine she required.

Sheryl felt heartbroken that her beloved horse was suddenly behaving in this way, reacting to her with what looked like fear and anger. Sheryl contacted Debbie to find out what was wrong.

The first thing Fering said to Debbie when she connected to her was that she was not completely blind. She said she could see occasional shadows and movement, but because she couldn't see exactly what the shadows were or where the movements were going, she was becoming more and more nervous, defensive, and frightened.

Debbie explained to Fering that Sheryl loved her and wanted to help her, that Sheryl would never hurt her and would do anything to make her feel comfortable and calm again. At once, Fering began to soften her tone. She had been so defensive for so long that it had become an automatic response.

Sheryl, Fering, and Debbie chatted for awhile, discussing the bond Sheryl and Fering shared and how much Sheryl wanted to help Fering have a calmer, happier life. Fering agreed to take her medicine, but wanted Sheryl to talk with her more when approaching and touch her body all over, focusing on the senses that were still strong.

Debbie still receives e-mails from Sheryl, who is delighted with the fact that Fering is like her old self, sweet and loving and accepting her medicine without a fight.

When Debbie communicates with an animal that has been abused or has deeply rooted fears, she senses an altered energy field around them. An animal with a lot of pain in the past often has an energy field or aura that actually appears to have holes in it. These animals tend to be very timid, ungrounded, and skittish. By helping them strengthen their energy field so that they don't absorb so much emotional energy from other people, animals, and their environments, these animals are better able to heal.

To help animals repair their own energy fields, Debbie visualizes a field of white light, thick and strong, all around the animal. Then, she asks them to do the same whenever they feel vulnerable or frightened, as a sort of psychic shield for protection and security. This technique has worked for many animals, including Fering.

> **Cat's Meow**
>
> Debbie's horse, Finnegan, composed this poem about healing (yes, animals can make up poetry, too!):
>
> | | |
> |---|---|
> | I was given a feather, | The middle of my back. |
> | A feather to heal, | She traced the outline |
> | Given to me by a girl | Of my energy field, |
> | Whose love I constantly feel. | Assuring me of its purpose: |
> | It came from the crows | To keep me safe, to shield. |
> | Who keep me in sight | Now I stand tall and |
> | And left me this magical feather | Look deep into the night, |
> | To save me from the night. | For I hold the medicine |
> | She tickled my nose | That frees me from my fright. |
> | With its velvety touch | —Finnegan |
> | And ran it across | |

Healing for Animal Athletes

People often call Debbie about show and performance animals who suddenly experience a problem, either physical or behavioral, that keeps them from showing or performing. Sometimes the animal seems injured but a vet can't find anything wrong. Sometimes the animal behaves as if he has no interest in an activity he has always loved.

Don, an active competitor in reining cow horse competitions, contacted Debbie about his Appaloosa mare, Wendy. He felt something was wrong and wanted to see if Debbie could find out anything.

When Debbie communicated with Wendy, Wendy showed her that bending to the right was difficult for her because her right front shoulder was stiff. She had a harder time recovering, or moving off her right front leg, than she did on the left, and this was impacting her performance, both physically and emotionally, as she was frustrated by not being able to do her best.

Don confirmed that he was having great difficulty trying to get Wendy to make quick turns to the right, and that it was costing him some points when working the cows. At times, it was even becoming dangerous. Wendy was also sensing Don's frustration at the loss of points and the inability to work together the way they once did. Don was glad to know exactly where the physical problem resided.

But Wendy also had some advice for how Don was riding. She told Debbie that Don tends to allow his right shoulder to twist forward more, so that there is a slight twist in his body in the saddle. This makes short stops to the right even more difficult for her.

Don went back to look at some videos of himself riding and saw that his body was indeed twisted just the way Wendy had described. Now he makes a conscious effort to remain straighter through his shoulders to help her balance into her stops and turns better.

At last Don knew that the performance problems he was having with Wendy weren't training issues, but physical ones. Don immediately took Wendy for treatment, and when her pain and stiffness was resolved, in conjunction with Don's altered riding style, this reining cow horse has become a real powerhouse!

> **Cat's Meow**
>
> I am afraid of falling. I have seen a horse fall before, and I don't want that to happen to me!
> —Nikki, a gray gelding, when asked why he was tentative on the cross-country course

How to Help Your Animal Heal

You probably aren't a vet, a doctor, or a chiropractor, and you can't heal your animal all on your own, but you can definitely help your animal to tap into the inner resources that will help her heal herself. In conjunction with responsible medical care, this kind of supportive healing can decrease healing time and repair relationships damaged from misunderstandings about the results of pain, injury, and sickness.

You can support your animal's healing in many ways. Here are a few tips Debbie has discovered over the years from the many animals who have helped teach her how animals need and want to be supported during healing:

◆ Many animals ask their people to send them healing light. Often, animals will even describe exactly which color of healing energy or light would help them most. Visualize this colored light surrounding your animal. Or, using your intuition, determine for yourself which color of healing energy your animal needs and wants.

◆ When sending healing energy to your animal, ask that your animal use it wherever they feel they need it most. If they become agitated, stop sending the energy and wait until your animal is more comfortable. You might be sending too much, or maybe you're sending it for too long. Picture the energy filled with love for your animal, encircling your animal's body.

♦ Sometimes animals ask that their people "see" them as healthy and well. When an animal is very sick and we look at him with pain and fear in our own eyes and hearts, this can compound his own fear and anxiety. If, when you look at your animal and you "see" him as healthy, he picks up on this energy and feels more optimistic.

♦ If your animal has a problem in a particular body part, you can focus on visualizing that body part in a healthy, working condition. For instance, Debbie's horse, Finnegan, had a colic episode that was not improving as quickly as Debbie would have liked. The vet was monitoring Finnegan (a must in such an emergency situation!), but rather than sit helplessly by, Debbie supported the vet's healing efforts by continually visualizing the impaction breaking up and passing through. By morning, Finnegan was fine.

♦ Feed your animal right! A lot of animal feed is highly processed and laden with chemical additives. The better food you feed your animals, the healthier they will be and the stronger their immune systems will be to fight off any problems. Poor diets are the cause of many illnesses that animals face today such as bladder infections, kidney disease, diabetes, and cancer. Choose the highest quality natural food or prepare a homemade diet (research how to do this so your animal's diet is nutritionally sound—see Appendix B for several books on the subject).

> **Cat's Meow**
>
> You know that we are scavenger birds, but our eating habits have changed. We find our food supply in human trash and the things we are eating are causing us strange health changes. Your trash is food for many, but it is a double-edged sword.
>
> —Victor, a black crow

Alternative Medicine for Animals

Debbie and Eve are both big advocates of alternative or complementary veterinary medicine. Holistic vets are easier and easier to find, and the American Holistic Veterinary Medical Association (AHVMA) maintains a directory of holistic vets on their website (www.ahvma.org), searchable by state, or check out altvetmed.com for another searchable database.

Alternative medicine treats the body as a whole to get to the root cause of the illness. This can be a successful and noninvasive way to treat animals and people, and is often less costly and has fewer side-effects than traditional medicine. In conjunction with conventional medicine, which can be best for acute and emergency situations, alternative therapies can help to balance your animal and keep her in a condition in which she is best able to heal herself.

Some of the more popular alternative therapies for animals include:

- **Chiropractic:** Basic alignment of the bones and joints for more correct mobility and function. Manual manipulation and the activator method are the two most common techniques used for animals. Some veterinary chiropractors are certified by the American Veterinary Chiropractic Association (www. animalchiropractic.org). Veterinary chiropractic care is now sometimes referred to as veterinary orthopedic manipulation.

- **Acupuncture:** Balancing of the body's energy flow by activating different energy centers along the body's energy meridians by inserting ultra-fine needles. Acupuncture is great for pain relief. Some veterinary acupuncturists are certified by the International Veterinary Acupuncture Society (www.ivas.org/main.cfm).

> **Horse Sense** _____
>
> Chinese herbal medicine is a separate category from "western" herbal medicine, using highly organized and specific techniques and ingredients that are popular in China. Some vets practice Traditional Chinese Medicine (TCM) on animals. One source of information is the Traditional Chinese Veterinary Medicine website at www.tcvm.com.

- **Herbal medicine:** Herbs are medicines in much the same way any other drugs are medicines. They can have a specific effect in the body that will help to mitigate the symptoms of a disease. Use herbs with caution under the advice of a professional veterinary herbalist, or those manufactured by reputable companies and made for pets. Don't use herbs made for humans on pets, as you might not know the correct dosage to give your animal. Find out more from the Veterinary Botanical Medical Association (VBMA) at vbma.org/index.html.

- **Homeopathy:** The use of highly diluted natural substances in minute amounts to stimulate the body to return to its normal function. Some veterinary homeopaths are certified by the Academy of Veterinary Homeopathy. Find out more about veterinary homeopathy at their website: www.theavh.org.

- **Animal massage:** This therapy has two uses: to prevent injury to the flexible parts of an animal's soft tissue structure, relaxing muscles so tendons and ligaments don't tear during activity, and to prevent the formation of scar tissue after a traumatic injury. Animal massage is very popular with performance horses, where it is sometimes called equine sports massage, but most other animals like dogs, cats, birds, and smaller animals really enjoy a good massage, too.

◆ **Flower essences:** We talked a lot about flower essences in previous chapters, especially Chapter 11. These gentle remedies contain the energetic essences of various flowers, bringing the body back into emotional harmony.

◆ **Reiki:** This energetic healing technique is similar to psychic communication because it can be accomplished face-to-face or long-distance. The Reiki healer channels universal energy to help balance and heal the animal's energy imbalances. Actually touching the animal isn't necessary. For more information on animal Reiki, see www.animalreikicare.com/symbols.htm.

Disease is a dis-ease in the body, a disharmony of process, both physical and emotional. Disease can manifest in any part of the body, mind, emotions, or spirit, but a healthy life and the balance that communication, love, and support invokes in both animals and people can help to heal everyone. That is, of course, one of the most beautiful and miraculous things that can happen when two sentient beings come together in a relationship characterized by love.

The Least You Need to Know

◆ You can help heal your animal by using psychic communication to get to the root of the problem.

◆ Body scan techniques enable you to move inside your animal's body to feel the same physical sensations your animal feels. This can help you to find the source of the problem. Asking the animal to send you images of his movement or other helpful pictures can also help to pinpoint a physical problem.

◆ Performance issues for animal athletes might be physical rather than training issues. Animal communication can reveal the difference.

◆ Support the healing efforts of professionals with visualizations of affected areas healing and working properly.

◆ A healthy diet and regular use of alternative veterinary medicine can help to keep your animal's immune system in top condition to help prevent or more quickly resolve health problems.

Chapter 19

Helping Your Pet Pass to Spirit

In This Chapter

- ◆ Does your animal know about death?
- ◆ How to know if your animal is ready to pass over
- ◆ Handling your grief
- ◆ Connecting to your animal in spirit
- ◆ A glimpse into life on the other side, as told by animals

Before Debbie started communicating with animals, death seemed so final. It was the end, and nothing more. The end of consciousness, the end of the self, the end of being. Now Debbie knows this is not the case.

Death is a transition. The spirit and personality continue on, it is only the physical body that is shed, like a snakeskin. Once animals or people transition into spirit, they aren't "gone." We might not be able to reach out and touch them or see them, but they are aware of us, and they remain with us to help us if we need them.

Do Animals "Get" Death?

Common wisdom has long told us that although we, as so-called intellectually advanced humans, understand what it means to die, animals live in the moment and know nothing of death. This is simply not true. More accurately, humans fear death because it is so unknown to them; animals have better access to their innate sense of the connectedness of the entire cycle of life, death, and rebirth.

Animals often tell Debbie how much fun it is to be in spirit form because now they can go with their people everywhere.

Debbie had the pleasure of doing a consultation with a little white pony named Penny. Penny had passed into spirit after a traumatic experience. Penny's people, Carole and Nadia, wanted Debbie to connect with Penny to see how she was doing on the other side. Carole was worried that her daughter Nadia was having a hard time dealing with Penny's death.

When Debbie connected with Penny the pony, she told Debbie that she was doing fine but that she was worried about Nadia. Penny the pony said that she visits Nadia every night. Penny showed Debbie that Nadia's room had carousel horses all around, and that Nadia kept a tuft of Penny's tail hair hung in her closet and that she would often go over and touch the tail hair and cry.

When Debbie relayed this information to Carole and Nadia, Nadia perked up. She said that her room did have carousel horses and that she did keep a tuft of Penny's tail hung up in her closet. Nadia thought it so cool that her pony was in her bedroom. Nadia eagerly asked if Penny had accompanied her on her trip to New York. When Debbie asked Penny, she said of course she did! Debbie asked Penny how Nadia would know she was there, and Penny showed Debbie that Nadia had peppermints in the pockets of her jacket. Nadia burst out laughing and said that it was indeed true, they were Penny's favorite treats.

It was comforting for Nadia and Carole to know that even though their beloved pony Penny had passed into spirit, she was still with them and enjoying their company in spirit form.

Animals will also sometimes show Debbie who they are with on the other side. Debbie got a call from a woman name Vivian. Vivian had contacted her about her Shih Tzu, Melvin, who had passed into spirit four months prior. When Debbie connected with Melvin, his personality was still as perky as ever. Vivian wanted to know who Melvin was with on the other side. Melvin showed Debbie a picture of a woman who was missing a hand, and a small man with a flannel shirt on, and toy trains all around him.

When Debbie relayed this information to Vivian, she was silent. Debbie admits she began to sweat a little. Could she be this far off? Then, quietly, the woman said that Melvin was with her parents. Her dad was a small man who had collected toy trains, and her mom had come to her in a dream after she had passed, and in the dream, she only had one hand.

For Vivian, this was a double confirmation that her beloved dog was being well taken care of with her parents on the other side, and validation that her mother had communicated with her from spirit through a dream. There is indeed great comfort in knowing that our animals have friends and relatives on the other side waiting for them.

 **Cat's Meow**

I still come to sleep on your bed at night, especially when you need it most.

—Carter, a black domestic short-

Haley called Debbie about her horse, Brewster. Brewster had passed over into spirit, and Haley was concerned about whether she made the right choice in helping Brewster pass over. When Debbie connected with Brewster, he said that his person had a lot of guilt over his passing but that it had been his time. He also wanted her to know that he had friends on the other side. He showed Debbie a dun horse and an older gray horse. The gray horse had been over there longer and was helping him.

When Debbie relayed this information to Haley, she said that that was a major concern for her, knowing whether he was with his friends. She said just a few weeks prior to his death, his friend, a dun colored horse, passed over as well. Before that, an older gray horse passed over. She was relieved to know they were all together.

Animals will often visit us in dreams after they have passed. It is the easiest way for them to communicate with us from spirit. Many times, they visit just to let us know they are okay.

Debbie's cat, Jimmy James, still visits her in dreams, and Debbie usually wakes up with a smile, knowing that she spent some time with him.

Is Your Animal Ready?

Knowing when your animal is ready to transition to the other side isn't easy, and it's the source of many of Debbie's calls. How do we honor our animals and know when they are ready to pass over? How do we know if they want help passing over, or if they want to pass on their own?

Each animal is unique and the decision is never easy. Our emotions run high, and this is the hardest time to tap into intuition. However, here is some advice to help you honor your animal and the delicate process of passing over, as well as how to better understand when the time has come to help your animals release themselves from the physical body:

♦ Some animals don't want more surgery or invasive drugs to keep them going. Some prefer to be left alone to handle the disease and the process naturally. Others want to fight with whatever means available. Ask your animals what they want. This can be a challenge, because what you want might not be necessarily what the animal wants. Take extra time to quiet your mind before you ask your animal these questions.

♦ Ask the animal to give you a sign that he or she needs help passing over. Some common ways animals let their people know it is their time are when the animal comes to them in a dream to say goodbye, becomes nonresponsive, has a vacant look in his or her eyes, prefers to sleep or remain in dark or out-of-the-way places, or refuses to eat or drink. Sometimes you will just know in your heart it is time.

♦ Give your animal permission to go. Many times after a person gives permission, the animal will pass shortly afterward, if they are able. It is important that you not just say this, but must also mean it from your heart. Allow your animal to make the journey with all the love in your heart. Death is a transition out of the physical body. It is freeing the spirit. It is not something to be feared.

♦ Remember the good times and share those memories with your animal. Thank them for being in your life. Prepare the other animals in the home by keeping them informed of what is happening.

♦ Ask your angels and spirit guides to help you and your animal through this process and to give you the courage to make the correct decision.

♦ Should you have to help your animal to pass over, be with them during the process. Many animals request that they not have to go back to the vets and would prefer to pass at home. Try to find a vet who will make house calls so your animal can pass in the comfort of a familiar place. If your only alternative is to go into the vet's office, you can make your animal more comfortable by bringing a familiar blanket or bed for them to lie on during the process. Use Rescue Remedy (see Chapter 11) for both you and your animal. Touch your animal throughout the process, knowing that it is a transition and that your friend will never really be gone.

♦ Some animals will pass on their own and will do it specifically when you are not around. Animals tell Debbie it is easier for them to pass when it is quiet and emotions are not running high.

The Aftermath: Your Grief

Losing an animal you love is extremely difficult, so don't ignore your own grief. Attend to it. Grieving for an animal can be one of the most difficult things to get through. Many people who do not have animals do not understand it. Seek support from others who do understand.

Grief is a process, so allow yourself time to grieve; and in time, make a commitment to move forward and heal. This doesn't mean you are forgetting about your animal, it means that you are honoring what they would want. Many people can't let go of their animal's physical presence and hold on to their grief, not wanting to heal. Animals report that this inhibits them from growing on the other side. When their people are unable to let go, it keeps animals more earthbound, fearing they are needed.

Also acknowledge the grief the other animals in the home might be going through. Try to grieve and heal together, understanding each animal's unique way of handling grief.

Flower essences can help, including Rescue Remedy, prior to the passing for both human and animal, and after the passing, for humans and other animals in the home.

Always remember that love transcends all boundaries and you will be reunited again! The ones left behind have the most difficult time. Your animal friend in spirit is in good hands and pain free.

Cat's Meow

When our editor Lynn's 15-year-old cat, Lui, started ailing, the cat stopped eating and drinking and would withdraw by going into a closet, as if she didn't want to be seen in that condition. When it became clear that Lui was not going to recover and was suffering, Lynn decided euthanasia was the best course. The morning of the euthanization Lynn had some time before the vet opened, so she drove to a nearby park and watched the squirrels with Lui. When she returned home that morning she spotted a rainbow outside the window, and she knew it was Lui telling her that she was finally okay.

Discovering and Accepting Transitions

Some animals leave this life, it seems, well before their time. This might be because they only have a short contract here on Earth, or they feel that they have completed their purpose here.

Sometimes an animal's death is a part of our growth. Animals will also sometimes leave to make room for another or to be on the other side to help a friend that has passed or will be passing. There is a reason for everything. Unfortunately, we can't always see the big picture, which may not unfold completely for us until we are reunited on the other side. Trust in the process and use your heart as your guide.

Carley called Debbie about connecting with her young filly, Sadie. Sadie had passed into spirit at the young age of two, and Carley had a lot of unanswered questions surrounding this young filly's passing. When Debbie connected with Sadie, her personality was as big as ever. Debbie expressed this to Carley, who confirmed that Sadie was a really outgoing girl with a big personality.

What Sadie said next answered a lot of questions for Carley. Sadie said that her condition and death were unavoidable, that it was a condition she was born with and that she was not meant to spend a lot of time on Earth. She said that it was nothing that Carley did wrong, but that it was her time to go. She said her passing was quick and peaceful. She said that she is doing just fine and comes to check on Carley many times at night. Sadie said that Carley could always know when she is there because she will get a whiff of her scent just under her nose.

Sadie also wanted Carley to know that she had a very important job on the other side. She said that she helps children who pass at a very young age to get adjusted. She says she works with a lot of children who have cancer who pass early and she helps bring them joy.

Carley was relieved to know that Sadie was doing well and continues to smell her presence in her bedroom.

Will Your Animal Be Back?

A frequent question people ask Debbie to ask their animals in spirit is whether or not the animal will incarnate back into their lives, and if so, as what. Some animals choose to rejoin their person's life as another animal. Many people report that a new animal has strikingly similar characteristics as the animal who had passed.

Horse Sense

How will you know when your animal has incarnated into another animal, and how will you find your animal? Quite simply, if your pet intends to find you, he or she will find you. Animals who are meant to be with us know how to get to us. There are animals who just adopt us, show up at our house, or come to us through unusual circumstances. Go with the flow and life will be a whole lot easier.

Some animals prefer to work with their people from spirit and wait for them to join them when their time comes. Still other animals may even choose to come back as wild animals, to learn a new lesson in a different body.

In Your Dreams

Sometimes our animals will come to us in dreams. Many times, an animal that has recently passed will come to us in a dream to let us know they are okay, or to simply visit with us. It is the easiest way for them to communicate with us.

People often try to demand that their animals come to them in a ghost form so that they know they are there, but these people don't realize that this can be very difficult for a spirit to do. Instead of paying attention to the small signs and miracles our animals send us, some people negate them, looking for something bigger.

Acknowledge the subtle signs. When you get them, smile and send your animal friend a big hello and a hug.

Gypsy, a chestnut standardbred mare, consistently told Debbie that she frequently visited her person during dreamtime. When Debbie asked Gypsy to tell her more about this, she said she would show her galloping across an open field, young and free.

Gypsy's person confirmed that approximately every other month, she had that exact dream. She said it was especially comforting because Gypsy had been very old and worn down when she passed, and to know she was young and free brought her great comfort.

When Animals Aren't Sure They Have Passed

Sometimes when Debbie is communicating with animals who are ready to pass over, they will show her angels all around them. This is usually a sign that they are preparing to pass rather soon, as these angels comfort and prepare the animal for the inevitable transition.

Sometimes, however, animals who have died might not realize they are dead. Animals who die suddenly, such as when they are hit by a car or attacked by another animal, might slip out of their body so quickly that they do not even realize they are in spirit.

In cases like this, Debbie gently explains to the animal what happened, and encourages them to go to the light, that friends will be waiting for them. She also asks that their angels and guides assist them through this process.

Cat's Meow _____

Once Debbie was driving down the road and noticed a dead skunk on the side of the road. Usually when she passes such a sight, she will say a quick prayer for the animal and tell them they are loved. This particular skunk, however, seemed to be hovering above his body, not quite sure what had happened. Debbie gently connected with him and explained that his physical body had expired and that now he was in spirit and needed to move toward the light. He thanked Debbie, and left the scene.

Debbie finds it comforting to think that when an animal passes, they cross a rainbow bridge to the other side that is so full of vibrant colors, beautiful sounds, and loving friends that it is pure joy. We can cross this bridge any time in our mind or through our dreams to visit our animal friends. And when our time comes, they will be there to greet us upon our arrival.

The Least You Need to Know

◆ Animals have an innate understanding of the cycle of life, death, and rebirth. They don't fear death the way many humans do.

◆ Psychic communication can help you to determine whether your animal needs your help in transitioning, or whether the animal wants to do it naturally.

◆ You can ease your animal's passing by being there, surrounding the animal with familiar things, and staying calm and loving rather than fearful and anxious.

◆ Your animal may come back to you in the form of another animal after death, or choose to stay near you in spirit. Or the animal may have a job to do elsewhere, and you might not actually see each other again until you, too, transition to the other side.

◆ You can help animals who haven't realized they have passed by gently explaining that their bodies have passed and that they now need to move into the light.

Chapter 20

The Sacred Bond Between Human and Animal

In This Chapter

- ◆ Your connection to the animal kingdom and Mother Earth
- ◆ How to spread what you've learned into the community to further enhance human/animal relations
- ◆ Sharing the gift
- ◆ Animal organizations to support

One of our goals in writing this book, in addition to allowing voices that fall silent to be heard, is to raise awareness about the incredible scope of feeling, love, and compassion animals have. Our animal friends, our fellow sentient beings living upon Mother Earth, are all connected to us in a chain of existence that is sacred. Protecting and preserving the earth and all of us who live here will help to honor and maintain this connection. Leave it behind, ignore it, and we may lose it.

The human race is awakening. This awakening goes deeper than each of us, individually, may realize. With the progressive surge in spirituality humans have experienced over the last decade, the human race has only recently rediscovered spiritual territory that has been dormant for centuries.

We are learning things the animal kingdom has always known, and although we may not be learning these things for the first time, we are relearning them in our current incarnations in this current time. This is new learning, a twenty-first century awakening, and yet, the animals have been at our side, assisting us in this transition all along.

Life Is Not as It Seems ...

When you look out the window, what do you see? So many of us only see with our eyes. It is time we see with our hearts and our souls as well. The world takes on new meaning when we look at it with a larger, more open consciousness. Spirit lies within each living thing, and each of us—human, animal, bird, fish, tree, flower—is here to learn, experience, and often, to teach.

The world is filled with miracles. Have you ever sat and admired the beauty of a flower, not just a casual appreciation in passing but a deep, focused, fully aware admiration for the color, scent, shape, texture, and essence of the flower? Have you ever felt the divine wisdom of a tree, admired its silent strength and seasonal transformations?

There are many worlds going on all around us. If we humans can finally recognize that we are not the center of the universe, but yet, an integral part, just like each other part, of the great cycle of life, we can re-enter our relationship with the planet and enjoy the transformation she has to offer us. It is time to honor the animals, the environment, the life cycle. It is time to teach our children to love and give thanks, to respect the beauty that is in each of us and all around us. This is what the animals want us to discover.

Giving Something Back

Animals do so much for us, and many of us have recognized that the time is right to return the favor. Here are some ways you can help. Only you can decide which of these ways are right for you to thank animals for the many ways they have enriched your life and saved your heart:

- Rescue or foster abused and abandoned animals.
- Volunteer at local animal sanctuaries or shelters.
- Find a way to educate others about the respect animals deserve.
- Pick up trash to keep the lands clean and healthy for wildlife.
- Recycle.

♦ Join an environmental activist group and get to work.

♦ Use your psychic animal communication skills to bring joy and peace to a scared animal in a shelter.

♦ Donate money to one of the many organizations that help and protect animals of all kinds.

There are many ways to give back to the animal kingdom. In doing so, you will be completing the circle and doing your part. When Debbie teaches workshops, she takes a portion of the proceeds and donates them to a local no-kill animal sanctuary, shelter, or rescue organization. It is her way of thanking the animals for helping her.

CAUTION

Doggone! _____

Each year in the United States, millions of animals including dogs, cats, rabbits, chimps, rats, and mice are confined in tiny cages as the subject of scientific experiments. Approximately 5 to 10 million cats and dogs die each year because they have no home, and more than 134 million animals who live in the wild are trapped and killed for "sport."

Thousands and thousands of mares are impregnated for the production of the estrogen replacement drug Premarin. As a result, most of these healthy foals are sent to slaughter. Premarin is made from the pregnant mare's urine. However, there are many synthetic and plant derived alternatives to this horrendous and needless procedure.

What can you do to help preserve animal welfare?

♦ Spay or neuter your animals.

♦ Contact various animal advocacy organizations for more information on what they do and how you can help.

♦ Educate your children, students, community, and friends.

♦ Write letters to companies who do animal testing, government officials, and newspapers.

♦ Buy cruelty-free products that are not tested on animals.

♦ Do not use Premarin. There are synthetic and natural alternatives to estrogen replacement.

♦ Donate to local or national organizations that support animal welfare.

- Make humane entertainment choices, avoiding circuses that use animals, sub-standard zoos, etc.

- Don't buy animals from pet stores that get their pets from puppy mills. Find a responsible and ethical breeder, or even better, adopt an animal from a shelter, rescue, or sanctuary.

- Volunteer for a day (or longer) at a local animal sanctuary or shelter. Get your family and children involved as well.

- Donate food, blankets, and pet supplies to local no-kill shelters.

- Do not buy fur or animal skin products.

- Avoid food from factory farms. Choose free-range organic foods instead.

- If you can't adopt an animal, why not sponsor an unwanted animal through the many organizations nationwide? This can make a wonderful gift for another animal-conscious friend.

Horse Sense

When a television show, company, ad campaign, or government official makes a ruling, decision, or public announcement showing compassion towards animals, write to them and thank them. Gratitude goes a long way in making a change. Acknowledge the good that is being done in the world—we hear enough about the bad every night on the news.

Finally, we would never, ever advocate violence to stop violence. Instead, send love to the animals who are being unfairly treated and use your strengths to bring about change. If you are a good writer, use that skill to make people aware of what is going on. A good speaker can attend town meetings or public events.

By throwing hate at a bad situation, you only give it energy. Hate fuels hate. If you really want to make a change, use that anger in a positive way. What many animals endure at the hands of humans is shocking and inexcusable, and it's easy to be driven into a state of rage, but in order to effectively make a difference, we have to harbor that energy and turn it around to make a positive change.

The Organizations Already Working

The world is a place where every soul has a chance to make a difference. It is the theater of life. Here are some helpful websites of organizations that promote animal welfare. These are just a few of thousands:

- **American Society for the Prevention of Cruelty to Animals (ASPCA):** www.aspca.org

- **The Coalition for Consumer Information on Cosmetics**: leapingbunny.org
- **Defenders of Wildlife**: www.defenders.org
- **EquineRescue.NET**: www.igha.com/ern.html
- **Friends of Feral Felines**: www.friendsofferalfelines.org
- **The Fund for Animals**: www.fund.org/animalfunding
- **Gentle Spirit Training**: www.gentlespiritllamas.com
- **Greenpeace**: www.greenpeace.org
- **The Humane Community of America**: saveourstrays.com
- **The Humane Society of the United States**: www.hsus.org
- **Mustang Rescue Ranch**: mustang-rescue.com
- **Purrfect Pals Shelter**: purrfectpals.org
- **Save the Elephants**: www.save-the-elephants.org
- **Save the Manatee Club**: www.savethemanatee.org
- **Save the Rainforest**: www.savetherainforest.org
- **Spring Farm Cares** (spay/neuter program): springfarmcares.org
- **Lifesavers, Inc. Wild Horse Rescue:** www.wildhorserescue.org
- **United Pegasus Foundation**: unitedpegasus.com

There are many small organizations and shelters locally that desperately need funding as well. Contact people in your area to see how you can help.

Cat's Meow

A symbol of success in this country is bringing the eagle back from extinction. But, my friends, it is a crime that he was put there is the first place.

—From an animal meditation of Debbie McGillivray

Interviews with Wild Animals and Animals in Captivity

Debbie has had many fascinating communications with wild animals. To help inspire you to understand the great minds and spirits of the animals that share our earth, Debbie has shared some interview transcripts.

Spotted Bottlenose Dolphins off the Coast of the Blue Lagoon Island, Bahamas

"When you humans are happy and experiencing joy, there is no room for prejudice, hate, or judgment. We take you away from this. If your heart is pure and free from distractions, you can experience this feeling of fitting in. We are here to show you the harmony that can exist between all beings. It has been said time and again that love conquers evil, and it can, if you are consistent. Be the catalyst. Be the one to conduct yourself within this realm of peace, harmony, and joy and you will affect others, for the feeling is contagious.

"Always keep your visions positive, they will bring you truth and prosperity in the form of happiness. You [humans] have cluttered the earth with so much in order to buy happiness. Go to the ocean and submerge yourself in its peace. Then search your soul for what lies beneath your flesh and bones, it is this light, this vibration of pure love that you need to nurture. Then you will see your world change before your eyes.

"Don't pass up opportunities when they present themselves to you that enable you to promote this inner dwelling of peace; seize the moment. Don't say you can't. See that you can. Feel the excitement around it, and make it materialize. See the world existing in harmony, even if for a day, even if for a moment."

Mother Elephant at a Well-Known U.S. Animal Park

Elephant: This is a life I have chosen, one free from poachers, free of undignified tricks and monotonous actions. Though the land is not vast, it is enough for us to pretend. I have my son by my side, and I know he is safe. I still do not trust all humans. I have seen the damage that they can do and the horrendous disregard for our families and our community.

Debbie: It hurts me to think about what you have endured, and I apologize for the careless and cruel actions of humans all over the world.

Elephant: Your apologies are just words. It is immediate action that is needed. The needless killings are frightening. I have lost many friends. My handlers are kind and try very hard. Many, however, still don't really understand our deep emotional bonds. We like to stay together and when one is separate, it upsets the group tremendously. It will take many lives to trust humans. We are gentle beings who only wish to live life harmoniously amongst ourselves. Our family structure is a bond that is strong; it is a part of us. When this is lost time and time again, the void is sometimes replaced by anger. This is what you may see when an elephant strikes. We mean no harm to anyone, unless our family circle is threatened. We fiercely protect our young and have lost our lives in this attempt. That is one of the reasons I am here.

Debbie: I wish I could promise you a future free of poaching and safety in your native Africa.

Elephant: The world has changed so much. We live in fear. Humans have become our biggest fear, which is sad because for years we enjoyed their silly existence and even enjoyed partnering with them. But they have selfishly removed us from our pack and in doing so, stripped us of our dignity and basis for existence, without so much as an apology. That is where our sadness begins.

Debbie: There are efforts being made to stop poachers. Is there something else we can do?

Elephant: You must start by changing people's hearts. I don't know how to do this or why people are motivated toward evil. It is evil to kill a member of my family for sheer selfish greed. Humans have to change humans. They need to open their hearts. When the heart is open, they cannot kill. Greed and disrespect are a closed, cold heart and this is dangerous to all animals.

Debbie: What would you like your son to grow up knowing?

Elephant: That there once was a land so spectacular and free. It is a place I can only show in pictures I send to him from my mind and stories I hear. Our life now, although safe, is very different. He must learn to get along with humans, despite the horrible stories he hears. This will be a challenge, I know. But he will keep his heart open and this will enable him to view each human encounter cautiously, but without a preconceived judgment. He will live a very different life than I. But I hope he never loses his pride of the species because captivity changes us. We lose a lot of our native instincts and behaviors. The wild would be frightening to him after living this life. We keep Africa alive in our hearts and minds, and this I want him to remember.

Debbie: Do you have a message for people?

Elephant: Our family is very important to us. Please don't remove us carelessly. It is so painful; it takes years to overcome. If you must put us in captivity, do not separate our family. We will happily cooperate, if you respect this wish.

Debbie: Any message for your friends still in Africa?

Elephant: Peace to them. They are our heroes. They are living dangerous lives, which we envy as well as abhor. Try to keep them safe from humans with cold hearts and evil hands. Save our children from the destruction that is taking place. If enough humans have good hearts, you can conquer the evil ones. Please try. We have such love to share, but you have shut that off temporarily with your destruction and killing. We want to live in harmony. This is not too much to ask.

Male Gorilla in Captivity

Gorilla: I am the one who is king of the jungle! I care for my family, that is my main focus. I watch over them closely, they are my focus here.

Debbie: How do you feel about living in captivity?

Gorilla: It is a home. I have not been in the jungle for a long time. I am used to this situation.

Debbie: How do you feel about your daughter growing up here?

Gorilla: I know it is safe. I am sad that this is all she will know, but also realize she will grow with a familiarity to humans and I realize the importance of this. It is a connection that will open hearts and minds.

Debbie: What is your message for humans and humanity in general?

Gorilla: Save the earth. We have been evicted from our homes, our natural habitat. You humans work so hard to put us in zoos and areas to duplicate our habitat. Put this energy into saving our land, our earth. When an animal becomes extinct, you cut off a link in the chain. When a link is gone, drastic changes will happen. I gladly represent my species for humans. I give up my privacy and social dignity for humans to see me. It is in hopes that they will want to save our world, to save us from extinction.

Debbie: So you realize your species is in danger of becoming extinct?

Gorilla: Sadly, yes. I chose to come here. I am the eyes, ears, and face for my species. I give up my freedom in hopes of freeing others from the suppression and ultimate death they will face.

Debbie: How do you feel about your daughter?

Gorilla: She enjoys playing hide and seek with me. I enjoy playing with her. I sleep while she jumps on me. She loves bodily contact; this is how we exchange our love and compassion with each other. She is my life now. She believes, as I do, that we are here to bridge the gap of unfamiliarity that exists and we accept this. We are a loving family with hopes, emotions, delight, gratitude, and respect. We relish each other's company beyond what your minds can understand. We nurture our young with love but must also be stern, that is where their mother comes in. She [daughter] is our future and serves a special spot in the world.

Debbie: Do you have anything else you would like to share for humanity?

Gorilla: Savor your young. Bring them up to follow their hearts, to keep their hearts open and let their hearts lead the way. Then maybe our world will cheat extinction and we can live harmoniously. I could live happily with my family without fear of termination from human neglect and disregard.

What the Animals Know

Animals have so much to give us, to teach us, to learn from us, to communicate to us. Every solid relationship is based on communication, so let animal communication become the foundation of your relationship, not only with the animals that share your home and your life, but with all the animals that share our world, our spirit, our essence. Just start talking. It's simple, and at the same time, it's a miracle.

The Least You Need to Know

- Humans are part of the animal kingdom. Recognizing this can help us feel more in tune with and more an integral part of the natural world.

- Animals and the environment need advocates to protect and preserve them.

- Many organizations already exist proactively working in the best interest of animals. Support your natural world and the universal spirit of all sentient beings by supporting an organization you believe in.

- Extended conversations with wild animals in captivity can reveal a lot about how intelligent and truly aware animals really are.

Power Animal Encyclopedia

What messages do the animals that cross your path have for you? What does your animal totem have to teach you? What powers can you draw from them?

By reading about the animals you are drawn to, or those who cross your path, you can gain a better understanding of your current situation and how to approach an upcoming conflict, decision, or endeavor. Here is a list of some animals that may either cross your path with a message to share, or ones you may have as your animal totem (or both!). Remember that many power animals come into and pass out of your life, according to when you need them. Stay attuned to the animal life around you, and refer to this Power Animal Encyclopedia for guidance when an animal brings itself to your attention. Find the lesson, and learn from the animals.

Different people attribute different meanings to various animals, so although this encyclopedia consists of Debbie's personal intuitions and connections with different animals, you might see different interpretations elsewhere. You might also feel, intuitively, that an animal you encounter means something different for you than we have written here, and that's fine. Use your own intuition and education about each animal to gain your own understanding of what the message may mean for you and in your life. Consider this a guide to get you started.

Alligator   Tap into ancient wisdom. Are you harboring secrets? Is your intention different than your perception?

Ant   It is time to take control of a situation that lacks social direction. You might need to impose a new order, dedication, or execution of a task. Pay attention to details.

Armadillo   Stop putting up walls and open yourself up. You are afraid of being hurt, or you're feeling vulnerable or subject to a social stigma. Face the world with an open heart and a happy face. You are strong enough.

Badger   Beware of someone's aggressive tendencies. Sharp words and thoughts harm. Beware of jealousy. Use positive thoughts to bring about the right results.

Bat   Disregard what others say about you. They might not understand your inner self, but you are you, so continue to be true to who you know you are. Do not get bogged down or held back by labels or conventional wisdom and gossip.

Bear   It is time to use your intuition to get answers. Do not rely so much on others. You deserve the honey in life, believe this.

Beaver   Your ambition can make you a builder of dreams and of your potential. Tap into your community consciousness. You can accomplish anything with the right tools and the right attitude.

Bees   It is time to reap the benefits of your hard work. Take time to reach out to family. Honor the elder woman in your life. Hasty decisions can cost you time.

Black panther   A change awaits you, and if you do not jump in with both feet, you will have difficulty adjusting. Trust in the direction you have chosen, and move forward with courage to the challenges you face. The mystery awaits you, and you are ready.

Blue heron   Do not forget to use your faith to overcome obstacles. Use the tools of your soul to rise above the mundane. Use song and dance to enlighten yourself or others.

Buffalo   Think about the sacred pacts in your life. Have faith in unknown forces and the power of prayer.

Butterfly   Prepare for transformation because change awaits you. You can integrate gracefully.

Cardinal   You are being acknowledged for your success and handling yourself with dignity and grace. Use both your male and female energy to achieve success.

Cat   Find your independence, and let a sense of mystery engulf you. Royalty runs deep within your bloodlines. You are tenacious.

Coyote   Don't take things too seriously. The elusive joker has appeared to remind you.

Crow   Someone is bringing you messages from the other side. Intelligence and companionship are important now. Your sacred partner in life is ready to find you.

Deer   Approach your life with gentleness and appreciation right now.

Dog   Remember the power of loyalty, trust, and love. These are the building blocks of a successful relationship.

Dolphin   Use your powers of communication, sound, and breath to achieve great things. Don't forget to access joy in your life. Water can heal you.

Dragonfly   Beware of false illusions in your life. You could experience a visitation from the other side. Harmony, hope, and joy will be delivered to you. You can tap into a different dimension right now.

Duck   Find the positive where others only see the negative. Rising above mundane consciousness with your optimism. Don't be afraid to speak your mind.

Eagle   Spirit is by your side and working with you. Soar to new heights. Now is the time to open up your intuitive self because spiritual tests await you.

Elk   Tap into your male energy. You feel strong and protective. Harness the energy of the moon to find renewal during the night.

Fox   Someone is silently intervening and supporting you. Remember that sometimes, blending into a situation works better than drawing attention to yourself. Try it.

Frog   You are about to experience a spiritual initiation, a leap in a new direction, or a change of path in your life. Tap into the joint power of water and earth.

Giraffe   Adaptability and flexibility will be your strength. Don't forget to stretch your limits to move forward.

Grasshopper   You have challenges ahead. Look before you leap. Tap into your intuitive wisdom.

Grouse   Indecisiveness need not apply. You are ready for bold decisions and a renewed confidence.

Hawk   This messenger from the sky asks you to prepare to be challenged, but assures that a wise interception will keep you on your sacred path.

Horse   Find your inner freedom of spirit. Draw on your childhood dreams to free your spirit.

Hummingbird   Open your heart. You can be sensitive now, and aware of the beauty and vulnerability in the world around you. Nurture it whenever you can.

Jaguar   It is time for quick action. Do not postpone until tomorrow what you must do right now! Speed and accuracy are essential. Don't wait too long.

Lizard   Change can be painless, you don't need to fear it. You have a wonderful opportunity for growth.

Lynx   Be aware of your surroundings and trust your intuition. Something is not as it seems.

Moose   Combine gentleness with power to achieve a healthy balance. You may be leaning more heavily one way or the other. It is time to get into balance. Pay attention to your inner rhythms.

Mountain lion   Tap into feminine power. Use your inner strength to climb high. Make the most out of your surroundings. A future promotion or success is imminent.

Mouse   Be selective in choosing your allies. In life you might have to savor the small bites along the way, knowing it will all lead to the big cheese someday.

Opossum   Do not be misguided by looks and appearances. True character lies within the heart. Look closer.

Otter   Now is the time to have fun, play, and enjoy the child inside yourself. The otter reminds us that play must be a part of a joyful life, so have fun. Also, remember that curiosity is healthy.

Owl   Be a patient observer and wait until the time is right. Set your sights high. Don't overlook the obvious.

Parrot   Use your power of speech appropriately. Be careful how your words might be interpreted. Mean what you say; say what you mean.

Peacock   You will experience sacred visions and rituals. You have spiritual guidance and support.

Pig   You have a sense of individuality and high self-esteem, but try not to harbor resentments for the poor choices you see someone else making.

Porcupine   Be careful what you project to others, it might not be necessarily what you intend. Don't be too cautious or you might lose out on something good. Realize what makes you unique and love it.

Rabbit   Envy may be standing in the way of your success. You can uncover your own power and talent, regardless of what others have. Do not fear or desire what you do not have. The rabbit helps us to feel satisfied and content with what we have within. Also a sign of fertility—could there be children in your near future?

Raccoon   Tune in to your inner creativity and flexibility. Someone needs you to look out for him. Face tough problems with a sense of creativity. Persistence pays off.

Robin   It is time for rebirth, renewal, and a new beginning.

Salmon   You may have to swim upstream to get what you want, but if you stay focused and believe you can do it, you will be successful. Tap into your power of determination.

Skunk   A flower of a different scent; things are not what they seem. Look beyond the physical in order to find the truth. Ignore conventional wisdom to gain spiritual insight.

Snake   What you fear takes away your power. Harness the power of your fear and use that power to transform yourself.

Spider   Pay attention to your dreams and tap into your feminine energy and your inner creativity.

Squirrel   It is time to prepare for the future. Don't expend all your time and energy on one endeavor or you may find other aspects of your life lacking. Prepare yourself for abundance by being thankful for what you have and by working hard. You will be rewarded. The squirrel might also signal the entrance of a mischief-maker into your life.

Swan   Slow maturity and a gradual blossoming is just fine. Your soul is progressing with a steady grace and ease. You are doing exactly what you are meant to be doing.

Tiger   You can find courage and passion.

Turkey   Be grateful and thankful for all you have. Practice unselfish generosity.

Turtle   Get in touch with the earth. Do something to help the planet. Spend more time in nature and preserving its divine essence. Tune in to your inner sense of motherhood and nurturing, or let someone nurture you.

Whale   Find and express an unselfish love of the planet and family. The whale helps to connect us with our purpose on the earth and our ability to make positive changes. Water is the vehicle from which you can draw power and intuitive renewal.

Wild boar   Do not be distracted by greed. Use your power to evoke positive change. Dig deep to get to the root of a problem. Don't just scratch the surface.

Wolf   A spiritual teacher will soon come into your life, or has recently come into your life; you have a lesson to learn about awareness of your surroundings or community abundance.

Woodpecker   Are you becoming too predictable? Perhaps it's time to shake up your routine. Don't get caught up in the mundane.

Pet Psychic Resources

Adams, Janine. *You Can Talk to Your Animals: Animal Communicators Tell You How*. Foster City, CA: Howell Book House, 2000.

Andrews, Ted. *Animal Speak*. St. Paul, MN: Llewelyn Publications, 1993.

———. *Animal-Wise: The Spirit Language and Signs of Nature*. Jackson, TN: Dragonhawk Publishing, 1999.

———. *The Animal-Wise Tarot*. Jackson, TN: Dragonhawk Publishing, 1999.

Bear, Jessica, Ph.D., N.D., and Tricia Lewis. *Treating Animal Illness and Emotional States with Flower Essence Remedies*. Atlanta, GA: Richman Rose Publishing, 1993.

Beck, Alan, and Aaron Katcher. *Between Pets and People: The Importance of Animal Companionship*, revised edition. West Lafayette, IN: Purdue University Press, 1996.

Becker, Marty. *The Healing Power of Pets*. New York: Hyperion, 2002.

Coquette, Sonia, Ph.D. *The Psychic Pathway*. New York: Three Rivers Press, 1994.

Edalati, Rudy. *Barker's Grub: Easy, Wholesome Home Cooking for Your Dog*. New York: Three Rivers Press, 2001.

Frazier, Anita. *The New Natural Cat*, newly revised and expanded. New York: Plume Books, 1990.

Kinkade, Amelia. *Straight from the Horse's Mouth: How to Talk to Animals and Get Answers*. New York: Crown Publishers, 2001.

Kohanov, Linda. *The Tao of Equus*. Novato, CA: New World Library, 2001.

Lingenfelter, Mike, and David Frei. *The Angel by My Side*. Carlsbad, CA: Hay House Inc., 2002.

Linn, Denise. *Quest: A Guide for Creating Your Own Vision Quest*. New York: Ballantine Books, 1997.

MacLaine, Shirley. *Out on a Leash*. New York: Atria Books, 2003.

Masson, Jeffrey Moussaieff. *Dogs Never Lie About Love*. New York: Three Rivers Press, 1997.

Moore, Arden. *Real Food for Dogs*. North Adams, MA: Storey Press, 2001.

Pitcairn, Richard H., DVM, Ph.D., and Susan Hubble Pitcairn. *Dr. Pitcairn's Complete Guide to Natural Health for Dogs and Cats*, new, updated edition. Emmaus, PA: Rodale Press, Inc., 1995.

Puotinen, C.J. *The Encyclopedia of Natural Pet Care*. New Canaan, CT: Keats Publishing, Inc., 1998.

Sams, Jamie. *Sacred Path Cards*. San Francisco: HarperSanFrancisco, 1990.

Sams, Jamie, and David Carson. *Medicine Cards*. New York, NY: St. Martin's Press, 1999.

Sherwood, Keith. *The Art of Spiritual Healing*. St. Paul, Minnesota: Llewellyn Publications, 2001.

Smith, Penelope. *Animal Talk*. Point Reyes, CA: Pegasus Publishing, 1996.

Swartz, Cheryl, D.V.M. *Natural Healing for Dogs and Cats A–Z*. Carlsbad, CA: Hay House, Inc., 2000.

Volhard, Wendy, and Kerry Brown, DVM. *Holistic Guide for a Healthy Dog*, Second Edition. Foster City, CA: Howell Book House, 2000.

Williams, Marta. *Learning Their Language*. Novato, CA: New World Library, 2003.

Wright, Michaelle Small. *Behaving as if the God in All Life Mattered*. Warrenton, PA: Perelanda, Ltd., 1997.

Animal Organizations

The Internet is a great place to find information about animal communication and the amazing world of animals. Please visit Debbie's website at www.animaltelepathy.com. We also find these other websites helpful:

Academy of Veterinary Homeopathy (the professional organization for veterinary homeopaths with a practitioner directory): **www.theavh.org**

Alternative Veterinary Medicine Practitioners (holistic vets listed by state): **www.altvetmed.com**

American Holistic Veterinary Medical Association (AHVMA) (a large professional organization of holistic vets with a detailed searchable database): **www.ahvma.org**

American Veterinary Chiropractic Association (AVCA) (learn more about veterinary chiropractic care and find a veterinary chiropractor in your area): **www.animalchiropractic.org**

Animal Talk (pet psychic pioneer Penelope Smith's web page): **www.animaltalk.net**

Animal Totems (learn more about animal totems): **www.spiritualnetwork.net/totems**

Animals in Our Hearts (information on grieving a lost animal): **animalsinourhearts.com**

AquaThought Foundation (dedicated to the exploration of the human-dolphin connection): **www.aquathought.com/index.html**

Cetacean Society International (an organization dedicated to eliminating all killing of whales, dolphins, and porpoises and to transforming all use of cetaceans by humans to benign uses): **http://csiwhalesalive.org**

Delta Society (information on therapy dog certification and programs): **www.deltasociety.org/dsa000.htm**

Heifer International (a nonprofit organization where your donation sponsors the gift of an animal or tree seedling to families around the world to help them become self-reliant): **www.heifer.org**

The Human Dolphin Institute (an organization dedicated to giving humans the dolphin experience): **www.whaleguide.com/directory/humandolphin.htm**

Humane Society of the United States (a national organization dedicated to supporting animal shelters and disseminating information about animal welfare): **www.hsus.org**

International Veterinary Acupuncture Society (find out more about veterinary acupuncture): **www.ivas.org/main.cfm**

Island Dolphin Care (a nonprofit organization that provides dolphin therapy to children with critical illnesses, disabilities, and special needs): **www.islanddolphincare.org**

National Animal Supplement Council (NASC) (lobbies to keep animal supplements on the market and competitively priced): **www.nasc.cc**

Veterinary Botanical Medical Association (find out more about botanical medicine for your pets): **vbma.org/index.html**

Pet Psychic Communication Tool Kit

In this appendix, you'll find hands-on tools for psychic communication: exercises, meditations, worksheets, and checklists, all pulled or adapted from this book and compiled here for your easy reference and daily practice—everything you need to get down to business and start talking with your animals!

Animal Communication Basics Exercise

Try this exercise every day for a week, to get you into the right mode for psychic communication with your pets:

1. Imagine you are having a conversation with your animal. It might sound strange, but this simple mind-expanding exercise will start to open the doors to your own telepathic abilities.

2. Reserve about five minutes after work each day, or first thing in the morning, or whatever works in your schedule.

3. Relax and focus on your pet for a few moments. Sit back with your pet, relax, and in your mind, say (for instance), "Hi, Frieda!" Then, just imagine that in your mind, you "hear" your animal saying, "Hi! I'm so glad you're back!" (or whatever).

4. Imagine asking your animal about her day, and imagine what she says back to you. Maybe she says, "Oh, it was the same kind of day I usually have, except someone knocked on the door right in the middle of my nap! Don't worry, I scared them away for you. Oh, and I'm hungry. When's dinner?"

5. Let an entire conversation play out in your mind as you sit relaxing with your pet. Look at her and notice how she acts, or reacts, as you do this. Even just imagining a conversation means forming thoughts that your pet might already be able to understand or "hear" in some way.

6. Let each day's conversation be different. In your mind, ask your pet questions. Imagine the responses. Don't worry about really trying to "hear" or "read" your animal's thoughts for now. Just keep imagining what they might say to you.

Modes of Psychic Communication Exercise

How do you communicate psychically? Stop what you are doing and sit very still for one minute. What is the first or most prevalent thing you notice?

A. The sounds: traffic, the white noise of a computer screen, birds singing.

B. Whatever object happens to be in front of me.

C. The smell of the air.

D. Physical sensations: a slight headache, an achy back, an empty stomach.

E. The feel of your tongue in your mouth. The taste of whatever you were recently drinking or eating.

F. Myself sitting quietly.

Now that you are tuned in to your senses, try this next worksheet, to see how your psychic communication taps into your senses.

Your Psychic Sensory Worksheet

How do you communicate psychically? The next time you communicate with your animal, notice what ways you receive impressions. Fill out this worksheet, then try it again a few months into your communication experience, to see if you are still receiving messages the same way, or if you have expanded or altered your sense impression tendencies for psychic communication:

◆ **Visual:** Do you see pictures or scenes with your mind's eye? For example, an animal might show you a scene or reenactment of something that happened. What did you see (if anything) when communicating with your animal?

_____

_____

_____

_____

◆ **Aural:** Do you hear words and thoughts with your psychic ear? You might actually hear your pet speaking to you in your mind, or you might hear sounds your pet heard. What did you hear (if anything) when communicating with your animal?

_____

_____

_____

_____

◆ **Tactile:** Do you experience physical or emotional sensations in your body that are coming directly from your animal, such as pain or vigor, strength or fatigue? Do you experience a sensation your pet experienced such as a shock, a chill, or heat? What (if anything) did you feel when communicating with your animal?

_____

_____

_____

_____

◆ **Olfactory:** Do you experience aromas as the animal would experience them? You might smell what your animal smelled: something burning, something delicious, something foul. What (if anything) did you smell when communicating with your animal?

_____

_____

_____

_____

◆ **Gustatory:** Do you experience tastes as the animal would experience them? You might get a sense of the great taste of your dog's favorite food, the horrible taste of those treats you thought your cat would love, or even a taste that could lead to uncovering a mystery about what your animal might have ingested. What (if anything) did you taste when communicating with your animal?

_____

_____

_____

_____

◆ **A general "knowing":** Do you ask a question, and you just know the answer, without being directly told through any of the five senses? Call it the "sixth sense" mode. What (if anything) did you sense when communicating with your animal?

_____

_____

_____

_____

Power Animal Meditation

What's your power animal? Use this meditation to uncover the animal, or animals, that have something to tell you at this time in your life. Have a friend read this out loud while you meditate, or record yourself speaking the meditation in a slow, gentle voice, and use it whenever you need it:

Inhale deeply. Fill up your belly, chest, and throat with breath, then exhale deeply. Repeat five times. Let all the tension flow from your body with each exhalation.

Imagine you are walking outside in nature, in a place that you love or a place you imagine: your own backyard, on a favorite trail, near the water, or whatever natural place inspires you. As you walk down the path, you see a bridge in front of you. Take a minute to look at the bridge. What does it look like? What is it made of? What is its shape? Slowly walk across this bridge. As you walk, hear the sound of the birds singing, and the smell of wildflowers in the air. Feel the bridge under your feet. Does it creak, or sway, or stand solid and silent?

As you reach the other side of the bridge, you see a path and decide to follow it. Notice the scenery along the path. What is the sky like? The trees, the plants? Spend some time envisioning the world around you.

At last, you arrive at a clearing where you see a bench surrounded by beautiful flowers. The sun is shining, but the air is crisp, cool, and clean, with a gentle breeze. You sit on the bench and close your eyes. You offer gratitude for finding such a beautiful place, and you know in your heart you can come here any time.

Today, you decide that you would like to meet your power animal, and you speak this intention. You close your eyes and say: "I want to meet my power animal, to help me better communicate with animals." Suddenly, you hear something coming towards you, and you await the appearance of your power animal with eagerness and anticipation. You slowly open your eyes and there is your power animal, approaching you. Take some time to appreciate the qualities of this being. What does it look like? What is it here to offer you?

[Take a few moments here to observe and meditate about your power animal]

Now you know it is time to bid farewell. You can return whenever you like. Thank the animal or animals you met and stand up from the bench. Slowly walk back down the path to the bridge. Notice the animals, birds, and insects you see along the way. Smile and inhale deeply and exhale deeply and cross over the bridge. Feel the earth below your feet and the sky above, and the way you move as an integral part of the natural world around you.

Take a few deep breaths until you feel grounded and centered in your body. When you feel you have fully returned, open your eyes, rest for a moment, and then if you wish, immediately write down the experience you just had so you don't forget.

Refining Your Psychic Skills Exercise

Debbie teaches this fun exercise in her workshops to help people determine their own tendencies. Debbie always starts with this exercise because it is somewhat difficult, and she can then tell her students that talking to animals is much easier than this exercise! To do this exercise, you will need a willing friend and a piece of paper and pen:

1. Sit facing each other. Decide who will be the sender and who will be the receiver.

2. Receiver: Close your eyes and relax your body by breathing deeply and exhaling through your mouth.

3. Sender: Write down the name of a color on your piece of paper. Write down if this color is hot or cold. Write down a simple object that is this color.

4. Sender: Quiet your mind so all you are thinking about is your color. Tell the receiver that you are going to send them the color, and then imagine it going over to the person. See the color all around the receiver like a thick mist.

5. Then, send the feeling of whether the object is hot or cool to the person. Let him or her feel the heat or the coolness. For example, if you chose the color blue, you would choose the feeling of coolness.

6. Then picture the object you wrote down and send this object right to the person's forehead. Try to stay focused and clear. For example, you might choose a blueberry or the sky as your object.

7. When the sender is done, ask the receiver what they perceived.

8. Receiver: As the sender is sending, try to remain quiet, relaxed, and open to whatever images might come into your mind.

9. Finally switch roles, so that the receiver gets to send, and the sender gets to receive.

Intuition-Expanding Exercise

This exercise will help you to get in touch with your own, very personal intuitive sense:

1. Write down a question for which you seek an answer, a decision with which you are struggling, or describe a situation you wish could be clarified or solved.

2. Sit quietly where you won't be interrupted: a bedroom with the door closed, a study, even in your car or the bathroom if that's what it takes to get privacy. Bring your notebook.

3. Verbalize your exact intention. Don't just think it. Figure out exactly how you would say it, then say it out loud. It might be something like, "My intention is to let my intuition help me to discover the answer to _____."

4. After you've spoken your intention, sit quietly. You'll surely hear thoughts racing through your mind. Don't try to stop this flow. Just observe it. Let it happen.

5. As you refuse to engage the mental chatter, you might find that what runs through your mind begins to change. You might start to get pictures, words, or feelings. Don't try to direct your thoughts. Just continue to observe them.

6. As your mind slows down (be patient, it will), you might keep coming back to certain images, sounds, or words. Keep watching, keep observing. What sticks with you, or makes a more distinct impression? Write down whatever seems significant or persistent.

7. If you feel you are getting nothing, write that down as well. Don't analyze what you are getting, or critique it. Don't worry about how well you write it, either. Just accept what comes, and write it down as honestly as you can.

8. Repeat this entire process, using the same stated intention, five different times on different days. However, each time, use a new page in your notebook. Do *not* look back at the previous pages until the five sessions are finished.

9. After the five sessions, go back and in one sitting, read all your notes. What themes continue to surface? Think about what your intuitive mind is trying to tell you about your problem, issue, or situation. Spend some time meditating on your summary of written reactions. See if you can find the answer pushing its way out from between all that written text. We're betting it's in there somewhere!

Exercise for Sending Telepathic Messages to Your Animal

Sending a message to an animal can be as simple as visualizing an image and mentally projecting it to your animal—a sort of talking to your animal without talking. Try this exercise to help you perfect your ability to send telepathic messages to your pet. This exercise is a good one to help you get started because it involves something your pet has strong positive feelings about: treats!

1. Think of a food or toy your animal likes—something you have on hand. Don't picture a treat you don't have or a toy you have lost. Make sure you have the object immediately available. For example, you might picture a delicious peanut butter dog treat, a small piece of chicken, or that favorite stuffed toy.

2. Picture the object of your animal's desire in your mind's eye. Try to picture it in as much details as you can, using all your senses. Imagine the object's texture, color, smell, shape, weight, volume, and anything else you can think of.

3. Say your animal's name in your mind a few times.

4. Send a picture of the treat to your animal. Imagine them eating the treat or playing with the toy.

5. When you are done, give your animal the treat or toy. You might or might not get any kind of reaction from your pet that tells you he or she got the message, but that doesn't mean it wasn't received!

6. Repeat the exercise daily until you feel comfortable with the process. Keep watching your pet for a reaction. You'll get one sooner or later!

The more you do this exercise, the more you can expand it, using different treats, toys, or even activities which you picture, then do with your dog (such as a game of fetch).

Sending Your Animal a Mental Postcard

Gone on vacation? Let your animal share in the scenery, the adventure, the experience, by sending a mental postcard. Here's how to do it:

1. When you find yourself in an interesting or picturesque spot, take a moment to breathe deeply and connect with your animal.

2. Look at the scene you would like to send your animal.

3. Tell your animal you are sending him or her an image.

4. Concentrate and imagine projecting that picture to your animal.

5. Explain where you are and what you are doing.

6. Take some time to stay open and receive an answer back from your animal. He or she might react to the image, or have other things in mind to tell you. Stay open to whatever comes through.

7. Write down the messages your pet sends back to you, and the time of day.

8. Do it again the next day!

9. When you get home, check with the person who was watching your animal to see if he or she noticed anything relevant that confirms the message you received back from your pet.

New Animal Interview

Thinking of bringing a new animal home? When considering a prospective new animal to join your family, you can learn a lot by connecting with the new animal and asking some questions:

- What is your personality like?

- What do you like to do?

- How do you get along with other animals in your species, and other animals in general?

- What do you think of children?

- Is there anything that makes you nervous or frightens you?

- What are your goals in life?

- What things do you want in a home or barn?

- What do you like and dislike?

- How does your body feel?

- Do you have any injuries or pains that come and go?

- How do you feel about showing/performance?

- Would you like to tell me anything about your past?

- How did you end up at the shelter, and how long have you been here?

Exercise for Connecting with a Lost Animal

Connecting with a lost animal can be difficult when both you and the animal are anxious, fearful, or stressed. When connecting with a lost animal, you will accomplish more if you ask very specific questions. Calm down, take some deep breaths, and try to connect. Here are some questions to ask:

- **How are you? How do you feel? How does your body feel?** This question can help you to determine your animal's mental state, and if your animal is injured or not. Remember to pay attention to any sudden feelings of pain or discomfort in your own body when you ask this question, because your animal might send you those feelings.

- **Can you hear anything?** Sounds your animal hears could give you a clue to where a lost animal is.

- **What does the ground feel like under your feet?** A dirt floor, a carpet, grass, concrete—these can all provide clues for locating your animal.

- **Is it dark? Can you see any light?** The lighting conditions can also be informative. Darkness in the middle of the day could mean your animal is stuck inside something: in a barn, under a porch, or in a basement.

- **Can I look through your eyes?** Can you look around for me? This can help you to get those flashes and images. If you see what your animal sees, you might be able to determine where your animal is.

- **How did you get here? Can you show me how?** A very frightened animal might not know or remember or understand what happened or how he got where he is. However, in some cases, animals know exactly where they are and exactly how they got there, and that can help you to find them and bring them home.

- **Did you leave for a reason?** Just like Precious, some animals leave on purpose because they are angry about something, or feel excluded, or got scared, or simply wanted to explore the neighborhood. Communicating with your animal about the issue can help resolve it so your animal feels willing and able to come back home.

- **Do you have a message for me?** Sometimes you might have trouble determining more concrete details about where your animal is, but you might receive a specific message, something your animal makes sure you want to know. This can also be important if your animal has passed on and needs to tell you he is okay or what happened, or if he wants to say good-bye.

- **How can I find you?** Your animal might not know where she is, but she might be able to tell you how to get to where she is, depending on what she remembers and how calm she is. If you ask this question, you might suddenly know exactly where to go.

Body Scan Exercise and Worksheet

To do a body scan, in which you go inside an animal's body to look for pain or dysfunction in order to better understand and treat your animal's physical state, you can use the same basic technique Debbie uses in here classes. Here's how it works:

1. Breathe deeply. Focus on your body, paying attention to what your body feels like, and whether you have any noticeable aches and pains. If you recognize what physical sensations are unique to you before connecting, you won't mistakenly attribute these to your animal.

2. Open your heart. Be ready to feel and accept anything at all.

3. State your intention. Verbalize in your mind exactly what you want to accomplish.

4. Call out the animal's name in your mind.

5. Ask for permission to do a body scan on your animal.

6. When you feel you have your animal's permission, ask if she can send to you any pain she feels in her body or to tell you where she hurts.

7. When you go inside the body, simply imagine that you are the animal, seeing through the animal's eyes, feeling what she feels.

8. When you're inside, visualize making your way through the body, starting at the tip of the tail or the crown of the head, whichever you prefer. Gradually work through the body, focusing on one part at a time and paying attention to subtle signals in your own body, such as a quick ache in your knee, an itch in your shoulder blade, a sudden awareness of your stomach.

9. Don't discount anything! Stay open.

10. Write down all the sensations you feel and all the things you feel draw your attention. Write as you go, so you don't forget anything. This is not the time to analyze your intuition. Just trust it, and write it down.

11. When you are done, imagine yourself coming out of the animal's body and back into your own body. Surround yourself with white light.

12. Don't forget to thank your animal for communicating with you in this way.

As you do the body scan, you can use this worksheet as a template to keep track of each part of the animal, as you focus on it.

Animal Body Scan Worksheet

Record what you feel while performing the animal body scan in the following spaces, or adapt this information to a format that works better for you. Remember to notice any feelings, sensations, words, images, colors, symbols, or anything else that emerges when you go into each body part. Trust that you are making an intuitive connection with your animal; consider all that comes up and document it faithfully—even if it might not seem to "fit." Each detail might prove valuable as you work to understand and heal the circumstances surrounding your animal's health.

Body Senses and Structure/Mobility (joints, muscles, tendons, and ligaments)

Head:_____

   Eyes: _____

   Ears: _____

Nose: _____

Mouth: _____

Teeth: _____

Neck: _____

Shoulders: _____

Front legs: _____

Knee: _____

Ankle: _____

Paw/foot/hoof: _____

Back: _____

Belly: _____

Hips: _____

Rump: _____

Tail: _____

Hind legs: _____

Stifle: _____

Knee/hock: _____

Ankle: _____

Paw/Foot/Hoof: _____

Misc.: _____

Body Functions/Organs:

Throat: _____

Esophagus: _____

Lungs: _____

Heart: _____

Blood: _____

Stomach: _____

Intestines: _____

Liver: _____

Spleen: _____

Kidneys: _____

Bladder: _____

More thoughts, impressions, sensations:

_____

_____

_____

Index